STUDIES

IN THE

SOCIAL ASPECTS

OF THE

DEPRESSION

Studies in the Social Aspects of the Depression

Advisory Editor: *ALEX BASKIN*

State University of New York at Stony Brook

RESEARCH MEMORANDUM ON SOCIAL ASPECTS OF READING IN THE DEPRESSION

By DOUGLAS WAPLES

ARNO PRESS

A NEW YORK TIMES COMPANY

Reprint Edition 1972 by Arno Press Inc.

Reprinted from a copy in The Newark Public Library

LC# 76-162847
ISBN 0-405-00850-3

Studies in the Social Aspects of the Depression
ISBN for complete set: 0-405-00840-6
See last pages of this volume for titles.

Manufactured in the United States of America

Preface to the New Edition

IN THE EARLY MONTHS OF 1932, newspapers in Detroit reported a proposed plan wherein patrons of the public libraries would pay for borrowing books. In its struggle for solvency, Detroit, hard-hit by the sharp decline in auto sales and auto production, examined a myriad of revenue-raising techniques. The response to the idea was immediate. Loud, indeed raucous, protests were heard from numerous individuals and interest groups and the library fee scheme was quickly abandoned. The temper of the citizenry was clear and no public official dared present the proposal again.

Libraries were a safe haven for the unemployed. The jobless, after futile hours of searching, could find warmth and escape in these generally hospitable surroundings. Books could waft one away to distant shores, lifting, momentarily at least, the burdens of reality. For those intent on examining the forces and the factors which contributed to the fiscal crisis, there were newspapers and journals, the works of scholars and polemicists. The literature was alive with plans, proposals, and panaceas.

In Highland Park, Michigan, home of one of Ford's large assembly line plants, men by the hundreds would gather daily at the employment office hoping for a chance to work again. Invariably the answer was the same: no openings, no jobs today. By afternoon the city's main library—the McGregor Public Library—a handsome and commodious structure built in a more affluent era, was filled to capacity, and those unable to find a seat lined the walls, reading, resting, and generally absorbed in some book or magazine. It is quite likely that libraries in other regions of the country served the unemployed in a similar fashion.

Diversion was essential if men were to preserve their sanity in those stressful years. The movies, with their bank nights and free dishes, offered some relief and, for those who owned a set, radio played an important role. But reading was, without question, one of the major outlets for one's time and energy. It is no accident that the paperback book became part of the American scene in this decade of Depression. The need and the reading public were present and while twenty-five cents was not easy to come by, it could be mustered and thousands bought the attractive shiny-covered tomes which bore the logo of a kangaroo with a book in its pouch. Not since Haldeman-Julius' Little Blue Book Series—which sold in the hundreds of thousands at five cents a copy—had soft-covered books been so popular and successful.

As might be expected, socially conscious and proletarian novels appeared, an understandable reaction to conditions. Most were of little lasting value but some, like Dos Passos' *U.S.A.*, Steinbeck's *The Grapes of Wrath*, and Roth's *Call It Sleep*, have a lasting place in American literary history.

In his study Douglas Waples describes the relationship of the Depression to the habits and practices of the American reading public. Drawing on a host of reports he has analyzed such items as the rise and decline of newspaper circulation in critical periods and the correlation of library book purchases to circulation. He examines those factors considered by publishers in determining which books will or will not be brought forth at a given time. Mr. Waples has explored the many facets of the printed word. One finds references to and statistics on publishing houses, book stores, libraries, newspapers, periodicals, distributing agencies, and the book trade in general. His research has been thorough and voluminous. The phenomena examined by Mr. Waples in the 1930's have in no way vanished from American life in the succeeding decades, and his findings are as pertinent today as when this study was first issued.

Alex Baskin
Stony Brook, New York, 1971

BULLETIN 37

1937

RESEARCH MEMORANDUM ON SOCIAL ASPECTS OF READING IN THE DEPRESSION

By DOUGLAS WAPLES
Professor of Educational Method
Graduate Library School
University of Chicago

PREPARED UNDER THE DIRECTION OF THE
COMMITTEE ON STUDIES IN SOCIAL
ASPECTS OF THE DEPRESSION

SOCIAL SCIENCE RESEARCH COUNCIL
230 PARK AVENUE   NEW YORK   NY

The Social Science Research Council was organized in 1923 and formally incorporated in 1924, composed of representatives chosen from the seven constituent societies and from time to time from related disciplines such as law, geography, psychiatry, medicine, and others. It is the purpose of the Council to plan, foster, promote and develop research in the social field.

CONSTITUENT ORGANIZATIONS

American Anthropological Association

American Economic Association

American Historical Association

American Political Science Association

American Psychological Association

American Sociological Society

American Statistical Association

FOREWORD

By the Committee on Studies in
Social Aspects of the Depression

THIS monograph on research pertaining to the social aspects of reading in the depression is one of a series of thirteen sponsored by the Social Science Research Council to stimulate the study of depression effects on various social institutions. The full list of titles is on page ii.

The depression of the early 1930's was like the explosion of a bomb dropped in the midst of society. All the major social institutions, such as the government, family, church, and school, obviously were profoundly affected and the repercussions were so far reaching that scarcely any type of human activity was untouched. The facts about the impact of the depression on social life, however, have been only partially recorded. It would be valuable to have assembled the vast record of influence of this economic depression on society. Such a record would constitute an especially important preparation for meeting the shock of the next depression, if and when it comes. Theories must be discussed and explored now, if much of the information to test them is not to be lost amid ephemeral sources.

The field is so broad that selection has been necessary. In keeping with its mandate from the Social Science Research Council, the Committee sponsored no studies of an exclusively economic or political nature. The subjects chosen for inclusion were limited in number by resources. The final selection was made by the Committee from a larger number of proposed subjects, on the basis of social importance and available personnel.

Although the monographs clearly reveal a uniformity of goal, they differ in the manner in which the various authors sought to attain that goal. This is a consequence of the Committee's belief that the promotion of research could best be served by not imposing rigid restrictions on the organization of materials by the contributors. It is felt that the encouraged freedom in approach and organization has resulted in the enrichment of the individual reports and of the series as a whole.

A common goal without rigidity in procedure was secured by requesting each author to examine critically the literature on the depression for the purpose of locating existing data and interpretations already reasonably well established, of discovering the more serious inadequacies in information, and of formulating research problems feasible for study. He was not expected to do this research himself. Nor was he expected to compile a full and systematically treated record of the depression as experienced in his field. Nevertheless, in indicating the new research which is needed, the writers found it necessary to report to some extent on what is known. These volumes actually contain much information on the social influences of the depression, in addition to their analyses of pressing research questions.

The undertaking was under the staff direction of Dr. Samuel A. Stouffer, who worked under the restrictions of a short time limit in order that prompt publication might be assured. He was assisted by Mr. Philip M. Hauser and Mr. A. J. Jaffe. The Committee wishes to express appreciation to the authors, who contributed their time and effort without remuneration, and to the many other individuals who generously lent aid and materials.

The present monograph, by Dr. Douglas Waples, differs somewhat from others in this series, since it presents, in Chapters III, IV, and V, a large and unique body of statistical information which the author had just completed tabulating at the time he was asked to undertake this volume. The data are

here published for the first time. The monograph will appear
also in a cloth-bound edition, entitled *People and Print: Social
Aspects of Reading in the Depression,* in the series "Studies in
Library Science," published by the University of Chicago Press.

William F. Ogburn Chairman
Shelby M. Harrison
Malcolm M. Willey

Preface

ALTOGETHER, about a score of professional associations, surveys, and foundations supported different parts of the work on which this book is based. To three institutions the obligation is direct: to the Carnegie Corporation of New York for a grant toward the volume as part of a study undertaken by the Graduate Library School of the University of Chicago to clarify the relationship of the public library to government; to the American Association of Adult Education, which largely financed collection of data used in Chapters IV and V, previously unpublished; and to the Social Science Research Council for critical assistance in preparing the volume in its present form.

The purpose of the 1933 Carnegie grant should be better served by the present discussion of the library in relation to other factors of reading behavior than by a report confined to the public library itself. Hence, public librarians should regard it as a companion piece to C. B. Joeckel's *The Government of the American Public Library*, published in 1935, and to Arnold Miles's *Problems of American Public Library Administration*, to be published later. The latter discusses the public library from the standpoint of the administration of municipal utilities as such. All three studies resulted from the same grant, and were planned as a trilogy which this volume completes.

Turning from organizations to individuals, I wish first to express obligations to Ralph W. Tyler, of Ohio State University, for his help to the series of reading studies continued since the establishment of the Graduate Library School in 1928. He was consulted on important questions of policy; he planned and supervised the statistical work, and supplied much of the interpretation.

William Weinfeld, working in consultation with Dean Malcolm M. Willey, University of Minnesota, supplied the facts and much of the discussion concerning the newspaper. Unpublished facts concerning *The Public Library in Depression* were largely furnished by Margaret M. Herdman, Director of the Library School of the Louisiana State University, whose dissertation by this title is doubtless the most adequate discussion yet to appear. Data concerning the interrelations of typical distributing agencies were organized by Ralph E. Ellsworth, whose dissertation, *Distribution of Print in Selected Communities,* contains much more detailed analyses. Further thanks are due William C. Haygood, for permission to use his reading sample from all New York Public Library branches in January 1936. This sample constitutes the best available evidence of post-depression reading to date.

Olga Adler supervised the secretarial work—a tough job—with customary grace.

Douglas Waples

CONTENTS

List of Tables

List of Tables in Appendix

Chapter I

Purpose and Plan

LIKE the facts about life, the facts about reading are too complex to fit any one scheme of presentation. They must be selected and ordered with direct reference to the questions to be met. In this discussion, the questions are those of interest to students. The plan of discussion comprises six chapters. The first states some primary assumptions: for example, that some cultural patterns have changed since 1929, and that the changes are to some degree indicated by changes in what people read and to some extent produced by their reading. Such hypotheses constitute a general frame of reference.

The second chapter outlines the field of reading as a field for research. The outline mentions problems confronting various academic, institutional, and commercial groups and suggests some possibilities to be realized by systematic and collaborative studies.

The next three chapters deal respectively with publications, distributing agencies, and readers. Each chapter states some questions relevant to the depression, indicates available evidence, and suggests investigations needed to complete the evidence. The final chapter cuts across the arbitrary distinctions among changes in publication, distribution, and consumption to identify social factors common to all three.

The discussion assumes that the various uses of printed matter reflect important changes in the cultural life of any community. During periods of economic stress one may expect changes in the subjects which certain groups find most interest-

1

ing. The changes are most likely to occur in the reading of groups who are habitually heavy readers and who suffered most during depression. The nature and extent of such changes, and their relation to changes in other social behavior and to successive stages of the depression itself are now unknown. The facts should show what different economic conditions have to do with the different social uses to which reading is put. Sociological analysis of reading behavior in relation to behavior of other types may in due time produce a reliable index of gross cultural changes. Some such index should simplify description of social changes resulting from a complex of causal factors too numerous and too obscure for separate identification by means of public records.

If some aspects of popular reading can be related to different economic conditions, we shall need hypotheses to explain the relationships. One might suspect relations between different patterns of reading behavior and different degrees of national anxiety, typical group tensions and pressures, and various types of social maladjustment. To establish such relationships involves extensive research in somewhat new directions. Typical cultures, social processes, and public opinions would be related to reading behavior as recorded by libraries, bookstores, and news agencies. Such agencies, to their own benefit and that of scholarship as well, might, if they chose, supply a valid and perennial commentary on current social change.

But so optimistic a statement may easily raise false hopes. The available facts come far short of the facts desired. Few individuals and institutions have sufficient use for adequate reading records to keep them systematically, and commonly lack the needed facilities. Hence existing records are sporadic and incomplete.

The scarcity of data is relieved in part by the values of the records we do have. The few thousands who read much and who can usually obtain whatever they prefer to read, tend to ex-

press themselves almost as well in their selection of current publications as they might in private talk. We can explain why such
people read as they do to the extent that we can identify the
social forces that move them. On this account the discussion depends heavily upon studies of other social changes for whatever
it contributes to a sociology of the depression. The effects of
depression upon popular interest in subjects like health, politics, crime, social service, fine arts, recreation, and religion
should be reflected to some extent in the reading of newspapers,
books, and magazines. To the extent that they are so reflected,
it becomes possible to describe some effects of depression upon
each of these areas in terms of what different social groups read
about them. Effects of depression upon interest in the fine arts,
for example, are suggested by the increased number of publications dealing with the arts, and by changes in the particular arts
about which most readers read.

The benefits to social science would be large indeed if such
changes in the cultural interests of society at large, or in the
interests of any one social group, were inevitably accompanied
by changes in their reading. If two very similar groups always
read the same things, and if two very different groups always
read different things, the sociological implications of reading
behavior could be taken directly from the record. We should
then have a sociology of the reading population, an analysis of
social patterns and forces limited only by the variety and range
of the publications read.

But the fact is that similarities and differences in reading
betoken similarities and differences among readers only to the
extent that the publications are equally available. Unless what
is read by any one reader is available for selection or rejection
by all other readers, it is plain that what each reader reads may
be determined quite as much by differences in the supply of
publications as by differences in the readers' preferences. Since
the diagnostic possibilities of reading data are based on the as-

sumption that the reader has free choice among existing publications, it is obviously essential to know how free his choice really
is before attempting the diagnosis. What meaning we attach to
the fact that a man reads nothing but his Bible depends upon
whether or not he has anything else to read.

Whenever the *supply* of reading matter is known to determine what is read by any social group, the record has a different
meaning for the student than when the reading is determined
largely by *demand*. We know that the relative influence of supply and demand varies widely from group to group. The following chapters accordingly stress the distinction, wherever the
causes of changes in reading behavior are discussed. To make the
distinction as clear as possible at this point should accordingly
simplify the later discussions.

The distinction between supply and demand is logical but not
sharp. In many cases, the two factors are inseparably confused.
They come clear only in extreme cases. But serious misinterpre-
tation of reading behavior is less likely if the student is ever alert
to the presence of both factors.

In general, the factor of supply is predominant when certain
readers are restricted to a few publications—the schoolboy to
his textbooks, the farmer to his local paper, the sailor to the
ship's bookshelf. It also predominates when certain publications are far better advertised or far more accessible than others
to the entire population—the metropolitan daily press, the *Saturday Evening Post,* the currently best selling novel. Again, supply is the more important influence when the community distribution of print is monopolized by a single type of agency—
whether it be the newsstand, the rental library, or the public
library branch. The publications not carried by such agencies
will be read by many fewer persons than read the available stock.

To explain changes in community reading which may be due
to changes in supply, one should examine the local conditions.
The conditions are objectively described by the number and

size of public libraries in the community; the number of local bookshops, rental libraries, and newsstands; the number and range of titles carried; the average prices charged by each commercial agency; the character and extent of advertising; and the rate at which each agency enlarges its clientele. Marked changes in any one or more of such conditions affect the supply of print and may affect both the quantity and quality of group reading.

New public library branches, for example, were established in 1936 with WPA funds in many urban and rural communities of Illinois. Most of the communities had previously shown less than normal interest in libraries. In some cases (e.g., Calumet City) previous studies had shown that comparatively few books were read. After the branch libraries opened, the circulation rapidly mounted to a normal figure for libraries in other communities of comparable size. Again, the dates when many large and well-established libraries (e.g., the Chicago Public Library) discontinued the purchase of new books, were followed by an impressive drop in circulation. Such changes in the amount and character of community reading are presumably due to changes in supply, since we have no evidence to indicate changes in demand.

Conversely, the influence of demand may be said to dominate whenever readers are physically close to large and varied supplies of reading matter from which they select for recognizably personal reasons. Publications read almost exclusively by members of a single group (e.g., *The Wall Street Journal*) reflect demand when there is evident connection between the content and the interests peculiar to the group. Demand may thus be gauged by the readers' discrimination among the types of reading matter available and among the available titles of each type.

This rather arbitrary definition of demand is somewhat stretched when applied to differences in the popularity of mass publications. The new magazine *Life*, for example, has enjoyed a meteoric rise in sales during its few months of publication. Does its instant and growing success imply popular demand, or the effect of supply, or both in about equal proportion? If the answer be approached with attention fixed on the social changes implied, the best answer would be "the effect of supply." A publication read by almost everybody is by that fact of small use in differentiating social groups. To find that the demand is "uni-

DEMAND AND SUPPLY

(Relative influence of each factor upon the reading of typical publications)

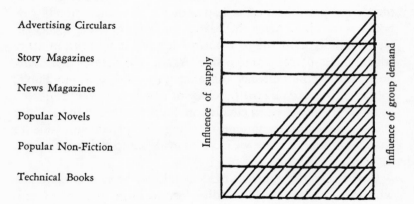

Group demand for particular publications shown by shading. Availability of publications shown by no shading.

versal" is for the student of social differences equivalent to no demand at all. To be read at all, any publication must meet a certain minimum of reader interest. Beyond that minimum, demand enters in to the degree that the reader's interest is specialized. The sensational radio advertising of *Life* and its wide distribution explain its phenomenal sales more satisfactorily in terms of changes in supply than in terms of changes in social demand.

Most of us are both "class" readers and "mass" readers at the same time. At times we choose our reading for clear personal motives; at others for reasons of mere convenience. The diagram on page 6 suggests that reading behavior is rarely explained either by the supply or by the reader's peculiar demands alone. The reading of advertising circulars received by mail is explained almost entirely by supply, i.e., by the fact that we must take them in hand, if only to extricate important letters. Yet the reader's peculiarities explain why some are read in full and others dropped at first glance. At the opposite extreme is the reading of highly technical publications, explained almost entirely by the reader's peculiarities. Take, for example, a scholarly monograph on the construction and orchestral uses of the baritone oboe. There are probably not over two hundred persons in the country who would read the monograph with any lively interest. But there are some few to whom its discovery would be an exciting event. They would take no end of pains to secure it, because of its probable effects upon their practice of music as a vocation and upon their intellectual mastery of their craft.

Between the two extremes is the normal type of reading behavior. It is due in part to availability, to the fact that the publication lies within easy reach because it has more interest for everybody. It is also due to purely personal motives. Among several news magazines in the dentist's waiting room we select according to preference; yet if the one selected had not been there, we should have read the next best with small sense of loss. To explain why people read as they do, we must know what they prefer to read and also from what publications they have to choose.

The distinction between relative supply and group demand as just defined has wide practical importance for researches in the sociology of reading. The student must resist the constant temptation to impute group differences in reading to differences in group culture patterns unless he can assume that the publications read by all groups are equally available to each. We know that city men read much more than country men with the same amount of schooling and read very different things. We know also that their cultures are widely different. But we cannot assume that the cultural differences are equally well *described* by differences in what they read, since the country folk are more dependent upon supply.

In short, reading selected from the whole universe of print may express culture patterns already formed; reading also, whether selected or imposed by restricted supply, may modify existing patterns not at all, some, or very greatly. In the former case we can more safely assume that cultural differences *cause* the differences in reading. In the latter case, we can not assume that differences in reading *cause* the cultural differences without specific evidence to that effect.

The sound interpretation of reading behavior thus requires the student to distinguish as clearly as possible among the following typical relationships: (a) The groups select their reading from an abundant supply that is equally available to each of the groups compared. In this case, reading may be used to describe group differences. (b) The group is restricted to reading of a certain character by the conditions of supply, and such reading plays a part in forming its attitudes. In this case, reading cannot be used to describe group differences. (c) The intermediate situation, in which reading can be used to describe group differences only in so far as the availability of the publications considered has been established, as, for example, in comparing different groups within the clientele of the same public library. Yet even here, of course, the reader's distance from the library would be a disturbing influence.

Assuming that both supply and demand as involved in reading behavior have changed in various ways during the depression, we may state certain hypotheses concerning the nature and extent of the changes.

*1. The depression affected both the number and the character
of publications read*

To demonstrate this proposition one must study the deviations during the depression period from the long time trend in the number and character of newspapers, books, and magazines published. It is practically impossible to interpret changes which occurred during the period from 1929 to 1935 as effects of the depression if the long time trends are unknown, although a positive or negative correlation with the segments of the business cycle which fall within this period might strongly support such an interpretation. In the preparation of this volume time and cost limitations have precluded the construction of long time series, and attention has, therefore, been focused on the period 1929 to 1935. Such treatment, it is hoped, will prove adequate to the purpose of this volume and should not result in similar restriction in other studies. If predepression data are not always available one should attempt to study the recovery period for comparison with the trough of the depression.

One must also show the relation of publications borrowed from friends or from the various types of libraries to publications bought and also to reading. If the publications bought and the publications read varied inversely, we could more safely assume the influence of depression. Then one should show corresponding changes in the amount of second and third class mail as against first class mail and telegrams. Second class mail is large in bulk, informational in character, often propagandistic (commercial advertising, appeals for charity, or for political support, etc.), and is less expensive and more accessible to the recipients than any other sort of print.

The evidence can be found in official documents, like the U. S. Department of Commerce *Census of Manufactures* and the reports of the Postmaster General. To some extent, the changes in the quantity and quality of publications indicate changes in the quantity and quality of material read. There are further questions, however, that demand careful attention.

Book production figures mainly concern the *new* books of each year, reprintings seldom amounting to one-fifth of the total. But the number of new books printed and sold annually may be so small a proportion of the books *read* per annum that the publication of new books might stop for some years without much effect upon the total number of books read. To estimate the lag, one should compare the ratio of new titles to old titles read in normal years with the ratios for depression years. Despite the size of the ratios, depression will have some qualitative effects upon the popular mind (possibly reactionary trends in certain areas) that may be due to the shortage of new publications.

In this connection it is important to know by how much annual losses in the number of new books and in the sales of all books were offset by increases in the patronage of libraries and by borrowings from friends. Various estimates point to a decline in book production and to a rise in library circulation from 1929 to 1933. More than twice as many copies of fiction books were published in 1929 as in 1933. Public libraries loaned 26 per cent more books (mostly fiction) in 1933 than in 1929. The loans by rental libraries, almost confined to cheap fiction, doubtless also increased. Hence there is good reason to distrust the evidence of sales as an index of reading during depression. Also, comparisons between books sold and books loaned may mean very little in terms of books read. One book sold probably reaches many more readers than a library book loaned for two weeks. With sufficient pains it should be possible to learn whether the depression actually saw an increase or a decrease in the number of book readers per capita and in the number of books read per reader, and similarly for readers of magazines and newspapers.

An answer either way would suggest interesting hypotheses concerning social aspects of the depression. An increase might imply that reading in general or reading of certain publications replaced other and more expensive diversions; or it might mean that the depression increased the number of those undertaking to extend their education by serious reading, or both.

A decline in book reading might mean that, on the whole, the depression tended to substitute the scrappier sort of reading, in magazines and newspapers, for the more deliberate reading of books. This question leads back to the production figures for magazines and newspapers. The available records show, for the magazines which carry advertising, the ratio of titles dropped to titles added, and also their spread by states. From the data one can estimate by how much the decline in *book* production was offset by the production of magazines, per year. They would also serve to compare annual ratios of book sales to magazine and newspaper sales. Further, by comparing the magazines which died with those which were born during depression, one can spot the more obvious effects of the advertisers' patronage upon the supply of magazines in different fields. Changes in magazine sales are significant as such. Since magazine readers are much more numerous than book readers, the changes in magazine production are a better indication of reading trends, both quantitative and qualitative, than are changes in book production. Newspaper production would furnish a still better indication, except for the standardized uniformity of newspaper content and the high cost of studies to determine what parts of the paper are actually read.

Gross changes in the amount of "mail literature" distributed per year are reported annually. Changes in the amounts read per year are very difficult to estimate. Most of us throw it away. But several million Americans probably read nothing but this mail literature, plus correspondence, business papers, and headlines, comics, sports, and one or two other sections of the newspaper. The pinch of the depression may also have so far increased the literature distributed gratis by advertisers in the "give-away" magazines or "shopping" newspapers, and by certain charitable and propagandist organizations, that their "literature" received more attention during the depression than before 1929. If so, the fact might affect the relationship between the national production and the national consumption of books, magazines, and newspapers.

2. Changes in popular reading are related to changes in the character of current publications

An abrupt decline in general prosperity might be expected to influence current publications in several ways. The first effect might be the discontinuance of class magazines with moderate circulation which operate mainly upon receipts from advertisers (e.g., *Vanity Fair*), or upon relatively high subscription rates (e.g., *The World Tomorrow*). Each such magazine withdrawn from the market tends to discourage other publishers from issuing new magazines aimed at the same group of readers and advertisers. Hence the failure of several *class* magazines during the depression doubtless increased the uniformity of magazine literature. This increasing uniformity might result first, from the suppression of the more highly specialized titles, second, from the tendency of new magazines to imitate the more lusty mass magazines which best survived, and third, from the reader's tendency to substitute the cheaper mass titles for the more expensive class titles he used to read.

The extent to which each of these tendencies appeared can be determined to some extent from data found in *N. W. Ayer & Son's Directory of Newspapers and Periodicals,* in the analyses of periodical circulation made by the Audit Bureau of Circulations and other advertisers' associations, and from analyses of the magazines themselves. The tendency toward uniformity in style and content of newspapers and magazines, which such analyses might reveal, is an interesting aspect of the depression. Uniformity is the obvious quality of mass literature in Germany and Italy today. Such literature tends to omit whatever ideas are considered unlikely to hit the dead center of current public opinions and tastes. The effect upon style is to increase the writers' use of unrestrictive verbal symbols and to discourage precise distinctions in meaning. The effect upon content is to exploit the popular prejudices and to disparage the fruits of scholarship. The effect upon society is the gradual regimentation of readers to a point at which they become less able to sense, and hence less able to resist exploitation by mass literature and other propaganda.

But the depression no doubt strengthened as well the contrary tendency for writers to say what they please, to write with eager conviction upon current social issues, to dramatize the problems of the day in fiction of every hue, and in non-fiction ranging from religion to economics. Such writings (whether in the form of articles, pamphlets, or books) are predominantly "class" literature. At best they represent a serious risk to the publisher in times of depression, unless the writers be well established. The decline in the number of new non-fiction books published since 1929, and more sharply since 1931, suggests the number of new writers whose books came short of publication.

The books which were published are available for analysis by any criteria. The analysis might show a preponderance of social criticism—levelled at government, the arts, the law, and education—during the first two or three years. Thereafter, when the writers had spent their fury and the publishers their money, the trend may have led away from experiments to define "the depression reader." Instead the effort was to define the persistent reader—that is, to identify the groups who spend most money for what they like to read in fair times and foul. Such trends away from the depression reader are justified in part by the flat failure of new radical publications to find a market during the depth of the depression, despite the presumptive increase in the number of their sympathizers. Trustworthy evidence of reactionary trends toward mass publications should benefit the canny publisher no less than the student of social science.

Between the two trends we have assumed to lead toward and away from the uncritical mediocrity of mass publications, the post-war period saw the rise of a tendency toward the popularization of class literature—e.g., E. E. Slosson's *Creative Chemistry*, Will Durant's *Story of Philosophy*, Van Loon's *Story of Mankind*, and the like. The movement was stimulated by studies (notably those of W. S. Gray) which showed the vogue of mass publications to be due in large part to their extreme simplicity of style and vocabulary. But those active in this direction are very little concerned with the mere translation of great literature into easy words. They are primarily concerned with such greater clarity in the writing of current non-fiction as may be achieved without violence to the writer's meanings. The success of their efforts should help to extend the range of substantial non-fiction to the number of readers eager for sound information and clear reasoning plus those who are now blocked by the unnecessary difficulties of the more authoritative works.

One must wait some years for evidence to show the effects of more readable books upon book consumption at large. One might, of course, find out by how much the number of such books has increased since 1929. Publishers' experiments have more recently been encouraged by librarians and teachers of adults, whose efforts to supply suitable reading to undereducated groups became more difficult when the depression largely increased the number of their clients. The tendency gained headway during the depression, and constitutes one effect of the depression upon publication.

The research here indicated clearly involves the identification of annual changes in the literature published during the depression, and the relation of such changes to changes in the literature read. To distinguish changes caused in part by depression from other changes not so caused, it would, of course, be necessary to determine fluctuations from the trend line extending much further back, say at least to 1920.

3. Changes in the publications read are related to changes in the distributing agencies

Evidence applicable to this assumption should describe separately the adventures of each agency during depression. Taking the public library as one social institution for the spread of good print, the desired evidence may be suggested by the following topics: (a) comparisons between the annual circulation totals of libraries whose appropriations were sharply reduced after 1929 and other libraries where appropriations were but slightly or not at all reduced; (b) like comparisons in terms of the relative circulation per year among different categories of books; (c) comparisons in terms of the relative circulation among different groups of borrowers; (d) comparisons in terms of relative circulation of different types of books to each group of borrowers. Similar data for other institutions—book stores, rental libraries, news agencies—are no less important.

The facts needed to show changes in public libraries are limited to the meager content of library records and to the analyses of circulation which students have made from time to time. Their application to the central problems of reading in the depression is also, of course, restricted to the relatively small (but also relatively more influential) proportion of readers who are book readers and who obtain some of their books from libraries. Yet despite these limitations, the basic question—who reads what books and why?—is more easily met by analyzing library records than by data as yet supplied by any other distributing agency. The other agencies are extremely difficult and expensive to cover. The reliability of books read by public library patrons as an index of books read by the population at large is suggested by a rank correlation coefficient of $+.65$ between the recent titles read by New York public library patrons and the titles reported as current best sellers by a sample of retail booksellers throughout the United States.

By analysis of the annual library patronage one can, of course, describe changes in the social composition of readers attracted to the library. The changing proportions of readers with much schooling and with little schooling, or of those on higher and lower economic levels, can be compared to estimate the relative cogency of different incentives to book reading in libraries. How true is it that the library became a refuge for the unemployed? To what extent did the local intelligentsia increase their patronage? Which elements in the library's clientele showed the largest and which the smallest increase, and why? Such questions bear directly on the library's sphere of influence in times of depression as in normal times. Similar questions should be asked and answered regarding the clientèles of other distributing agencies.

Also, the data serve to compare changes in the books bought by the libraries with changes in the circulation of each book. Those who come for new books will cease to come if the books are not there. Others who come for "something to read" may read the old as cheerfully as they read the new. Hence useful distinctions appear when the readers are compared before and after certain libraries ceased to purchase new books. By such comparisons one can infer some social effects of reduced library appropriations in terms of changes in the publications supplied by libraries to different population groups.

Library reading has been compared with the total book reading in a few metropolitan centers. Publications obtained from libraries and publications obtained from all sources are enough alike to justify the hope of weighting library records so as to sample community reading. To determine the proper weights one must of course have comparable data regarding the press, the publishing industry, the book trades, the magazine subscription agencies, and other important distributors. Each institution was affected by depression in ways which inevitably affected the amount and character of the publications supplied to its changing clientele.

4. Changes in the reading behavior of different social groups reflect different means and degrees of resistance to the depression

To this point we have suggested changes in popular reading during the depression which may have resulted from changes in the character of the publications available. We may now suggest changes resulting from differences in the cultural, social, and economic status of readers. The two must be combined to explain reading trends.

There is much testimony and some respectable evidence to show that reduction or loss of income affects both the individual's satisfaction in reading anything at all, and the relative satisfaction he finds in reading different sorts of print. If true, the fact should emerge whenever the employed and the unemployed members of the same social groups can be compared to note differences in the amount and character of their reading. The differences, in turn, may be analyzed to discover the major incentives toward or away from reading which fit the progressive stages of depression.

Sudden unemployment may, for example, stimulate reading about share-the-wealth schemes, bonus legislation, or political attacks on special privilege. As the shock wears off, the reader may turn to educational programs for vocational adjustment, then to religious doctrines that offer consolation, then to light fiction which inspires pleasant day dreams, and finally, to whatever helps to kill time and demands no mental effort—like tabloid photographs. Thus each change in the reading of some groups may imply a progressively weaker resistance to the economic environment, an increasing acceptance of spiritual defeat; or it may imply an intellectual dominance of adverse conditions.

Evidence sufficient to differentiate group solidarity in terms of reading behavior should be an important contribution to social science. To know what each economic group reads in order to meet its difficulties and also what it reads to escape them, would make any continuing survey of community reading an important social diagnostic. Conversely, the same evidence might enable publishers and distributors of print better to supply the publications useful to the readers of each economic level. It is therefore much to the point to consider the practicability of securing the facts needed.

Relevant studies would record and compare the publications read annually during the depression and recovery periods by groups selected to represent wide differences in the conditions known to influence reading. Among such conditions it is well to distinguish those not affected by depression from those which are affected by depression. The former may be called "fixed" conditions. They include sex, nationality, amount of schooling, age, vocational competence, and others, which largely determine the individual's ability to resist the enervating effects of unaccustomed economic distress. The latter class include amount of income, security of income, type of occupation, social prestige, amount of leisure, and variety of available diversions that compete with reading. Such conditions are useful for experiment, as against the fixed conditions useful for control.

The fixed conditions are entirely objective and hence can be used to classify individuals whose reading has been recorded. This means, for example, that American readers might be grouped in several classes, ranging from a class of mature persons of each sex, who held professional degrees and responsible positions in 1929, to a class of immature youths who had left high school for blind alley jobs. To go lower on the educational scale would take us below the level at which any considerable amount of reading is done, hence a sample would need to be impossibly large to catch enough reading to show socially significant annual changes.

With readers so grouped, one might first estimate the mere

number of books and magazines read per group per year. To the
limits of the sample, the comparisons would show which groups
found relatively more, and which found relatively less satisfaction in reading as such, as the depression wore on. The comparisons would also show qualitative changes.

Next, one might classify the publications read by all groups
into categories representing various degrees of scholarship, literary excellence, or technicality. The percentages which the publications in each category are of the total reading by each group
per year might then be compared. The comparisons should reveal the presence and the extent of tendencies on the part of
groups representing different levels of social competence to read
progressively "easier" or "harder" publications than they read
in the predepression period. One would expect, for example, that
the reading of professional men in general changed less, both
in quantity or quality, than the reading of stenographers; but
the comparisons suggested would tell the amount, the difference,
and the direction of the changes that actually occurred.

Similar analyses might be carried much further to refine the
interpretation of the evidence. One need merely categorize publications to meet more specific hypotheses. Enough has been said
to suggest the practicability of indexing depression resistance by
records of community reading. Procedures for neutralizing the
effect of differences in the availability of publications are suggested in later chapters. The results of the studies here mentioned should meet the two central questions: What social
groups used reading as a means of resisting or of easing the
shock of the depression? and what departures from their predepression reading did such uses require?

*5. Shifts in the status of individuals within any social group
differentiate their reading interests from those of the
group as a whole*

We have just discussed some social implications of possible
depression changes in the reading behavior of groups that range

from high to low in socio-economic status. Despite the greater difficulty of defining them, the intragroup changes, as contrasted with the intergroup changes, doubtless afford the more precise indications of what the depression actually did to the hopes and fears of the population at large, as reflected by changes in their reading.

When an entire community is gradually depressed by bank failures, reduced income, uncollected taxes, mounting relief bills, inadequate social services, and the rest, one may suppose that the normal response in this country will be a more or less cheerful acceptance of the common lot—not unlike the response to other acts of God like drought, tornado, earthquake, and war. Because a general calamity is no respecter of persons, the companionship in misery persuades the conflicting social groups to declare a truce and to proceed for a time along parallel if not converging lines, toward "recovery." Investigation of the hypotheses already stated will probably disclose this trend toward fusion of group interests, during the early thirties, as reflected by the greater similarity of current publications and also by the larger number of publications read by rich and poor alike.

But the tendency to forget group differences is born of emergencies. When the shock of the emergency wears off, either the old differences reappear or else new differences are discovered in the new setting. Collective solutions which the community applies to the general problem will not help everybody to the same extent. Many individuals, on each economic level, will benefit less than their fellows. It matters little, from the standpoint of morale, whether the majority remains the same and the minority rises above it, or whether the minority falls below the majority. In either case the members of one group will lose prestige, and will accept new loyalties in the hope of regaining prestige. Essentially this means that the former group equilibrium is destroyed, the basic attitudes of predepression groups are complicated, and new groups are formed for self-defense and for the expression of common sympathies which cut across the former distinctions among different socio-economic groups.

To describe this process of realignment in terms of reading behavior, we should identify changes in the character of groups reading different sorts of publications. Changes in the status of individuals, in their respective culture groups, may be reflected by changes in their reading. If so, we should also explain why such changes occurred. There are two theoretical answers to the why. One is that the change in status produced the change in reading. The other is that the change in reading did something to change the status. To differentiate the two implications, especially in community reading during recovery, would greatly enrich the interpretation of all future, and of much previous data concerning the publications read by different social groups.

The study of individual departures from group tendencies in reading is practicable in so far as the individuals representing different degrees of variation from the central tendencies of their respective groups can be adequately sampled. Selection of the samples demands a knowledge of the individual's changing status in the group, which can seldom be obtained by methods less laborious than the case study.

Occasionally, however, it is possible to find groups, ready formed, which represent progressively longer periods of unemployment. Such are ideal for analyses to describe the effects of depression upon the disorganization of former group reading patterns. Ready formed groups of this character may sometimes be found in a selection of the same departments in the same industry in different cities wherein the industry occupies different levels of prosperity at the same time; in a selection of small one-industry communities, representing different employment ratios, or in a single nationwide industry which records changes in the economic status of individual employees in sufficient detail. Possible sources are cited later.

The hypotheses to be evaluated by data concerning the individuals thus sampled are of several different sorts. Probably the more important, for the purposes of this monograph, can be classed as political, if we understand "political" to cover the competition among minority groups for status among the élite, with all the economic and prestige values which such status implies. Generally speaking, political rivalries are sharpened by social inequalities. They are accordingly intensified by the depression, in so far as differences in income affect the individual's security and prestige.

We may then venture the following political hypotheses, suggested by Harold D. Lasswell, which lend themselves to investigation in terms of reading behavior: (1) collective rather than private solutions are favored during the initial phases of depression; (2) a later phase is marked by the individual's greater attention to himself and to his immediate surroundings than to ideas and issues more remote in time or place; (3) a third phase sets in when the prospect of recovery seems all but hopeless and the individual tends to escape his problems; (4) during the later stages the conflict between conservative and revolutionary sympathies grows keener; (5) members of the predepression elite are concerned with threats by underprivileged groups.

How these hypotheses relate to changes in the symbols met in depression reading has already been suggested by occasional illustration. Their validity can, of course, be studied by analyzing many of the other changes in popular reading as mentioned in the foregoing pages. But what deserves emphasis at this point is the importance of checking these and other similar hypotheses against the reading behavior of individuals whose group status is known to have suffered most from the depression. Such changes in group status usually affect reading behavior by the operation of such factors as amount of income, security of income, type of occupation, social prestige, amount of leisure, and the variety of available diversions that compete with reading. Whenever the reading data yield evidence relevant to the hypotheses, the findings should supply a useful analysis of the "protest" attitudes at each stage of transition. They should also indicate the several uses of literature by groups identified with the typical attitudes implied. Recognition of such uses should benefit publishers and distributors of class publications, by whom the problems should be studied.

6. *The most persistent readers before, during, and after depression are found in the same social groups*

This assumption is perhaps more important for technical than for other considerations. If and when established, the fact would greatly economize description of the social attitudes expressed in reading at any particular time. To identify certain groups— for example, students, housewives with high school or college education, and professionals like teachers and clergymen—as the groups best representing the large consumers of books and magazines, might justify almost exclusive attention to such groups in sampling any community. Also, where large-group reading behavior is the field of study, it is probable that relations between the reading of major and of minor groups can be established to the point of predicating changes in the minor groups from samples of the major groups. Recent experiments to develop and compare reading indexes for entire communities and for the constituent groups in each community, show that community reading can be sampled far more selectively than is generally supposed.

Furthermore, the assumption that the bulk of community reading is confined to a few groups in good and bad times alike is sufficiently plausible to encourage careful study. The data needed to test it will consist of reading records for groups formed to represent different combinations of traits known to influence reading—sex, schooling, occupation, age, and others. Such records over periods of different social and economic tension will show whether changes in the reading behavior of groups that read little are consistent with and predictable from changes in the groups that read much. The amount of group reading per reader changes in the groups that read much. The amount of group reading per reader obviously limits the degree to which the analysis of any group is reliable. To learn as much about trends in the reading of a group of light readers as can be learned from a sample of heavy readers, one must record the reading of a much larger number of light readers in order to obtain an adequate number of cases.

Attention to this assumption should also distinguish changes in reading behavior that are properly ascribed to the depression, as such, from other changes occurring within the depression years. For the fact that reduced incomes do not reduce the *amount* of reading by certain groups (if it be a fact), makes it possible to identify other conditions than the depression per se which affect the nature, the source, and other significantly social aspects of group reading. Such "other conditions" have been classed as historical incidents (e.g., wide vogue of the *Readers Digest*), "secular" changes (e.g., repeal or lax enforcement of censorship legislation), and "cyclical" changes (e.g., the re-crudescence in presidential years of campaign biographies and political apologia).

It is clearly more efficient to work with heavy-reading groups than with light-reading groups in the attempts to distinguish the depression from other contemporary factors in the reading changes observed. It is equally clear that unless such distinctions are made, the student may easily impute certain changes in reading to changes in economic status for no better reason than that both occurred at the same time. More accurate appraisal of the depression's influence upon reading demands a search for the economic factors behind each change. Whenever they are not clearly identified as a sufficient explanation, the search for better explanations should go farther. Many changes, of course, imply economic factors in almost hopeless confusion with others of the historical, secular, or cyclical sort. While the confusion can usually be resolved by patient analysis, the relative importance of the different factors is not easily estimated.

One conspicuous change in popular reading, for example, is the swing to the *Readers Digest* since 1929. That a non-fiction monthly periodical, priced at a quarter, and devoid of advertising, should attain unexpected mass sales during depression, suggests that many who formerly subscribed to several magazines turned to the *Digest* to save money. But it is entirely probable that the depression did as much to restrict the sales of the *Readers Digest* as to increase them. Its success may be due to the secular change in public preference from the long article to the short among articles of equal merit. Secular preference for the short article is consistent with the vogue of the tabloid, news reels, news magazines, and other trends. The fact that the *Readers Digest* has so far outdistanced its many competitors is further explained by an historical fact. When the magazine began publication in the middle twenties, it secured exclusive rights to reprint what it chose from some twenty-five of the nationwide magazines of general interest. Social aspects of the depression are therefore as likely to appear in the changing content of this magazine since 1929 as in the fact of its mounting circulation.

The analysis required to distinguish the effects of economic hardship from the effects of other contemporary conditions upon the reading of different social groups, should increase the value of reading studies to student, practitioner, and commercial agencies alike. The student of social change should welcome objective description of the relative weight of current publications upon different social issues, of the predominant social traits among their readers, and of the relative importance of different distributing agencies, as factors in the direction of popular reading at different levels of prosperity. Conversely, such evidence should give the student a fuller understanding of the culture patterns consistent with any given level of prosperity.

The practitioner—whether editor, librarian, teacher, publicist, minister, or statesman—should utilize the same data to identify the subjects and types of publication in which his clientele reads most, as contrasted with the subjects in which he wants them to read more—whether because he believes they would benefit more from reading on new subjects, or because he can tell, from reading they now do, what else they would read with persuasion.

The commercial agent—publisher, jobber, bookseller, book club manager, rental librarian, magazine salesman, news agent, and his peers—is primarily concerned with sales. But because his attention to sales impels him to distribute publications as acceptably as possible, he is best able to collect the facts to show what methods of distribution are most acceptable to each type of reader. His knowledge of readers' preferences should be intimate. To convince the distributor that data of interest to the student are worth his trouble to collect is the most efficient means of promoting research in the sociology of reading. By due attention to the data already assembled and interpreted by students, the distributor might learn to adapt his methods of marketing to different levels of prosperity, and profit accordingly. But the distributor who takes the pains to fill the wide gaps in the data will benefit himself and also students and practitioners who seek a fuller knowledge of reading behavior.

It is important to know more than we now know about the social uses of reading. Additional facts will not only help us to mark changes in the consumption of different sorts of publications by different social groups, in periods of prosperity and depression; they should also designate publications useful to each group for different purposes in each period. They can scarcely fail, therefore, to describe the intellectual and emotional patterns—in terms of hopes, fears, and resignations—of all like-minded groups who do any considerable amount of reading. If they do as much, the facts to answer the questions—who reads what and why—will enrich our understanding of socializing processes.

Chapter II

Reading, a Field for Research

DESPITE their contributions to literature, history, politics, publishing, education, sociology, and much else, the facts about reading do not fit any one academic discipline, profession, or governmental agency. Yet, when effectively organized, with reference to hypotheses which overlap existing social sciences, the facts about reading should help to explain the formation of social attitudes in general, and the distribution of attitudes among different social groups. Political decisions increasingly show the weight of public opinion, not so much by the ballot as by congressional and other lobbies, pressure group activities, and the expanding rôle of the literate masses in forcing political decisions distasteful to the elite. Public opinions have become sharper and more potent with the rapid and recent growth of literacy. The time is ripe for the several social sciences to pool their interests in a fuller knowledge of reading, and also of the other important arts of communication, in their social aspects.

The present chapter sketches the field of reading with chief attention to its structure, as indicated by the work done to date. The outline thus has no particular relevance to the depression. It applies about equally to any time or place. But cross-fertilization with established social sciences is plainly needed to make the fruits of reading studies more abundant and more satisfying, and studies of the depression of the early '30's serve well to integrate the facts of reading with other facts of social change.

Since this chapter proposes to examine the phenomena of reading in a social vacuum, so as to describe their interrelations more clearly, it is important to insert a brief note on reading in its total setting. Our attention to reading as such should never become so close as to minimize the fundamental fact for social science, namely, that the social uses of reading can be understood only in so far as reading is studied in relation to other social activities and influences. The social scientist's first interest in reading is probably to estimate its effect upon the attitudes and behavior of different groups as compared with other means of communication and forms of social contact. It is obvious that reading plays an insignificant part in forming the attitudes of some people, a large part in forming the attitudes of some others, and for most of the population a part that is at present unknown, probably immeasurable, highly variable, and ever dependent upon the number and appeal of other kinds of experience, education, and propaganda. In the following review of research problems in the field, this problem of defining the relative status of reading carries only one reference, the study by Butler, which as a pioneer attempt to develop appropriate methods of attack deserves close attention.

Reading involves three major elements: the material read, the source from which the reader obtains what he reads, and the reader. Information about any one of these elements means a great deal more when it is related to the two others.

Studies of *publications* must take account of both readers and sources. Studies of publications range from commentaries on classical manuscripts to reviews of current writing or lists of best sellers.[1] Because the facts are hard to obtain, such studies seldom show by whom each publication is read, nor how its means of distribution affect the number and selection of readers. Yet such facts are needed to analyze publications sufficiently to explain differences in their consumption by, and effects upon different social groups and the population at large.

---

[1] E.g., the lists prepared by *The Publishers' Weekly, New York Herald Tribune,* and others.

Studies of *distribution* are made by advertisers, publishers, booksellers, news agencies, and libraries. They range from careful to slipshod, depending upon whether the market analyses are used by the agency itself or are passed on to outside groups who need to be impressed by the number and importance of the readers.[2] Few studies made by any distributor to date contain reliable facts concerning the types of publication, even from its own stock, which are read by different groups of readers.[3] They have mainly described the titles most widely sold or circulated, without evidence to explain the differences in demand.

Finally, many groups of *readers* have been carefully described. School children, perhaps, have received most attention.[4] The more important studies of children's reading show the relation between what is read and what is available. They also show the relative importance of school library, public library, friends, home library, newsstand, and other sources of supply to the children of each sex and grade. One such study[5] is being continued over a sufficient period of time to establish and analyze tendencies in the reading of individuals. Each of these relationships must be known to explain *why* school children or other like-minded groups of people read as they do.

The piecemeal character of reading studies to date requires that facts about publications, sources, and readers be *integrated*. Synthesis has lagged far behind analysis. Until they are integrated, the incomplete data will mislead those concerned with

[2] A study serving both purposes well is Palmer, James L. *Survey of Daily Newspaper Home Coverage in Metropolitan Chicago.* The Chicago Daily News, Inc. 1934

[3] Cheney, O. H. *Economic Survey of the Book Industry, 1930-1931.* New York: National Association of Book Publishers. 1931

[4] See Gray, W. S. "Summary of Investigations Relating to Reading." *Supplementary Educational Monographs.* No. 28, and annual supplements to date. Chicago: University of Chicago Press. 1926

[5] Progressive Education Association's eight-year study of reading in thirty selected high schools.

particular groups of readers, or with particular types of publications, or with the efficiency of one or more distributing agencies. The unrelated facts are ambiguous. To the extent that observations are confined to separate sections, the field of reading remains a wilderness.

The importance of interrelating the three elements may be emphasized by a few typical problems. Taken all together the problems may suggest a possible structure for the field as a whole.

PUBLICATIONS

Publications have been studied for a longer time and more systematically than readers have been studied. Before the "yellow" journal (cf. James Gordon Bennett's *New York Herald*, 1835, and still more sensational Joseph Pulitzer's *New York World*, 1883) began a new era of "mass literature," the reading population of most western countries was restricted to minorities of better than average literacy. There was consequently more reason to ascribe differences and changes in the character of reading to the changes in current publications, than to the changes and differences among their readers. But since the introduction of compulsory elementary schooling by almost all western nations has had time to take effect, both literacy and the influence of the literate masses upon governments have increased in spectacular amounts. The character of current publications is thus increasingly affected by changes in their readers.

Technical Improvements

As subfields of research, the problems involving the technical processes of printing, illustration, and manufacture stand in sharp contrast to the problems of critical analysis. The two types of problems have perhaps no more in common than the present eagerness of the book trades to learn what sorts of printed matter can be most widely sold. The publisher is sometimes no less eager to learn what types of format are preferred by different purchasers than he is to learn what subjects and modes of stylistic treatment they prefer. Otherwise the technical problems are distinct from the critical problems. They differ in scope, in their dependence upon capital to finance experimental ventures, and in the number of students competent to study each type of problem.

The best documented of the book arts is probably the field of printing.[6] The mysterious origins of the craft have stimulated historians no less than the demand for mechanical improvements has stimulated the technicians. Related research concerns the manufacture of paper and its many substitutes, the preservation of books, the arts of illustration and binding, and, recently, the troublesome problems of photographic reproduction.[7] The adaptation of format to the uses of different types of publication and to publication costs has been applied to many sorts of merchandising.[8] This has directly influenced the relative volume of different sorts of publications through the years.

Criticism

Studies to distinguish various literary qualities and their presence or absence in publications appealing to different groups of readers are so varied as to defy brief description. By ignoring the shadings, one may divide the major types of criticism into two categories—critical theory and classification.

(1) Critical theory.—It is not easy to say whether any given description of publications should be classed as criticism or as a contribution to the history of literature. We are here concerned mainly with the literary description which becomes more convincing and more permanent as it becomes more objective. Ob-

[6] Condit, Lester. *Studies in Roman Printing Types of the Fifteenth Century*. University of Chicago. Ph.D. thesis. 1931; and Willoughby, Edwin Eliott. *The Printing of the First Folio of Shakespeare*. Oxford: Oxford University Press. 1932

[7] See American Library Association *Bulletin* and *Proceedings*, recent volumes.

[8] See *The Publishers' Weekly. Passim*

jectivity, in this case, increases with the number of criteria which any odd assortment of honest critics can apply to the same publications with very similar results. Objectivity and impressionism occupy opposite ends of the scale.

The contribution which students of reading can make to the corpus of critical theory is made by checking the pronouncements of impressionistic critics by facts concerning the actual responses of different groups of readers to the publications criticized.[9] Few authors write only for the critics. Those who address the public at large are entitled to a hearing before a larger, though less articulate jury than the corps of professional reviewers. To record the verdict of this larger jury is to record the present social importance of each author and publication.[10] To obtain and to interpret such records demands of the student an acquaintance both with the given field of literature and with the techniques of sociological analysis.

(2) Classification.—The second purpose of describing publications is the more practical one of helping readers to find what they want to read. The obvious means of affording such help is to put similar publications in the same class and label the class. But the usefulness of any classification clearly depends upon the basis of similarity chosen. The publications may be classed logically, with reference to size, subject matter, authorship, language, date, or other self-evident characteristics. They may also be classed psychologically, with reference to the peculiar appeal that each makes to readers of a given description. The psychological classification is far more difficult than the logical. It can only be attempted when the classifier knows what it is that different sorts of readers seek in the particular publications or authors. A different scheme of classification may thus be required for each distinguishable group of readers. Hence it is

---

[9] Foster, Jeannette Howard. *An Experiment in Classifying Fiction Based on the Characteristics of Its Readers.* University of Chicago. Ph.D. thesis. 1935

[10] Waples, Douglas and Lasswell, Harold D. *National Libraries and Foreign Scholarship.* Chicago: University of Chicago Press. 1936

probably safe to say that few satisfactory classifications upon the
psychological basis exist, if we except the purely academic classifications wherein the logical and the psychological bases are almost identical.

Psychological classification is feasible to the extent that readers are accurately described in terms of their uses for different
publications. The importance of such classification will be plain
to any one sensitive to the problems of publishers, educators,
librarians, publicists, and all others who try to reach particular
audiences with print.

The difficulties in securing the necessary facts about readers
largely explain why classifiers have not paid more attention to
psychological categories. There is, however, the further reason
that the problems of classing publications in libraries are mainly
problems in efficient filing. Classification of individual authors
has been undertaken by critics and literary historians; classification of books has been the task of librarians. Neither group has
much reason to make the sort of functional classifications made
by other sciences. The physical scientist classes phenomena according to observed similarities which define their essential characteristics. In short, classification is the accepted method of showing what the phenomena mean. The librarian's problem is rather
to organize a given collection for the reader's convenience than
to find meaningful differences among publications as such.[11]
Hence the problem of "psychoanalyzing" publications by means
of experimental classifications has not yet been squarely faced.

But the classing of publications may serve many other uses.[12]
It may give the prospective reader or custodian of any collection
a picture of its contents—whether they be the annual publica-

[11] A noteworthy exception is found in the annotated catalogues on subjects
of known interest to different social groups as developed by Walter Hofmann of
Leipzig; see his *Die Lektüre der Frau*. Leipzig: Quelle und Meyer. 1931

[12] See the excellent discussion in Rice, Stuart A. *Methods in Social Science*.
Chicago: University of Chicago Press. 1931. Pp. xiii+822. Case Analyses Nos.
36, 40, 43, 49, and 52, and Appendix B

tions of an entire nation or the stock of a single library or book store. By counting the items classed under each subject, author, language, date, selling price, and other rubrics one may learn the *nature, scope,* and *trends* of any sort of publication to the end of fuller knowledge.[13] Subject classifications alone describe the character, variety, and changes through time of ideas available in print. The difficulty lies in making the subject classes sufficiently discrete without making them so fine as to destroy their value as a diagnostic of social trends.

Estimates of Public Opinion

It is widely assumed that different amounts of reading on various subjects reflect differences in the readers' interests. On this assumption students have compared the number of publications on different subjects to estimate differences in public attention to each subject. But the hypothesis may be only half true. Its validity depends upon the sorts of readers considered. How valid it is cannot be told until the amounts of newspaper space, the number of magazine articles, and the number of books devoted to given subjects are compared with the publications on each subject that are actually read. Of this, more later.

Space counts are more useful when they are dated and continued over a period of years. Studies like that by Hornell Hart[14] to show the ratios of magazine articles for and against specific issues like birth control from 1890 to 1930, suggest the possibilities. The *New York Times* space counts of press items are also important. Large benefits to groups ranging from publicists to sociologists should follow similar analyses in the many classes of publications to which they have never yet been applied. They should show the groups of readers whose interests receive most space in each type of publication, through time.[15]

[13] Hulme, E. Wyndham. *Statistical Bibliography in Relation to the Growth of Modern Civilization.* London: Grafton and Co. 1923

[14] *Recent Social Trends in the United States.* New York and London: McGraw-Hill Book Co. 1933. Vol. I. Chapter VIII

[15] Hulme, E. Wyndham. *Op. cit.*

Technical studies here have been stimulated by political scientists at work on propaganda.[16] Similar studies have a place in other fields. The social and cultural implications of classic English fiction might be described, for example, by correlation between the estimated sales of each author and various objective indications of social change, over considerable periods of time. Did Charles Dickens really stimulate or merely echo a popular sentiment for prison reform, as shown by comparison of dates? So also with best sellers, persistent mass publications (e.g., the tabloid press and crime magazines), forthright propaganda organs, and prohibited books.

The last involves the broad field of literary censorship, in which statistical analysis is rare. It should be useful and practicable to determine by *whom* given sorts of publications are read, before they are censored. Many censored publications may never have reached those whom the censorship seeks to protect. Political censorship needs likewise to be studied by descriptions of content *in relation to readers,* and particularly in the postcrisis period when repressions are likely to occur.[17]

Histories of Publications

Cutting across the three aspects of publications we have mentioned—the technical, critical, and diagnostic aspects—is the history of publications and publishers. The study by E. Wyndham Hulme, just cited, is classed by its author as "statistical bibliography." The label is a good one. It serves to distinguish factual accounts of the development of each science through the

---

[16] Lasswell, Harold D., Casey, Ralph D., and Smith, Bruce Lannes. *Propaganda and Promotional Activities.* An annotated bibliography. Prepared under the direction of the Advisory Committee on Pressure Groups and Propaganda, Social Science Research Council. Minneapolis: University of Minnesota Press. 1935

[17] Of particular interest here is Foster, H. Schugler, Jr. "Charting America's News of the World War." *Foreign Affairs.* 15: 311-319. No. 2. January 1937. The extensive literature on censorship defines important problems more clearly than it defines effective research techniques.

years, as recorded by relative amounts of publication at different times, from bibliography in the narrow sense.

The account of successive changes in amount and character of publication in different fields greatly needs to be written. It should permit the evaluation of many different influences upon the progress of knowledge in any field. It would enrich the field of comparative science by indicating the conditions which enabled certain sciences to prosper better in certain countries and at certain periods than in others. It would also clarify the process whereby the class reading of one generation sometimes becomes the mass reading of the next—e.g., psychoanalysis. It would also produce a history of institutional growth as contrasted with the history of particular institutions—e.g., a history of the library and librarianship, as contrasted with the separate histories of individual libraries.

Investigation of the history of publications, with appropriate reference to their influence upon contemporary thought and, conversely, with reference to their reflection of contemporary thought, is clearly conditioned by the results of previous research in the contributing fields of reading behavior and reading distribution.

SOURCES OF SUPPLY

The second subfield of reading concerns the variety of conditions and services which bring publications and readers together. *Accessibility* largely explains why people read as they do. Hence the distributing agencies probably determine what is read no less than the interests of literate people or the character of current publications determine it.

The term "accessibility" has many implications not easily distinguished. From the standpoint of any one distributor, it first implies that certain publications are selected from the universe of print for local distribution. The particular titles carried, whether in stock or in the catalogue, are more accessible than others to the patrons of the agency.

Yet to pass from the stacks of a library or from a jobber's warehouse to the reader's hands, the publication must be advertised—by separate display, by insertion in selected reading lists, or by the many devices of subscription book agencies. It must escape the oblivion of the general catalogue or open shelf and come to the prospective reader's attention. Next, it must find the reader under conditions that best suit his particular convenience. This usually means that the delivery must be made with least trouble to the reader, at a minimum cost, at an appropriate time, in a convenient place, and under circumstances conducive to reading—such as privacy, quiet, and comfort. Since readers differ in such preferences no less widely than they differ in taste for subjects, styles, and formats, each distributor has much to learn if he would give more efficient service even to a single group of like-minded patrons.

The major problems confronting the distributor are thus how to select his stock, how to advertise it, and how to deliver it acceptably. The problems are essentially the same whether the distributor is obliged to *spend* money (like the library) or to *make* money (like the commercial agencies). The librarian with money to spend and the commercial agencies with money to make are alike in that efficient administration for both means the reduction of the overhead. The selection of stock which does not move, the advertising which fails to attract readers, and the conditions of delivery which irritate more customers than they please, are problems for research. But excepting empirical approaches to book selection by libraries,[18] studies of display and other advertising,[19] and book dealers' experiments with different methods of delivery,[20] there have been few systematic studies by private distributors.

---

[18] Wellard, James H. *Book Selection: Its Principles and Practice*. London: Grafton and Co. 1936

[19] *The Publishers' Weekly. Passim*

[20] Cheney, O. H. *Economic Survey of the Book Industry, 1930-1931*. New York: National Association of Book Publishers. 1931

The literature concerning typical distributors is meagre, even from the standpoint of the trades themselves. Speaking generally, the accounts of American distributors—publishers, jobbers, libraries of all kinds, booksellers, subscription clubs, and news agencies—are confined to descriptions of policy, organization, and administration. Because it is so difficult to identify the readers served by each agency, their policies of administration have, as a rule, been determined by financial considerations, and especially by past sales. Records by any publisher which might offer a means of predicting future sales have probably not met the elementary standards of reliability which any competent student would seek. Nor has any group of publishers or other distributors made their sales records available to qualified students. Until publishers do supply their sales figures, there is small hope for an adequate analysis of the book market as such.[21]

So long as the prospect for a science of book distribution depends upon the research initiative of individual agencies, each concerned exclusively with its own financial problems, the omens are bad. Too few of them know what data are relevant. The situation plainly invites the sort of collaboration prerequisite to useful studies in any field that overlaps two or more others. The extent to which the distributing agencies are willing to pool their information will determine how much each can learn about conditions affecting them all.

The purpose of the cooperative studies would be to identify the consumers of different sorts of reading matter, to indicate how much of each sort the community will normally consume, and to suggest the lines of specialization (whether by types of readers served or by types of publication carried or by both) that are most profitable for each distributor. Such local studies[22] suggest the possibility of displacing the present cutthroat and

[21] But see Unwin, Stanley. *The Truth about Publishing*. Boston and New York: Houghton Mifflin & Co. 1927

[22] Fair, Ethel M. *The Public Library versus Other Sources of Books*. University of Chicago. Unpublished M.A. thesis. 1935

often ruinous competition among local agencies by intelligent division of the field.[23] By describing the distribution of newspapers, magazines, and books throughout an entire community, past studies have defined various problems in the distribution of print that should appeal to academic faculties.

Market Analysis

One such problem is whether potential readers of this or that, and non-readers as well, can be identified by data supplied by the census and other periodic analyses of population.[24] Recent studies of reading distribution in different cities suggest an affirmative answer. They show a discrepancy between what certain of the better educated population groups now read and what they undoubtedly would read if distribution services were improved. They have also identified other groups as virtually beyond the reach of any books, no matter how resourceful the distributor may be.

Book Selection

Studies of separate conditions affecting reading behavior (e.g., sex, schooling, occupation) have as yet been too limited in scope to benefit the distributors. The different values of current publications to different social groups must be identified and tested before they can yield efficient criteria for book selection. Meanwhile the facts pertinent to book·selection do not interest the general distributor, however much they may interest students of the social problems involved.

Adaptation of Services

Problems of "merchandising" arise in the public library as well as in the book store or other trades. Customers differ in

[23] Cobb, Mary Elizabeth. *The Collateral Reference Function of the Teachers College Library as Affected by the Holdings of Other Local Libraries.* University of Chicago. M.A. thesis. 1930

[24] Winslow, Amy. *A Study of Data Pertinent to the Advising of Adult Readers.* University of Chicago. M.A. thesis. 1929

their preferences for different kinds of service. The antiquarian bookseller or the librarian of a highly specialized collection may perhaps satisfy energetic collectors or zealous students by operating on the come-and-get-it principle. The purveyor of current novels may need to spoon-feed his clientele to retain it. The problem for study here is to discover the types of service preferred by the type of customer attracted by the publications carried. Plainly, the more the service can be varied without too much overhead expense, the sooner the clientèle should expand to its normal limits.

American libraries forbid smoking because it is often distasteful to a majority of their readers. Some German libraries maintain a special reading room for smokers, thereby attracting readers who otherwise stay home with newspaper and pipe. There are doubtless many conditions which discourage library patrons and book store customers to the same extent. Some of the conditions may apply to book service in general. More diversified service methods should justify the studies of customer preference that have been made to advantage in other trades.[25]

Advertising

The ingenuities of advertising have long been applied to the book trades. Some experiments with merchandising by mail have made money. But the advertising of publications to *discriminating* readers has not been studied with the attention that the advertising of mass publications has received. The reader in search of a particular title and the seeker for "something to read" are generally well cared for. But the impressive number in between, readers with tastes well developed by the better class of reviews or by conversation with well read acquaintances, stand at present without much benefit from screaming posters on the one hand or from general catalogues on the other.

---

[25] Charters, W. W. *How to Sell at Retail.* Boston and New York: Houghton Mifflin Co. 1923

Cooperative studies may well establish means of affording such readers, each according to his kind, a perspective of publications available and chosen to fit his needs.[26] Their success, as with all studies of marketing, will depend upon how skillfully the differences among customers and differences in the merchandise are integrated and brought to bear upon the problems of selective advertising.

Cost Accounting

Pending the precise definition of such terms as "book," "magazine," "good literature," "reference works," and "reader," it is visionary to discuss the adoption of cost accounting methods by agencies for the distribution of print. The records now maintained by both commercial and institutional agencies are in general so meagre and so unstandardized as to require the introduction of new records. The recording of transactions, whether by libraries or by sales agencies, should be such as to yield reliable and comparable estimates of cost for each unit of reading matter supplied.

Cost accounting on a cooperative basis is clearly utopian in the United States, where trade secrets are guarded so jealously. It is not, however, too much to suggest that the relative efficiency of typical distributors in different localities can be estimated in terms of population units.[27]

The need is again a synthesis of facts supplied by community reading studies. It would show what publications are obtained by each distinguishable group of readers from each local source in several communities, and at regular intervals of time. One might then relate monthly expenditures to the number of read-

---

[26] Wheeler, Joseph L. "Methods for Making Known to Inexperienced Readers the Resources and Facilities Offered by American Public Libraries." *Library Quarterly.* 5:371-406. No. 4. October 1935

[27] Wilson L. R. and Wight, E. A. *County Library Service in the South.* Chicago: University of Chicago Press. 1935; Miller, Robert A. *Cost Accounting for Libraries.* University of Chicago. Ph.D. thesis. 1936

ers supplied with different amounts and kinds of reading matter. By comparing the data for several communities of similar size and wealth, one might arrive at useful estimates of relative costs per reader and per publication distributed.

Research upon problems of distribution, in short, would study distributing agencies in terms of the publications carried, of the type and amount of reading matter supplied to each important group of readers, and of the aims and scope of the important agencies in each place.

READERS

An effective description of readers presents the facts which explain why they read as they do. Differences and similarities among people may sometimes be used to explain differences in their reading.

A major frame of reference is geography. People who live together are more conveniently studied. They also tend to read alike, in so far as they are the same sorts of people and have much the same things to read. Hence, geographical descriptions of reading help to contrast regional attitudes and cultures. The influence of geography becomes less, of course, as the units decrease in size through international, state, county, city, community, and neighborhood groups.[28] International differences are highly important.

Within or across the geographical groupings, readers respond to many other influences. The degree to which different sorts of people read different publications is thus a basis upon which to evaluate each influence. Among such influences are nationality, race, sex, age, schooling, occupation, income, marital status, language, and others, to the limits of the sample.

The adequacy of the sample determines the number of fac-

[28] Cf. Wilson, L. R. *The Geography of Reading.* Chicago: University of Chicago Press. 1937; Purdy, George Flint. *Public Library Service in the Middle West.* University of Chicago, Ph.D. thesis. 1936

tors that can be evaluated.[29] Suppose that all ten thousand residents of reading age in a given community have reported their reading in accurate detail. The ten thousand are at once reduced to about five thousand of each sex, to one thousand of each of five age levels, to an average of two hundred and fifty of four different levels of schooling, and to fifty of each of five occupational groups. Fifty is usually a number too small for statistical reliability when the data concern actual reading, depending of course upon how much the individuals read. But there are other important influences not covered, such as nationality, income, marital status, and place of residence, which affect reading appreciably. Thus, if the factors first mentioned are held constant, even a complete return from a community of ten thousand inhabitants would fail to show how differences in nationality, income, or marital status affect the nature and amount of reading in the same community.[30]

Readers are accordingly best studied with reference to hypotheses concerning particular influences. A few examples will illustrate.

The importance of reading depends upon the cultural pattern of the community.—The values of reading may be compared with those of other group activities to estimate its local importance, to determine the present importance or status of reading in the community life. Differences in the amount and character of what is read by different groups reflect the deference paid by each group to literature as such.[31] European groups probably read larger amounts of more substantial publications than cor-

---

[29] *Cf.* Waples, Douglas and Tyler, Ralph W. *What People Want to Read about.* Chicago: American Library Association and University of Chicago Press. 1931. Chaps. II and III

[30] For a discussion of reliabilities in sampling reading behavior see Waples, Douglas. "The Relation of Subject Interest to Actual Reading." Library Quarterly. 2:42-70. No. 1. January 1932

[31] See Butler, Helen. *The Status of Reading as a Means of Communication: An Experimental Approach.* University of Chicago. M.A. thesis. 1933

responding groups in the United States. The relatively greater
American aversion toward serious reading is partly explained
by the youth of American culture. The "builders of empire" who
became national heroes were engaged in the development or exploitation of natural resources. They had small use and less time
for the literary pursuits which lend prestige to the élite of
older countries. The status of reading as such is widely variable,
as data reported in later chapters will show.

Like-minded people read the same things.—There are, of
course, many reasons for describing what different social groups
actually read. It is sometimes taken for granted that "like reads
like." But different sorts of specialists have different reasons for
asking how like-minded the readers must be to read the same
things. The distributor seeks to learn what sorts of publications
he can best sell to each group through the same agency.[32] The
educator seeks to learn what subjects in print appeal most
strongly to various student groups and why.[33] The advertiser
seeks the most profitable medium.[34] The librarian seeks to define
the types of respectable writing most appealing to each of the
groups comprising its present clientele.[35] The sociologist seeks to
explain social processes and social changes in terms of group
preferences for different sorts of reading matter.[36] The political
scientist seeks the evidence which reading behavior affords concerning the response of political groups to the issues carried in
the public prints.[37] Other academicians have further specialized

---

[32] See Conklin, Groff. *How to Run a Rental Library.* New York: The R. R.
Bowker Company. 1934

[33] See Carnovsky, Leon. *The Reading Needs of Typical Student Groups, With
Special Attention to Factors Contributing to the Satisfaction of Reading Interests.*
University of Chicago. Ph.D. thesis. 1932

[34] Palmer, James L. *Survey of Daily Newspaper Home Coverage in Metropolitan Chicago.* The Chicago Daily News, Inc. 1934

[35] Carnovsky, Leon. "Community Studies in Reading. II, Hinsdale, a Suburb
of Chicago." *Library Quarterly.* 5:1-30. No. 1. January 1935

[36] Lynd, R. S. and H. M. *Middletown.* New York: Harcourt, Brace Company. 1929. *Passim*

[37] Wright, Quincy. (Editor) *Public Opinion and World Politics* (Lectures on

interests in the facts of popular reading. The student of reading per se seeks to check his assumptions concerning the types of reading associated with different sorts of people.[38]

There are thus many compulsions toward more precise knowledge of what sorts of writing are read in different amounts by particular social groups. By comparing the reading of groups that represent wide differences in traits like age, schooling, and occupation one can estimate the relative influence of each trait upon the corresponding differences in reading.[39] The importance of describing what is read by different social groups makes it essential to develop efficient techniques. How to devise better and simpler methods of recording what people read is thus a major problem for research.[40] The methods used to date range from the comparison of sales and circulation figures, through the inefficient questionnaire, to highly laborious and expensive programs of interview and observation.

The normal reader's interest in a given subject is but dimly reflected by what he actually reads.—It is easily assumed that we read most upon the subjects of most interest. The assumption is highly dubious. It has been found that for most readers there is a wide discrepancy between the subjects in which they express most interest and the subjects they read most about. The discrepancy is somewhat analogous to that between a man's hopes and their actual fulfillment. Most desires exceed our grasp. Actual reading is more influenced by the reading matter available than by the reader's curiosities. Only few of the reader's curiosities may be satisfied by publications within reach. It is

the Harris Foundation) Chicago: University of Chicago Press. 1933. Pp. xiii+236; Lasswell, Harold D. *The Strategy of Revolutionary and War Propaganda.* Chicago: University of Chicago Press. 1933

[38] Waples, Douglas. "Social Implications of the Popular Library." "Public Libraries." *Encyclopaedia of the Social Sciences.* 12:662-664. 1934 ed.

[39] Miller, Robert A. "The Relation of Reading Characteristics to Social Indexes." *American Journal of Sociology.* 41:738-756. No. 6. May 1936

[40] Crompton, Margaret. *A Technique for Describing the Reading Interests of Adults.* University of Chicago. M.A. thesis. 1929

well to define both the commercial and the educational possibilities of research to define subject interests for the particular reading groups now least content with the publications available.[41]

The normal reader is more attracted by the style than by the subject matter of his reading.—This implies that important publications would find more readers if unnecessary difficulties were removed. The difficulty often lies in overcomplexity of style.[42] But many readers are equally disturbed by the oversimplicity that comes short of precise distinctions in meaning. One should note, however, that most readers' failure to understand writing on the subjects of most interest finds a psychological explanation in deficient verbal imagery, visual defects, school aversion to reading, and slow rates of comprehension—which explain dissatisfaction with all writing of normal difficulty. The definition and evaluation of such hindrances go far to explain the cultural limitations of print. Gray's "Summary" (*op. cit.*, p. 29) names the relevant studies.

The effects of different sorts of reading can be evaluated.—Educators sometimes ascribe certain types of behavior to certain types of reading, despite the fact that reading is never the sole cause of any behavior. To show that an individual followed printed directions in effecting a rescue or in making a cake does not make reading the sole cause, for all of his previous experience and present motives play a part. The effects of group reading are still more complex. Yet, because no direct effects of reading on behavior have *yet* been objectively described, the description is not impossible. The studies of Blumer[43] and Thur-

---

[41] Waples, Douglas and Tyler, Ralph W. *What People Want to Read About.* Chicago: American Library Association and University of Chicago Press. 1931. Chapter I; Carnovsky, Leon. "A Study of the Relationship Between Reading Interest and Actual Reading." *Library Quarterly.* 4: 76-110. No. 1. January 1934

[42] Gray, W. S. and Leary, B. E. *What Makes a Book Readable?* Chicago: University of Chicago Press. 1935. See also, for techniques of measurement, Thurstone, L. L. *The Measurement of Attitudes.* Chicago: University of Chicago Press. 1929

[43] Blumer, Herbert. *Movies and Conduct.* New York: The Macmillan Company. 1933

stone[44] to define the emotional effects of motion pictures on children suggest that the solution of several technical difficulties will permit at least equally satisfactory results in the field of reading. Promising leads have also been developed in the similar problems of radio listening.[45] When such techniques are developed, the educator, propagandist, advertiser, and other manipulators of public opinion through reading may enjoy a conspicuous rise in the estimation of scientists. Meanwhile there is urgent need for studies to define the extent of co-variation between the publications read and the behavior patterns of readers.

The causes of reading can be explained by individual and group motives.—Reading motives defy close description, and can seldom be analyzed without risk of mere verbalizing. The same reader may read the same publication for different motives at different times. The extent to which reading is undertaken deliberately—as against capricious or random impulse—depends upon a combination of the reader's curiosities and the reading matter available, which can seldom be disentangled without violence to the actual situation. Hence the results to date of studies to specify causes or even purposes of reading are disappointing.[46] They call for new techniques or for more skillful use of familiar techniques. Questionnaire, check list, interview, and case study methods each tell only part of the story. Readers tend to rationalize their motives for reading, they are often unwilling to state genuine motives when they do know what they are, and they are often unable to describe their motives with sufficient precision when they are both able and willing to describe them. Observation, a far safer method, has not as yet been applied to a fair sample of homogeneous groups to identify such widely

[44] Peterson, Ruth C. and Thurstone, L. L. *Motion Pictures and the Social Attitudes of Children.* New York: The Macmillan Company. 1933

[45] Lumley, Frederick H. *Measurement in Radio.* Columbus: Ohio State University. 1934

[46] Pendleton, Charles S. *The Social Objectives of School English.* Nashville, Tenn.: The author. 1924

different motives as intellectual curiosity, thrill seeking, news interest, or sheer boredom. The next decade should show large advances.

Individual vs. group studies.—Studies of *individual* readers are needed to check many hypotheses not yet amenable to group study. It would be illuminating, for example, to study all the publications—newspapers, magazines, and books—read by the same individuals over periods of twenty years or more.[47] The analysis of such records in relation to psychiatric studies and case histories might disclose the social implications of reading in several directions that lie beyond the present reach of group statistics. Studies to this end[48] have shown a correspondence between type of psychosis and type of reading done. Further study may eventually relate types of literature to particular emotional disturbances, to the ends both of diagnosis and of cure.

RELATED FIELDS

This sketch of the field of reading is plainly incomplete. The publication, the distributor, and the reader may be analyzed indefinitely. Each may be analyzed far more than has been the case and yet stop short of pedantry. It is particularly desirable from the research standpoint that such analyses be *continuous through time.*

But what will chiefly justify such analysis of separate elements is their *interrelation,* also through time. Studies to this end will require the attention not only of students of reading per se, but of all academic fields, that can either interpret reading data or apply them to the illumination of their own conventional prob-

[47] The writer has collected several such reading diaries. Many more can be obtained from biographies, published correspondence, and private journals. The current investigation by R. W. Tyler of Ohio State University for the Progressive Education Association is recording the reading of several hundred individuals during the eight years between high school entrance and college graduation. Such records are being analyzed in relation to most other important influences of school, home, community, personality, and other important factors.

[48] *E.g.,* Dollard, Victorine. MS. Files of Graduate Library School. University of Chicago

lems. This means, of course, that the implications of reading in relation to other means of information, persuasion, and recreation will be examined by different groups of specialists. The academic departments involved in such collaboration and the direction of their respective interests in the field may be briefly suggested.

By "related fields" we mean university research departments interested in one or more aspects of reading. Thus far we have implied that the field of reading should be studied because of its intrinsic meaning and practical uses. But the fundamental problems of reading require literary, historical, political, sociological, educational, religious, economic, psychological, and other explanations which no one field can supply. Hence to isolate the field of reading is to sterilize it. Conversely, the field is enriched and the fruits of its study become more abundant when the contributory departments are cross-fertilized. Research will succeed to the extent that the sources and techniques of related fields are applied to reading problems by interdepartmental studies.

CLASSIFICATION OF FIELDS

Different academic departments have interests in the facts of reading which range from immediate to remote. They may accordingly be grouped under three heads: (1) fields whose contributions to and benefits from the study of reading are about equal, (2) fields that contribute more than they receive, and (3) fields that contribute less than they receive.

Such grouping of fields merely punctuates the present description. In practice, the personal interests of one or two individuals in a faculty will determine how far the department enters into any program of reading research. The present grouping is thus based upon assumed departmental interests that are relevant to the reading problems already mentioned. Furthermore the grouping is of course only temporary. Some departments now indifferent may become active when the reading problems to which their sources apply have been more sharply defined and more fully documented.

Departments of the First Group

Several departments are already attentive to reading problems. What their studies contribute to the field of reading and to their own fields is about equal in extent. The collaboration of such departments with students of reading per se is mutually advantageous. It is natural to find such departments among the social sciences.

1. Psychology.—Psychology and reading are supplementary to the degree that the psychologist seeks to explain the reading behavior of individuals. Students of reading must depend upon psychologists to explain why people read as they do, whenever differences in reading behavior imply differences in mental organization and function.

The active interest of psychologists may be assumed from the large attention paid to the description of reading processes in psychological literature. But such processes are not fully described by the psychological data alone. The problem of explaining individual differences in the amount of reading done, is a fair example. Much research has assumed that non-readers have not developed the necessary skills and attitudes. But to explain the cases in which readers and non-readers have the same mental equipment, the psychologist must go beyond his proper field. He must ask how far differences in amount and character of reading are due to the amount and character of reading matter available, how far they are due to group attitudes toward reading as such, how far they are due to competing diversions and to other conditions which other departments are more competent than psychology to describe.

Similar help from other departments is needed in psychological studies of the response by different types of personality to different sorts of reading under various conditions of social stress, political changes, racial difference, economic status, and

other influences upon which certain departments have specialized knowledge.

Psychology is plainly the field in which the effects of reading
will be defined with increasing precision, thanks to the progressive analysis of school children's reading. Differences in reading
behavior are related to rates of development in the various
school subjects, command of reading skills, acquaintance with
contemporary affairs, literary appreciation, resistance to propaganda, and other partly measurable traits. Such studies have
gone far to define principles applicable to any age level and are
certain to go further, as hypotheses regarding adult reading are
investigated with cumulative results.

2. *Sociology.*—The sociologist's attention to certain reading
problems is no less direct than the psychologist's. Nor are the
sources and techniques of sociology less important.

Sociology describes group processes at work in different societies through time. Most sociologists pursue the facts of social
change that any given social group may experience. Hence sociology provides hypotheses to explain the changing character of
reading behavior from group to group; for example, popular
preference for fiction of different sorts at different times.

Students of reading may benefit the sociologist to the extent
that they too are obliged to describe the phenomena of group
differences and their changes through time as reflected in reading. The student of reading cannot escape the task of sampling
all the reading done by different groups. Such records supply
the sociologist with data by which to check his own hypotheses
concerning the factors that make for changes in other types of
social behavior. The assumption, for instance, that social disorganization is characterized by the individual's indifference to
the community at large, may be checked by the extent to which
various "disorganized" groups read about the community's problems in local newspapers and magazines.

In so far as students of reading can show what the given social
group wants, how its wants change, how well informed it is on

matters vital to its own interests, and how it tends to regard the larger communities of which it is a part, it is clear that sociology benefits by collaboration with students of reading. Records of community reading can be treated to show the direction of community attitudes; provided, of course, the groups do some reading and that differences in the availability of reading matter are controlled. Studies of community reading should apply as directly to many conventional problems of sociology as the sources and techniques of sociology apply to the interpretation of differences in group reading.

3. *Other social sciences.*—Various other social sciences bear the same reciprocal relation to reading as a field of research. In the nature and amount of reading by contemporary immigrant groups representing different national and racial cultures, anthropology finds a type of data directly pertinent to the present trend of its research in several American institutions. Conversely, the differences in reading behavior found by students of reading to exist among various racial and ethnic groups at different stages of adjustment to American civilization require interpretation by the anthropologist and sociologist.

Departments of geography have no interest in the relation of social institutions to each other but have much interest in the relation of particular institutions, like reading, to the physical differences among regions. Their techniques in mapping areas to show differences in the availability of typical publications, and the like, are particularly useful.

Departments of political science and government have a use for data concerning the reading done by different social groups, at different times and places, on various political or cultural issues, and in various sorts of publications. Students of reading no less require the help of political scientists to explain differences in reading behavior by means of the same hopes and fears that explain political behavior. Both are equally concerned with studies of censorship and propaganda in their many phases, under different governments, and in different periods of time.

Departments of the Second Group

Other departments contribute much to the study of reading, but to date have received little in return. Of such, a good example is history. Historical research supplies the sources, techniques, criteria, and hypotheses without which the evaluation of social communication can neither be described nor understood. Facts about the reading done by different social groups at different periods are meaningless without the background which historical research supplies.

The histories of particular institutions which have stimulated and distributed writing (like monasteries, libraries, publishers, book-dealers, and literary guilds) are by no means complete. Such histories largely remain to be written, with the possible exception of early printing. Far too little is known about the differences among readers of particular writers. How did the contemporary readers of Voltaire differ from those of Rabelais? What are the origins of mass reading—of the *Police Gazette* type? How do literary fashions evolve? Lacking research on previous reading populations, we can only make inferences from the types of writing as such—inferences which when applied to modern publications like mystery stories are clearly false. It is seldom that wise men read only wise books and that fools read only foolish books.

The point here stressed is that historians themselves are better qualified to investigate historical aspects of reading and of the several institutions concerned with literary activities than are students trained in other fields. While historical studies are much needed to clarify contemporary problems in reading, it is not easy to see how historians themselves may be moved to undertake them. Collaboration with non-historians is perhaps more useful to historians of modern periods, where sources are more numerous and easier to interpret, than to historians of earlier periods. For earlier periods historians themselves are the best students of reading behavior.

The relation between economics and the field of reading is

also one-sided. Economists have little reason to expect students of reading to supply facts useful in defining economic values. The student of reading, however, must depend upon the economist for hypotheses needed to explain relationships between economic conditions and trends in reading behavior. Economic interpretations go far to explain major differences in the reading of different groups and communities at different times, as the foregoing chapter testifies. Recent comparisons among European cities, selected to represent different degrees of prosperity, suggest that the social attitudes responsible for different sorts of reading are closely related to differences in economic status. While the student of reading must check the hypotheses proposed by economists, the economic interpretation of reading is a task for the economist himself.

It is possible that the economist may later have his return in the form of hypotheses which bear upon the entire economic policies of different communities. In so far as economic values depend upon what men want, and in so far as reading behavior serves to express such wants, the analysis of community reading through time may be expected to explain changes in economic values—a type of evidence that may prove useful to economic theory. In short, it should interest the economist to know to what extent economic values are determined by ideas obtained by certain groups of people from different sorts of publications.

Other social sciences bear much the same relations to the field of reading that history and economics bear. They afford the student of reading new methods of approaching his problems and new hypotheses for the interpretation of his findings. The entire group of physical and biological sciences doubtless belongs at present in the same category.

Departments of the Third Group

We are here concerned largely with the humanities and professional schools, like journalism, law, and medicine, which are affected by trends of public opinion or in other ways by the recreative and informational values of reading. But while the findings of reading studies apply directly to certain of their professional interests, the schools are not as yet much disposed and are in some cases unable to collaborate effectively.

Philosophy, for example, does not generally employ hypotheses and criteria that bear upon the evaluation of what is read by different sorts of people. Philosophical distinctions are remote from the empirical values defined by contemporary reading studies. Studies by schoolmen to define the values of experiences useful to the school curriculum come much closer home. The philosopher, however, should have a use for facts concerning the attention of different sorts of people to the ideas obtainable from print. Presumably the present hiatus between the two fields, whose objectives are clearly related, can be closed when the benefits are recognized. It is the philosopher and other normative scientists who can best supply the student of reading with what he needs to construct a theory of literary values applicable to popular reading. Such a theory should differ markedly from conventional standards of literary criticism.

The several humanistic departments of literature and language are similarly detached and yet equally concerned with common problems. In so far as students of reading can analyze print to explain its appeal to different groups of readers, they need guidance by those who know the literature. So also the student of literature may reasonably improve his standards of criticism by taking account of values that become explicit in trustworthy records of group reading. So described, the publications preferred by different social groups should help to check hypotheses concerning literary trends that have been formulated without reference to such data.

Departments of law, medicine, business, and journalism bear a similar relation. What legal research might contribute of value to the student of reading is hard to imagine. What legal research might receive is considerable. The jurist's interest in modes of behavior as related to court decisions should extend to popular sanctions of dubious conduct as reflected in current novels, where the arts of persuasion are used to the full in defense of current standards. The relation between popular fiction and popular standards of justice may be close or it may be opposite.

Medicine is another field of application. The therapeutic values of reading have been proclaimed by the medical profession far more than they have been investigated. Yet the problems of selecting reading matter according to the patient's temperament and mental condition should respond readily to the sorts of collaboration here urged. Hospitals should make ideal laboratories for the study of reading in relation to pathological conditions. None to date has permitted such investigation.

Departments of business administration may apply the results of reading studies to many of their typical problems—specifically the merchandising of publications, and also the manifold problems of advertising. Students of community reading should supply the facts and students of business should supply the criteria for efficient administration of commercial propaganda. There is also the more general application of reading trends to the description of business trends. Such description is possible to the extent that analyses of community reading show relationships between types of publications read by different groups and the markets which distinguishable reading groups patronize.

This chapter presents an informal brief for the development of reading as a field of research. The contention throughout is that the field of reading is too extensive and too complicated for any one faculty to occupy. Whether the emphasis be placed, as it is here, upon the social implications of reading in times of crisis, or upon any other broad aspect of the field, substantial progress demands the systematic collaboration of a wide range of specialists. Cooperative research is necessary not merely for the development of an adequate theory regarding reading behavior but also for the application of such theory to the many institutions and social problems that would benefit.

Chapter III

Publications

THE amount and character of what is published each year go far to determine what the various agencies have to distribute. Annual changes in what each agency distributes will naturally affect what is read. We may thus regard changes in publications, distributing agencies, and readers as concentric and progressively larger fields of research in the wide area bounded by people and print.

Publications constitute the innermost circle. Conspicuous changes in the books, magazines, pamphlets, newspapers, and leaflets printed each year have a radiating influence, first upon the shelves of the distributing agencies, and then upon the readers. But the influence extends both ways—from the inside out and from the outside in. Social changes that alter the readers' demands will partly determine what the agencies stock and hence what the publishers print. Only by following the influences in both directions can we distinguish differences in reading behavior due to changes in people from those due to changes in the publication and distribution of reading matter.

Economic adversity affects publication, distribution, and reading—all three, though the effects may appear at different times and in different degrees. Depression hits the publisher hard when his operating capital and credits are threatened or seriously cut. It hits him gradually as the public deletes the item "books" from the domestic budget. Depression has different effects upon the publishing house and upon the publications produced. A newspaper, magazine, or book publisher might conceivably ride the depression without loss by changing his publications to meet changing demands. Or he might suffer reverses which necessitate a thoroughgoing reorganization of his business and still continue to produce about the same publications. The depression probably afflicted the publishers who depend upon advertising more than it afflicted those depending upon sales; but the effects upon the business and the effects upon publications should be distinguished in either case.

In view of the impracticability of dealing more fully with the predepression period in this study, we shall first ask what changes occurred in the publications from 1929 to date. Such changes may imply hypotheses related to the successive stages of the depression. The hypotheses should, in turn, suggest the problems more urgently in need of study to determine social aspects of depression as implied by changes in publication.

BOOKS

The description of books published in any one year may be carried to any desired degree of detail. The titles issued by each publisher appear in their respective announcements, which are conveniently collected in the *Publishers Trade List Annual*. Current books are also listed under various schemes of classification in a wide variety of catalogs, the *Book Review Digest* being one of those more widely used for qualitative description of general books. The *Technical Book Review Index* is no less important in its special field. Thanks to such aids, the student may readily identify whatever titles may express social changes of any suspected character, and then analyze the books themselves for as complete data as he needs regarding the nature and direction of each change. While sociological analysis of literature has received more attention in Europe,[1] the field is not neglected in America.

---

[1] *Cf.* references in Kohn-Bramstedt, Ernst. *Class Distinctions as Reflected in the German Novel of the 19th Century: Aristocracy—Middle Classes—Intellec-*

To analyze each author's reflection of his social environment is a highly specialized and laborious means of defining the social tendencies of contemporary books.[2] Sociology must usually make the best of grosser data. At the farthest remove from analyses of individual books and authors, we have analyses of changes in the number of books published annually in different categories. For an indication of major changes in book production, such data are easier to interpret and are available for each year.

The question, How many books were published each year? may be answered by the number of copies printed, by the number of new titles published, by the number of old titles reprinted and the number of new editions, or by various combinations. Table I permits the comparison of the three categories indicated. All three imply that book production fell with the depression, reaching its depth in 1933-34. As one might expect, reduced sales and other depression conditions are reflected first by the printing of fewer copies, next by fewer new editions and reprintings, and last by fewer new titles. The changes indicated in Table I relate to the first two of the hypotheses stated in the first chapter, that the depression affected the number and character of the publications read, and that changes in popular reading are related to changes in the character of current publications. We are here concerned merely with changes in the number and character of publications, and to the extent of suggesting problems for study.

Table II shows magazine circulation to have resisted depression more successfully than book sales did. Book sales declined from 1929 to 1933 (Table I). They probably declined steadily, though we lack the facts for the even years. The low in 1933 is about half of the 1929 book production. Magazine circulation,

_____

tuals (1830-1900). A study in sociology of literature. University of London. Ph.D. thesis. 1936

[2] For an interesting series of illustrations, see Weeks, Edward. "What Makes a Best Seller?" *New York Times Book Review.* December 20 1936

TABLE I

NUMBER AND INDEX NUMBERS OF BOOKS PRODUCED:
UNITED STATES, 1929–1935

	NUMBER						
	1929	1930	1931	1932	1933	1934	1935
New book titles[a] . . .	8,342	8,134	8,506	7,556	6,813	6,788	6,914
New editions and re-printings[a]	1,845	1,893	1,801	1,479	1,279	1,410	1,852
Total new titles, editions, and reprints. .	10,187	10,027	10,307	9,035	8,092	8,198	8,766
Total number of new copies (in thousands)[b]	214,334[c]	—	154,462	—	110,790[c]	—	140,652[c]

	INDEX NUMBERS (1929 = 100)						
New book titles[a] . . .	100	98	102	91	82	81	83
New editions and re-printings[a]	100	103	98	80	69	76	100
Total new titles, editions, and reprints. .	100	98	101	89	79	80	86
Total number of new copies (in thousands)[b]	100	—	72	—	52	—	66

[a] *The Publishers' Weekly.*
[b] *Biennial Census of Manufactures.* United States Department of Commerce, Bureau of the Census.
[c] These figures from mimeographed release. *Census of Manufactures: 1935.* "Printing and Publishing" (industries numbers 508 and 510). Released April 14 1937

TABLE II

NUMBER AND INDEX NUMBERS OF MAGAZINES PRODUCED AND
CIRCULATION OF SELECTED MAGAZINES: UNITED STATES, 1929–1935

	NUMBER						
	1929	1930	1931	1932	1933	1934	1935
New magazines[a]	202	274	229	245	251	160	226
Discontinued magazines[a] . . .	54	105	96	61	108	52	32
Magazine circulation (in thousands)[b]	57,897	60,894	63,566	58,730	57,785	59,052	60,314

	INDEX NUMBERS (1929 = 100)						
New magazines[a]	100	136	113	121	124	79	112
Discontinued magazines[a] . . .	100	194	178	113	200	96	59
Magazine circulation (in thousands)[b]	100	105	110	101	100	102	104

[a] *Bulletin of Bibliography.* Boston: F. W. Faxon Co.
[b] *Standard Rate and Data Service, Inc.,* Chicago

however, was much tougher. The selected magazines represented
by the index numbers of Table II never yielded beyond the
1929 base line.

From the 1935 release of the *Biennial Census of Manufactures*, "Printing and Publishing," we learn that much the same

TABLE III

NUMBER AND INDEX NUMBERS OF PERIODICALS PRODUCED, BY FREQUENCY
OF PUBLICATION: UNITED STATES, 1929–1935[a]

FREQUENCY OF PUBLICATION	NUMBER (IN THOUSANDS)			
	1929[b]	1931	1933[b]	1935[b]
Weekly	34,495	30,782	39,365	42,648
Semi-monthly	9,168	6,375	4,593	5,508
Monthly	133,048	122,671	103,193	102,194
Quarterly	20,605	19,576	23,238	23,277
Other	2,346	1,978	1,742	2,161
Total	199,662	181,382	172,131	175,788

INDEX NUMBERS (1929 = 100)

Weekly	100	89	114	124
Semi-monthly	100	70	50	60
Monthly	100	92	78	77
Quarterly	100	95	113	113
Other	100	84	74	92
Total	100	91	86	88

[a] *Biennial Census of Manufactures*. United States Department of Commerce, Bureau of the Census,
[b] These figures from mimeographed release. *Census of Manufactures, 1935*. "Printing and Publishing," (industries numbers 508 and 510). Released April 14 1937

is true of all periodicals published. The circulation of the nation's periodicals, classed by frequency of publication, is presented in Table III. The index for total periodical circulation
in 1933 drops only to 86 as against the drop to 52 for books.
The fortnightlies, a very small class of periodicals,[3] suffered
most and fell to 50 in 1933. The monthlies fell to 78, and the
"other," the smallest class, fell to 74. The quarterlies and the
weeklies both rose, to 113 and 114, respectively.

[3] Only 224 of them in 1929 as against 2,799 monthlies

The stronger resistance of magazines to depression may be due partly to loyalties born of habitual reading, to the sales pressure of advertisers which books do not enjoy, to the lower cost of magazines, to the variety and brevity of their articles (which make môst magazines fit more moods than most books will fit), and to their easier availability—whether purchased or merely read. Each of these incentives to reading during depression and several others will be noticed as the discussion proceeds. We are here only making the point that comparisons between annual book and magazine publication since 1929 supply many interesting hypotheses for studies to determine shifts in the relative strength of various influences upon publishing during depression.

Another obvious comparison of Tables I and II concerns the annual fluctuations of book reprints and new editions as related to the number of magazines discontinued each year. One may suppose that both, to some extent, reflect the publishers' conviction that the depression reduced the demand further for certain existing books and magazines than for others.

From the second rows of index numbers in Tables I and II it is plain that old books found it much easier to survive then old magazines. The book reprintings fell to 69 in 1933 but the "discontinuance" of magazines rose to 200. In 1935 the magazines made a far better recovery; for each 100 magazines which died in 1929 only 59 died in 1935, and for each 100 new magazines in 1929 there were 112 in 1935. The book reprintings in 1929 and 1935 were the same, and the new book titles in 1935 rose from its low point in 1934 only to 83. The social implications of this contrast are red meat to the student of reading. They imply that the magazines' appeal is more mercurial; that the substantial book has a more persistent social appeal; that the success of most magazines, depending largely upon advertisers, responds more promptly to fluctuations in purchasing power;

that the psychology of the recent depression, which drove most readers to the distraction of the magazine and a few readers to the solace of the solid book, was more receptive to the magazine. Each of these implications can be evaluated by the relation of facts suggested by Tables I, II, and III to the available evidence concerning reading behavior.

A third obvious comparison involves the top row of index numbers in the two tables. The implications are much the same as those first noted. The birth of books and the birth of magazines during depression result from some common factors and from some peculiar factors. It would be useful to sociology to differentiate the factors tending to produce new books and new magazines respectively. The common factors represent the publishers' opinions as to what depression readers as such most want to read. Such opinions are important in so far as they are valid. Their validity can be checked to some extent by relative sales. Their importance lies in the effects of publications upon social attitudes and the effects of social attitudes upon what is published.

It is evident from the tables that in each year reported except 1934 the index of new magazines was above the 1929 level. In contrast the index of new book titles surpassed that of 1929 only in 1931. Moreover, the number of new magazines each year is at least over twice as large (and in 1932 it is four times as large) as the number of magazines discontinued. Hence changes in the character of new magazines should be a more sensitive index of changes in the publishers' diagnosis of depression demand than changes in the character of new books.

The corresponding comparison of the two upper rows of index numbers in Table I supports a similar generalization concerning books: the index of new titles exceeded that of the reprintings for each of the years reported, excepting 1930 and 1935. The new titles express the publishers' idea of the depres-

TABLE IV

NUMBER AND INDEX NUMBERS OF NEW BOOK TITLES AND NEW EDITIONS AND REPRINTS, BY SUBJECT CATEGORIES: UNITED STATES, 1929–1935[a]

Subject Category	New Titles							New Editions and Reprints						
	1929	1930	1931	1932	1933	1934	1935	1929	1930	1931	1932	1933	1934	1935
Fiction	1,340	1,348	1,272	1,384	1,317	1,356	1,362	802	755	670	604	489	543	677
Sociology and economics	450	472	580	610	573	622	616	34	51	52	40	48	52	75
Fine arts and music	154	265	277	230	254	198	258	22	27	24	24	14	18	31
Games and sports	114	123	156	174	147	110	152	16	19	14	8	7	24	23
History	380	386	421	420	434	433	359	37	45	66	45	30	54	88
Philosophy and religion	1,021	1,029	1,009	904	782	765	690	91	100	73	47	69	50	83
Juvenile	788	771	873	579	523	466	532	143	164	145	139	103	135	138
Biography	667	699	699	603	506	435	471	71	93	76	82	39	50	77
Travel and geography	313	314	287	234	213	220	174	60	71	100	44	30	44	38
Science, medicine	685	607	686	619	556	578	527	141	173	185	148	161	156	206
Poetry and drama	1,065	1,027	1,049	831	684	785	845	234	208	156	129	112	135	195
All others	1,265	1,093	1,197	968	823	820	928	194	187	240	169	177	149	221
Total	8,242	8,134	8,506	7,556	6,812	6,788	6,914	1,845	1,893	1,801	1,479	1,279	1,410	1,852

Index Numbers (1929 = 100)

Subject Category	New Titles							New Editions and Reprints						
	1929	1930	1931	1932	1933	1934	1935	1929	1930	1931	1932	1933	1934	1935
Fiction	100	101	95	103	98	101	102	100	94	84	75	61	68	84
Sociology and economics	100	105	129	136	127	138	137	100	150	153	118	141	153	221
Fine arts and music	100	172	180	149	165	129	168	100	123	109	109	64	82	141
Games and sports	100	108	137	153	129	96	133	100	119	88	50	44	150	144
History	100	102	111	111	114	114	94	100	122	178	122	81	146	238
Philosophy and religion	100	101	99	89	77	75	68	100	110	80	52	76	55	91
Juvenile	100	98	111	73	66	59	68	100	115	101	97	72	94	97
Biography	100	105	105	90	76	65	71	100	131	107	115	55	70	108
Travel and geography	100	100	92	75	68	70	56	100	118	167	73	50	73	63
Science, medicine	100	89	100	90	81	84	77	100	123	131	105	114	111	146
Poetry and drama	100	96	98	78	64	74	79	100	89	67	55	38	58	83
All others	100	86	95	77	65	65	73	100	96	124	87	91	77	114
Total	100	99	103	92	83	82	84	100	102	98	80	69	76	100

[a] *The Publishers' Weekly*

sion demand, even though less clearly than new magazines and for a different area of the population. The titles reprinted, of course, reflect actual sales, a far more trustworthy indication of demand than the appearance of new titles. Analyses of particular books not reprinted by a few of the leading publishing houses might define changes in demand more clearly.

Table IV advances the discussion by showing what changes occurred during depression in the character of books published. Here also the contrast between new titles and reprintings or new editions of old titles implies cultural changes during depression, although conclusions of this type are necessarily tentative until checked against the long time trends.

The changes in new book titles may be classified under three captions: slight change, increases above the 1929 level, and decreases below the 1929 level.

The only entry under "slight change" is fiction. Although the index numbers for fiction fluctuate somewhat, they at no time exceed the 1929 level by more than 3 per cent nor drop below it by more than 5 per cent.

The influence of depression upon the publication of fiction books is most evident in the fluctuations of reprints. The index numbers for reprints steadily decline from 1929 to 1933, and decline farther than the index numbers for all reprints. It would be necessary and useful to examine the relation of new titles to reprints over a longer period of time to learn how much the falling off in reprints is due to a general trend toward more fiction titles with smaller editions and how much to a change in popular taste that may have occurred during the depression.

In two categories, sociology and economics, and fine arts and music, the indexes of new titles stand above the 1929 level throughout the period. This is true of games and sports except for 1934 and of history except for 1935. From the index numbers, the largest increase in new titles above the 1929 level in any year occurred in fine arts and music, the next largest in games and sports, the third in sociology and economics, and the fourth in history.

The fine arts category is naturally interesting because it suggests the hypothesis that cultural interests rose in popular esteem as business activity fell off. The index numbers of 180 in 1931 and 165 in 1933 are impressive. To carry the hypothesis into a study of the particular aspects of the fine arts on which most books appeared would be very much worthwhile. The operation of a depression influence is further implied by the fact that the reprintings of fine arts, which increased 23 per cent in 1930, dropped to 9 per cent above the 1929 level in 1931 and 1932, and then fell below the 1929 level. Despite the fact that the number of reprints was small throughout the period it is apparent that the depression caused publishers to issue different sorts of books on the fine arts; and the same is true of games and sports, which has a somewhat similar pattern.

In sociology and economics, in contrast, new editions and reprints show even larger increases than new titles. This is also true of history except for 1933. Social, economic, and historical subjects were clearly of interest to writers and publishers during depression. Whether they held the same relative interest for readers we shall ask later.

The remaining seven categories of books all lost more than they gained in new titles. The index numbers raise many hypotheses on effects of the depression which should justify research. The research should relate changes in publication within each category to contemporary events that seem likely to have changed the complexion of popular interest or changed the publishers' estimates of the interest, and should also check the changes which have occurred during the period studied, with the long time trends.

It is possible, for example, that the apparent lack of correlation between the index of new book titles in fiction and the business cycle is due only to the absence of a longer time series.

If the long time trend in new fiction titles was upward, the apparent stability of this index might actually represent a positive correlation with the business cycle in that an increase in new titles was checked. The student must be exceedingly cautious in interpreting depression effects from limited data of this type.

Some hypotheses taken at random that might be posited from the data presented are as follows: (1) Juvenile new titles fell off because they are generally regarded as luxuries. The increase in new titles in 1931, and the only annual increase, represents a publishing experiment to reach well-to-do book buyers who were least frightened by the depression. (2) Biography is aimed in general at the same market that buys books on travel. It has much the comforting and distracting effect of fiction and sold well, especially in reprints, until the beginning of recovery, 1933. Thereafter it was displaced by new titles on current affairs. (3) The reprintings in travel and geography which flourished until 1932 reflected good sales to persons eager but too poor to travel but not too poor to buy travel books. The falling off thereafter, in both new titles and reprints, was due, as in biography, to a shift toward the exciting current publications of the presidential year and to other subjects which publishers considered of more immediate interest. (4) Poetry and drama were not pushed because publishers anticipated losses except for the gift book and school markets. (5) The total column of index numbers in Table IV implies that publishers were adding more titles in 1929 than the market would stand and that they are making the most of the market for reprints and new editions. (6) The categories in which publication of new titles was most affected by depression as against the long time trend are those in which the 1935 index numbers are the highest and the lowest, namely, fine arts and music, sociology and economics, and games and sports for the highs; and travel and geography, philosophy and religion, juvenile, and biography for the lows. This hypothesis is not so obvious as to discourage investigation, because the long time trend and various conditions affecting publishers, which were unrelated to the depression, may prove the better explanations. All six hypotheses deserve investigation.

Table V raises further interesting questions by shifting attention to the number of copies produced annually as related to changes in new titles and reprints. The index numbers show patterns very different from those of Table IV. To determine the normal relation, if any, between number of new titles and number of copies produced in typical categories would greatly simplify analyses of book production. New titles are more easily dealt with because they are promptly announced by each publisher, whereas the number of copies is very hard to determine accurately. The marked discrepancies between number of titles and number of copies of fiction books, for example, suggest widespread experimenting with small editions. It would thus be useful to study the causes and effects of this experimental policy.

Hypothetical relationships between the number of new titles and sales have no validity, of course, until sales conditions are studied directly and in terms of the various economic, sociological, political, and psychological differences among the buyers of different books. The salvation of the publishing industry may well depend upon such studies, which have yet to be undertaken by any one publisher or group of publishers, excepting only the Association of German Book Publishers[4] in Leipzig. The student who does determine how closely the number of new titles published annually in any one field is related to the number of copies sold, will have made an important step toward the knowledge of conditions which determine the successful book.

Coming at Table V directly, we may use the data presented to compare publishers' opinions of public demand, as suggested by the number of new titles, with actual sales, as suggested by

[4] The best account in English of *Der Börsenverein von Deutschen Buchhändler* is probably Unwin, Stanley P. *The Truth about Publishing.* Boston and New York: Houghton Mifflin Co. 1927

the number of copies printed. As a basis we may compare the total index numbers in the odd years for the categories shown in Table V. They are:

	1929	1931	1933	1935
Total New Titles	100	104	88	90
Total Number of Copies	100	72	45	52

It appears that new titles for these categories increased in 1931 while total number of copies (of new titles, new editions, and reprints) decreased, and although new titles were fewer in

TABLE V

NUMBER OF COPIES AND INDEX NUMBERS OF BOOKS PUBLISHED FOR SIX SELECTED SUBJECT CATEGORIES: UNITED STATES, 1929-1935[a]

SUBJECT CATEGORY	NUMBER (IN THOUSANDS)				INDEX NUMBERS (1929 = 100)			
	1929[b]	1931	1933[b]	1935[b]	1929	1931	1933	1935
Fiction	26,880	19,249	11,528	15,240	100	72	43	57
Sociology and economics . .	1,052	620	1,114	1,013	100	59	106	96
Philosophy and religion. . .	17,626	13,181	7,430	6,639	100	75	42	38
Biography	2,714	2,176	1,449	2,575	100	80	53	95
Fine arts and music	1,134	724	335	166	100	64	30	15
Poetry and drama	4,048	2,590	1,990	2,268	100	64	49	56
Total	53,454	38,540	23,846	27,901	100	72	45	52

[a] *Biennial Census of Manufactures*. United States Department of Commerce, Bureau of the Census.
[b] These figures from mimeographed release. *Census of Manufactures, 1935.* "Printing and Publishing," (industries numbers 508 and 510). Released April 14 1937

1933 and 1935 than in 1929, they did not decrease as much as the number of copies decreased.

Taking the categories separately, we note that new titles in fiction held close to the 1929 figure throughout, whereas copies of fiction lost 28 per cent in 1931, 57 per cent in 1933, and 43 per cent in 1935. This discrepancy is most natural in fiction, since the publishers are always groping for a best seller that will recoup a score of novels that do not repay the costs of production, thus producing many titles in experimental editions. It would be helpful to compare these ratios of titles to copies with similar ratios for pre- and postdepression years.

In sociology and economics the number of copies fell in 1931 to 59 per cent of the 1929 number, when new titles rose 29 per cent above the 1929 level. This again may imply the publishers' overestimate of popular interest in the why's of the depression. Sociology and economics differ, however, from the other categories in that new editions and reprints were strong, as we have noted, and also in that the number of copies as well as the number of new titles actually rose in 1933 above the 1929 base. The bad year 1933 tended to discourage publishing experiments, of course, but it also tended to sharpen the book reading public's curiosity to learn what was coming next. Thus book publication in sociology and economics does show a depression spurt as one might expect it to do. But, as in all such cases, the changes in sociology and economics publications since 1929 should be related to the trend line since 1920 or earlier to learn how wide the depression deviations really are. It is likewise important to break down the category to see whether some particular phase like New Deal legislation is not mainly responsible for the apparent rise of the entire category in book production.

Much the same comment applies to biography as shown in Table V, though only in 1935 does biography match sociology and economics in relative number of copies produced on the base of 1929. The actual number of copies in biography are shown by Table V to be two and one half times as many as in sociology and economics in 1935. Only in 1933 do the two categories yield comparable numbers of actual copies, and then biography produced 335,000 more. It would be good to know whether good or bad times do more to stimulate book production in biography. It is easier to suppose that bad times do, since the timely choice of biographical subjects by publishers offers a book that fairly combines the "escape" interest of fiction with the analysis of social change to be found in current sociology.

The steady shrinkage during depression of book copies in philosophy and religion, from seventeen to six million, is somewhat astonishing. The number of titles also decreased but not so much. In 1931 and 1933 the index numbers for copies printed are about the same as those for the total of all six categories shown in Table V. Philosophy and religion printed two-thirds as many copies as did fiction in 1929, and copies in both categories fell off at about the same rate until 1935, when the two part company. We cannot therefore impute any sinister effect of depression peculiar to book production in religion and philosophy. Here again we need to know what sorts of books figured largely in the 17 million copies of 1929, and why the publishers failed to capitalize the depression in the interests of books on philosophy and religion as they apparently did in the much smaller field of sociology and economics. A fair guess at the latter question is that the purchasers of the more technical books on sociology and economics were more prosperous throughout the depression than the purchasers of books on the popular philosophies.

Fine arts is the field in which the depression saw the largest increase in the number of new titles since 1929, yet the index of copies decreases more than any of the six categories shown in Table V, and the 1935 number was only 15 per cent of that printed in 1929. The fine arts pattern is not unlike that of philosophy and religion and the two may have similar explanations. In so far as number of copies is an index of sales, it may be that the depression encouraged the contemplation and even the production of art and discouraged the former book buyers from reading about it. If so, the fact might explain the apparent recklessness of publishers in the number of new titles produced in the hope of directing the apparent increase in artistic interests since 1932 toward the purchase of books on the arts. This hypothesis would not be hard to check.

Poetry and drama also reduced copies during the depression to about the same extent as the six categories combined. The pattern resembles those of philosophy and religion, and fine arts. It invites the same sort of further analysis, to the end of fuller knowledge of the depression's escape psychology as book publishers tried to exploit it.

MAGAZINES

Surveys in predepression years have found at least two magazine readers to one book reader. The ratio of those who read something in some magazine to those who digest any one substantial book is not less than six to one, and probably much larger. Hence changes in social attitudes should be more reliably inferred from changes in magazine production than from changes in book production from 1929 to date.

But such advantages in the numerical superiority of magazine readers to book readers are somewhat offset by the miscellaneous content of most magazines. The advertisers' considerations sometimes overshadow the readers' preferences and may have more effect upon editorial and production policies. Advertisers want wide circulation within one or more consumer populations. Hence general magazines seek to attract every sort of reader by extending the variety of their contents. When a general magazine makes a sudden spurt in sales one seldom knows whether the spurt is due to a single popular feature (e.g., stories by a certain author), to the peculiarity of the magazine as a whole (e.g., the new *Life*), or to the variety of content as such (e.g., the many digests). The interpretation of group changes in magazine preference is also hindered by the fact that most "regular" readers of a general magazine skip more than they read. The greater uniformity of content in "class" magazines (e.g., the *Spur*, the *Christian Century*) simplifies interpretation of changes in sales. These considerations suggest the value of analysing magazine circulation in order to clarify sociological implications. Many readers of the more widely circulating magazines probably read them for reasons irrelevant to the type of interest implied by the titles. We need to know what the reasons are.

An approach to the interpretation of changes in magazine production since 1929 can be made by comparing the production of books and magazines in categories where both figures are available. Tables V and VI permit such comparisons in a few categories which are roughly comparable, namely, fiction with the fiction magazines; sociology and economics with monthly reviews, weekly news, and liberal and radical; philosophy and religion with religious magazines; fine arts and music with fine arts magazines. It is usually dangerous to class magazines and books in the same categories. Most of the widely read magazines defy classification under any of the headings used to report gross book production. But it would be important to determine the possibility of relating book and magazine production in common fields of interest. Properly refined comparisons should show whether the depression stimulated a taste for piecemeal publications as against the more sustaining book, or vice versa, in each field, and, where the data are still obtainable, for different groups of readers.

Table VI gets at the social implications of magazine production, by showing the production of magazines each year in the period from 1929 to 1935. To describe the influence of advertisers we need facts concerning annual changes both in the volume and in the lineage cost of advertising in each category of magazines. Table VII says that changes in lineage cost do not affect circulation. The Audit Bureau of Circulation, Chicago, the standard source of data on advertising *volume,* has thus far confined its reports to newspapers, but intends to report on volume of magazine advertising beginning January 1937. To interpret changes in magazine circulation, it is clearly essential for students to show the effect of changes in receipts from advertising upon changes in selling costs, and hence upon sales.

Changes in magazine production are pointed by the index numbers of copies sold for the twenty-two classes of magazines shown in Table VI. Theoretically one might expect relationships

TABLE VI

NUMBER OF COPIES AND INDEX NUMBERS OF MAGAZINES SOLD, FOR SELECTED SUBJECT CATEGORIES: SELECTED CITIES, 1929–1935[a]

Subject Category	Number (in thousands)							Index Numbers (1929 = 100)						
	1929	1930	1931	1932	1933	1934	1935	1929	1930	1931	1932	1933	1934	1935
True Story and other love	2,995	3,185	2,930	2,526	2,889	3,330	3,905	100	106	98	84	96	111	130
Detective and adventure	2,370	3,442	4,554	1,473	2,939	3,590	3,277	100	145	192	62	124	151	138
All radio and movie	1,443	1,527	2,387	2,503	2,428	2,498	1,994	100	106	165	173	168	173	138
Five cent weeklies	6,816	7,597	7,654	7,303	7,191	7,303	7,422	100	111	112	107	106	107	109
Mediocre and medium priced monthlies (stories and articles)	4,906	4,684	4,697	4,388	4,312	4,352	4,572	100	95	96	89	88	89	93
Humorous weeklies	313	294	248	216	186	194	205	100	94	79	69	59	62	65
Religious	396	381	320	300	321	292	288	100	96	81	76	81	74	73
Fine arts (non-technical)	262	192	175	192	193	163	164	100	73	67	73	74	62	63
Parents', women's, home	18,083	18,926	19,252	19,110	18,045	18,433	18,530	100	105	106	106	100	102	102
Juvenile	1,719	1,420	1,451	1,531	1,521	1,315	1,564	100	83	84	89	88	76	91
Quality	569	596	501	407	354	282	509	100	105	88	72	62	50	89
Elite	164	180	212	208	199	346	448	100	110	129	127	121	211	273
Monthly reviews	332	472	480	171	292	294	317	100	142	145	52	88	89	95
Popular science and mechanics	1,586	1,579	1,581	1,558	1,511	1,645	1,667	100	100	100	98	95	104	105
Weekly news	2,521	2,892	2,759	2,699	2,242	2,546	2,594	100	115	109	107	89	101	103
Liberal and radical	221	206	253	160	160	140	166	100	93	114	72	72	63	75
Sports and outdoors	872	756	852	829	827	925	844	100	87	98	95	95	106	97
Fraternal	2,265	1,881	2,402	2,492	2,137	1,849	1,951	100	83	106	110	94	82	86
Farm	7,524	8,050	8,319	8,255	7,965	7,745	7,706	100	107	111	110	106	103	102
Travel and foreign lands	1,389	1,437	1,387	1,245	1,102	1,042	1,121	100	103	100	90	79	75	81
Business, commerce, and finance	781	820	796	750	673	433	726	100	105	102	96	86	55	93
Health	372	380	357	416	298	337	346	100	102	96	112	80	91	93
Total	57,899	60,897	63,567	58,732	57,785	59,054	60,316	100	105	110	101	100	102	104

[a] *Standard Rate and Data Service, Inc.*

of three types: a positive correlation with the business cycle, a negative correlation, or no correlation. Examples of changes in production positively correlated with the business cycle are furnished by the categories true story and other love, mediocre, and medium priced monthlies, humorous weeklies, juvenile, quality, monthly reviews, liberal and radical, travel and business, commerce and finance. Of these magazines true story and other love recovered most quickly and by 1935 were 30 per cent above the 1929 level. On the other hand, humorous magazines

TABLE VII

NUMBER AND PERCENTAGE DISTRIBUTION OF SELECTED MAGAZINES BY STATUS OF ADVERTISING RATES AND CIRCULATION: UNITED STATES[a]

Status of Advertising Rates and Circulation, 1929–1935	Number	Percent of Total
Magazines increasing regularly in both circulation and advertising rates .	12	24
Magazines decreasing regularly in both circulation and advertising rates .	19	38
Magazines maintaining same circulation and advertising rates	8	16
Magazines decreasing in circulation with same advertising rates	7	14
Magazines incomplete, i.e., not published continuously	4	8
Total	50	100

[a] Compiled from *Standard Rate and Data Service, Inc.*

recovered most slowly and in 1935 stood at only 65 per cent of their 1929 level. Instances of changes in production negatively correlated with the business cycle are radio and movie magazines, parents', women's and home, and farm. Each of these was still above its 1929 level in 1935. The remaining categories of magazines (detective and adventure, five cent weeklies, religious, fine arts, elite, popular science and mechanics, weekly news, fraternal, and health) show no definite relation to the business cycle. This observation, however, and also the relationships described above, should be checked against the long time trends in order to isolate the depression influences. In this last class of magazines are to be found instances of publications which showed a fairly continuous increase throughout the period studied, e.g., elite; publications with a fairly continuous decrease, e.g., religious; publications which remained relatively constant, e.g., popular science and mechanics; and finally, publications which were irregular in their production, as exemplified by detective and adventure magazines.

Each of these relationships raises interesting questions which we lack the facts to answer. Assuming as we must that our classifications are valid, we wonder whether humorous magazines lost as they did because the depression found no relief in humor, or because the subscribers found too little fun in them and the advertisers too small returns to justify the expense. Again, why should magazines on religion and the fine arts sell so much better in 1933 than did books on both subjects as inferred from copies printed, of which the index numbers are 42 and 30 respectively? Were the books and magazines bought by the same people? What satisfactions can be found in the magazines but not in the books? Or was the difference due to difference in price?[5] Most interesting of all, perhaps, is the performance of liberal and radical magazines. They reached their peak in 1931, lost about 42 per cent of their circulation the following (election) year, and also in 1933, lost 9 per cent more and hit bottom in 1934, and regained some of the loss in 1935. Dependable information on the annual turnover among subscribers to liberal magazines during these years might explain such changes. The changes in Table VI invite one sort of interpretation if we assume that the magazines were read by the same sort of readers in different amounts between 1929 and 1935. They invite a very different sort of interpretation if we assume a large turnover in their readers, say from 1931 to 1933 and from 1934 to 1935.

Another interesting group consists of the four magazine types which clearly prospered during depression or recovered quickly from a temporary setback, to new highs, namely, true story and love stories, detective and adventure, radio and movie, and elite.

[5] See Table X

The last caters to readers whose ability to pay for magazines was least affected. The other three types represent the cheapest magazine reading thrills obtainable by literates. The large consumption of such undoubtedly explains much of the loss of other publications. The rise of the three mass fiction types is explained by the increased leisure of those who prefer them and also by their low cost—10, 15, or 20 cents. The spectacular rise of the élite, smart, or swank magazine is largely due, of course, to phenomena like the *New Yorker* and especially *Esquire*. It would be highly useful to study the new magazines that did not prosper.

In general, Table VI provokes many important questions. It invites studies to distinguish the psychological from the purely commercial factors responsible for the changes shown, to examine the psychological factors in relation to hypotheses like those presented in the first chapter, and to estimate the validity of magazine sales as an index of cultural change.

The wide difference in the number of magazines in each category makes it risky to deal with categories instead of individual publications. Statistical corrections by which magazines of similar type might be compared by a standard unit of circulation have not been made because the categories are plainly incomplete. The many magazines for which circulation data are not available (e.g., scientific journals, ".courtesy" or controlled circulation magazines, pamphlets that carry no advertising, and many purely local papers) should be included before annual changes in selected classes of magazines, as sampled, can explain changes in the character of magazine production as such. The urgent technical problem is the collection of sales and circulation data that will meet the needs of the student as distinguished from the needs of the advertiser.

The facts of Table VI concern only some two hundred of the better known magazines in the twenty-two categories in selected cities. It is well therefore to conclude this reference to magazine production by noticing the behavior of *all* magazines as reported by the *Biennial Census of Manufactures.* (See Table VIII.) The discrepancies between apparently similar categories

TABLE VIII

CIRCULATION OF MAGAZINES AND INDEX NUMBERS OF CIRCULATION, BY SUBJECT CATEGORY OF MAGAZINE: UNITED STATES, 1929–1935[a]

SUBJECT CATEGORY OF MAGAZINE	CIRCULATION (IN THOUSANDS)				INDEX NUMBERS (1929 = 100)			
	1929	1931	1933	1935	1929	1931	1933	1935
Agriculture, stock raising, etc. . . .	20,285	21,581	19,974	19,135	100	106	98	94
Art, music, and drama	1,297	888	673	389	100	68	52	30
Automobiles, motor boats, etc. . .	2,105	2,057	2,159	1,397	100	98	103	66
Commerce, finance, and insurance .	3,130	2,046	1,775	2,165	100	65	57	69
Educational	2,848	4,416	4,058	5,536	100	155	142	194
Fraternal	9,412	8,453	5,848	5,901	100	90	62	63
Labor (by labor organizations) . .	3,344	3,146	1,940	3,125	100	94	58	93
Legal	177	206	161	186	100	116	91	105
Medicine, surgery, and dentistry. .	1,961	1,232	1,218	1,323	100	63	62	67
Motion pictures	2,316	4,434	3,456	3,365	100	191	149	145
News summaries, general literature, and fiction	62,880	62,339	59,897	60,201	100	99	95	96
Religion (denominational)	41,629	36,581	45,704	45,756	100	88	110	110
Science and technology	2,989	3,579	2,118	3,403	100	120	71	114
Society, fashion, beauty culture, etc.	22,600	13,652	11,059	7,839	100	60	49	35
Sports, games, and amusements . .	2,302	2,376	1,997	3,550	100	103	87	154
Trade journals not elsewhere classified	7,806	8,415	6,176	6,732	100	108	79	86
University and college	973	879	729	636	100	90	75	65
Miscellaneous	13,705	7,238	5,819	7,975	100	53	42	58
Total	201,759	183,518	174,761	178,614	100	91	87	89

[a] *Biennial Census of Manufactures.* United States Department of Commerce, Bureau of the Census.

in Tables VI and VIII, respectively, are attributable to variations in category content and to possible bias in the sample. Four types of periodicals produced the largest number of copies in 1929, namely, (1) news summaries, general literature, and fiction; (2) religion; (3) agriculture, stock raising, etc.; (4) society, fashions, beauty culture, etc. All four declined in the number of titles published,[6] and all but the religious magazines (which gained 10 per cent) lost circulation by 1933. However, the losses of the first and third classes were negligible (5 and 2 per cent, respectively). The other large category (society, fashions, beauty culture, etc.) lost half (51 per cent) of its 1929 circulation by 1933. Three small categories—(1) educational, (2) motion pictures, and (3) automobiles, motor boats, etc.— sold more copies in 1933 than in 1929: 42 per cent, 49 per cent, and 3 per cent, respectively. All other types of periodicals printed less in 1933 than in 1929. Some (agricultural, educational, legal, motion pictures, science, sports, and trade journals, circulated more in 1931 than in 1929, but lost all or part of their gains by 1933. Some types (automobiles and religion) lost in 1931 but gained in 1933 over 1929. In each case students should meet the question, Why? The sociological implications warrant further study.

NEWSPAPERS

Data annually reported by *Editor and Publisher* and by *N. W. Ayer & Son's Directory of Newspapers and Periodicals* show the number of daily newspapers to have decreased since about 1917. In 1920 there were 2,042 dailies. In 1929 there were 1,944. (See Table IX.) During the depression years the number reached a low point of 1,911 in 1933, the smallest number of English language daily newspapers printed in the United States at any time during the present century. Even in 1900 there were more than two thousand daily newspapers published.[7] After 1933 the number increased, and by 1935 *Editor and Publisher* listed 1,950 daily newspapers, the largest number since 1927, when the total was 1,949.

---

[6] For years indicated see *Biennial Census of Manufactures*. U. S. Department of Commerce, Bureau of the Census.

[7] The number of daily newspapers in 1899 was 2,167. This figure was obtained from page 36 of a study by Masche, W. Carl. *Factors Involved in the Consolida-*

The decrease in number of different English language daily newspapers through 1933 contrasts sharply with the increased circulation of the same papers through 1930. From 1920 to 1930, inclusive, when the number of dailies declined from 2,042 to

TABLE IX

NUMBER OF DAILY AND SUNDAY ENGLISH LANGUAGE NEWSPAPERS, AND TOTAL AND PER CAPITA CIRCULATION: UNITED STATES, 1920–1935[a]

YEAR	DAILY NEWSPAPERS			SUNDAY NEWSPAPERS		
	NUMBER	CIRCULATION (IN THOUSANDS)	CIRCULATION PER 100 POPULATION[b]	NUMBER	CIRCULATION (IN THOUSANDS)	CIRCULATION PER 100 POPULATION[b]
1920	2,042	27,791	26.1	522	17,084	16.0
1921	2,028	28,424	26.3	545	19,041	17.6
1922	2,033	29,780	27.1	546	19,713	17.9
1923	2,036	31,454	28.2	547	21,463	19.2
1924	2,014	32,999	29.2	539	22,220	19.6
1925	2,008	33,739	29.4	548	23,355	20.3
1926	2,001	36,002	30.9	545	24,435	21.0
1927	1,949	37,967	32.1	526	25,469	21.5
1928	1,939	37,973	31.7	522	25,771	21.5
1929	1,944	39,426	32.4	528	26,880	22.1
1930	1,942	39,589	32.1	521	26,413	21.4
1931	1,923	38,761	31.2	513	25,702	20.7
1932	1,913	36,408	29.2	518	24,860	19.9
1933	1,911	35,175	28.0	506	24,041	19.1
1934	1,929	36,709	29.0	505	26,545	21.0
1935	1,950	38,156	30.0	518	28,147	22.1

[a] The figures are those of the annual editions of the *International Year Book Number* of *Editor and Publisher*. They appear every year as part of a single page summary table indexed under the title "Ready Reckoner." The number of paper is as of December 31 of the given year.

[b] Population estimates as of July 1. Data from *Statistical Abstract of the United States*, United States Department of Commerce, 1935. For a more refined analysis of per capita circulation the population 10 years of age and over, or the literate population 10 years of age and over, can be substituted for the total population.

1,942 (a loss of 4.9 per cent), circulation of the same dailies increased from approximately 28 million to 40 million (a gain of

tion and Suspension of Daily and Sunday Newspapers in the United States Since 1900: A Statistical Study in Social Change. University of Minnesota. Unpublished M.A. thesis. 1932. Pp. 190. The figures are compiled from *Ayer's*. The available *Editor and Publisher* figures since 1920 differ from the *Ayer* figures by amounts that vary from year to year. In 1920 *Editor and Publisher* listed 2,042 dailies, and *Ayer's* listed 2,324. In 1933 *Editor and Publisher* gave 1,911 and *Ayer's* gave 1,902.

43 per cent). From the peak year[8] of 1930 the circulation fell to a low of 35 million in 1933, but rose again both in 1934 and 1935, reaching 38 million in the latter year. Although this was still one and one-half million less than the peak circulation of 1930, the indications are that the 1936 daily circulation figures will equal or exceed those of the previous peak year. It is interesting to note that per capita circulation increased steadily through the twenties (with a very slight recession in 1928). Changes subsequent to 1929 did not differ greatly from changes in total circulation.

It would appear that, prior to the depression, the number of newspaper titles decreased and the circulation increased, suggesting a trend toward the concentration of newspapers in fewer hands. Such concentration would seem to be distinguishable from the growth of chain ownership, which involves a concentration of newspaper properties as well as circulation, and from increase in the number of newspapers because of population increases in the cities of publication. The comparisons should show which papers are disappearing—whether the small paper in the small town, the small paper in the larger cities, or the medium sized papers. The facts will relate to cultural changes in so far as the three types of paper differ in content. The problems in analysing changes in circulation are sociologically important to the degree that differences in content are

---

[8] The *International Year Book Number* of *Editor and Publisher* gives *annual* total circulation which is in terms of the aggregate average circulation per issue over a six-month period ending September 30. The regular issues of *Editor and Publisher* give data on circulation for the six-month period ending March 31, although the figures are not available for every year. The highest calculated circulations for total daily and Sunday papers were recorded for the six-month period having its midpoint on January 1, 1930. The actual peak in circulation was, therefore, reached somewhere between July 1, 1929 and July 1, 1930. The peak calculated circulations for the six-month period ending March 31, 1930 (the midpoint being January 1, 1930), were 40,078,892 for total daily and 27,488,682 for Sunday. See *Editor and Publisher*. 63:12. July 19 1930

known. Far too little work has been done to differentiate the presentation of the same news by different papers.

From 1930 through 1933 the previously increasing total and per capita circulation fell sharply. But in 1934, when the circulation rose for the first time since 1930, the number of papers, instead of continuing its long time downward trend, showed an increase. In 1935 when circulation rose again, the number of dailies also rose.

The increase in circulation is patently due to the improvement in business conditions. But does the increase in the number of papers indicate the rise during depression of new factors which upset the trends before 1930? Has the trend toward concentration changed? Here again the answer probably lies in analyses of the number and circulation of daily newspapers in relation to population trends by years since 1920 at least. The analysis can be made from the *International Year Book Numbers* of *Editor and Publisher.*

The trends in the number and circulation of the Sunday editions of English language daily newspapers are like the trends in the dailies, but a few minor differences deserve comment. While the number of dailies declined since about 1917, the number of their Sunday editions has increased at least since 1900.[9] The number of Sunday papers continued to increase until 1925, then slowly declined through 1934. The per capita circulation steadily increased until 1930, reached its low in 1933, and regained the 1929 figure in 1935. In general, the depression seems to have scarcely affected either the number of dailies or the number of their Sunday editions. The ratio of four dailies to one Sunday edition has been steady from 1920 or earlier to 1936. Again it should be stressed that studies to show changes in content are needed to give importance to these figures.

---

[9] Masche, W. Carl. *loc. cit.* The trend in the number of Sunday papers shown by Masche checks with the trend shown by *Editor and Publisher,* but his actual figures are much less than both *Editor and Publisher's* and *Ayer's.*

Changes in circulation imply changes in the social influence of the press, whether the content changes or not. But changes in content are always likely to have more social influence than changes in circulation as such.

Sunday circulation, like daily circulation, increased after 1920, despite the depression of 1921-22. Yet the depression decreased both Sunday and daily circulation in 1930.[10] In 1920 the Sunday circulation was over seventeen million. The peak year was reached in 1929 with a circulation of about twenty-seven million. Substantial losses occurred each year through 1933. Then came a turn. During the next two years the Sunday circulation gained so fast that in 1935 it had reached over twenty-eight million copies, an all-time "high" for American journalism, although the per capita circulation was the same as in 1929. Such resilience from depression goes far to prove the soundness of the fourth estate. It also implies that the newspaper is a necessity for large numbers of people. But finer implications must wait for studies to explain the annual changes in terms of contemporary social and economic conditions.

One can scarcely describe the adventures of print during depression without comparing the production rates of publications which differ in price. The comparisons should show the relative importance of cost to the consumer as against the importance of other factors conditioning the number and character of publications read. One might expect the newspaper, the cheapest publication, to survive the depression best. Table X shows the production rates of five types of publications by year—ranging from the two cent daily to the two dollar book. Between 1929 and 1933 book production declined 48 per cent, pamphlets

---

[10] The fact that according to Table VII the daily circulation peak came in 1930 and the Sunday circulation peak came in 1929 is not significant because, when the circulations are recorded for six-month periods instead of annually, both the daily and Sunday circulations appear to have reached their peak circulation in the six month period ending March 31, 1930. See *Editor and Publisher*. 63:12. July 19 1930

TABLE X

NUMBER OF COPIES AND INDEX NUMBERS OF BOOKS, PAMPHLETS, MAGAZINES, AND DAILY AND SUNDAY NEWSPAPERS PRODUCED: UNITED STATES, 1925–1935[a]

YEAR	BOOKS		PAMPHLETS		MAGAZINES			DAILY NEWSPAPERS			SUNDAY NEWSPAPERS		
	NUMBER (IN THOUSANDS)	PER 100 POPULA-TION[b]	NUMBER (IN THOUSANDS)	PER 100 POPULA-TION[b]	NUMBER	CIRCULA-TION (IN THOUSANDS)	CIRCULA-TION PER 100 POP-ULATION[b]	NUMBER	CIRCULA-TION (IN THOU-SANDS)	CIRCULA-TION PER 100 POP-ULATION[b]	NUM-BER	CIRCULA-TION (IN THOU-SANDS)	CIRCULA-TION PER 100 POP-ULATION[b]
1925	200,997	175	232,214	202	4,496	179,281	156	2,116	37,407	32.6	597	25,630	22.3
1927	227,496	193	242,879	205	4,659	153,954	130	2,091	41,368	35.0	511	27,696	23.4
1929	214,334	176	215,865	178	5,155	201,760	166	2,086	42,015	34.6	578	29,012	23.9
1931	154,462	125	216,054	174	4,882	183,519	148	2,044	41,294	33.3	555	27,453	22.1
1933	110,790	88	143,487	114	3,459	174,759	139	1,903	37,630	29.9	489	25,454	20.3
1935	140,652	111	194,610	153	4,018	178,614	141	2,038	40,871	32.1	520	28,684	22.6
INDEX NUMBERS (1929=100)													
1925	94	—	108	—	—	89	—	—	89	—	—	88	—
1927	106	—	113	—	—	76	—	—	98	—	—	95	—
1929	100	—	100	—	—	100	—	—	100	—	—	100	—
1931	72	—	100	—	—	91	—	—	98	—	—	95	—
1933	52	—	66	—	—	87	—	—	90	—	—	88	—
1935	66	—	90	—	—	89	—	—	97	—	—	99	—

[a] *Biennial Census of Manufactures.* United States Department of Commerce, Bureau of the Census. Data for the years 1929, 1933 and 1935 from mimeographed release, *Census of Manufactures,* "Printing and Publishing" (industries numbers 508 and 510). Released April 14, 1937.

[b] Population estimates as of July 1. Data from *Statistical Abstract of the United States,* United States Department of Commerce, 1935. For a more refined analysis of per capita circulation the population 10 years of age and over, or the literate population 10 years of age and over, can be substituted for the total population.

declined 34 per cent, magazines declined 13 per cent, Sunday newspapers declined 12 per cent, and daily newspapers least of all, 10 per cent.

The figures imply that what and how much we read during depression depended upon how much it cost. But much evidence suggests that the same depression which decreased the *production* of the more expensive publications also supplied many incentives toward reading which doubtless increased the number of readers (and the number of pages read) per book, magazine, or newspaper sold. Such incentives undoubtedly produced the peak of public library circulation recorded in 1933.[11] They swelled the proportion of magazines and books which readers of the more depressed classes borrowed from their friends. And they certainly increased the unrecorded number of persons who read the same copy of newspapers, magazines, and books.

The instinctive attraction of novelty or timeliness is one explanation, and perhaps the best of several that might be offered, for the fact that daily newspaper production decreased less than the production of any other type of publication. Yesterday's newspaper is almost as dead as last year's Annual. The far greater decline in book production may be explained by the notion that books improve with age, like wines and violins. Old books and even old magazines are certainly read so much more than old newspapers that we might have reduced our purchases of new books and magazines and continued to buy newspapers, even though all three publications had sold at the same price.

PROBLEMS FOR STUDY

The foregoing facts about book, magazine, and newspaper production are perhaps sufficient to show what might be naturally assumed, namely, that all three had their downs and ups like other commercial products; that the gross totals, described by number of copies, show parallel trends, excepting magazines; that divergent trends appear in the number of new publications

---

[11] See Chapter IV. Table XVI, p. 104.

of each type per year; and that (whether described by number of copies or by number of new titles) the curves of book and magazine production in comparable categories are sufficiently inconsistent to suggest the effects of changes both in marketing policies and in sales receipts during successive stages of depression.

We are primarily concerned with the nature and extent of such effects; hence it remains to state some assumptions and hypotheses which students of publication may investigate to distinguish the more strictly "social" factors from the other factors implied in the annual fluctuations.

1. *The figures obtainable from the standard sources—Editor and Publisher, The Publishers' Weekly, U. S. Census of Manufactures, N. W. Ayer & Son's Directory of Newspapers and Periodicals—are valid.*

This assumption is clearly basic to any thoroughgoing analysis of the data. To check it one would need to consult enough publishers to estimate the uniformity and reliability of their reports, especially of reports on the number of titles published in the specified categories. The fact that some of the other estimates of annual printings are larger than the figures of the *U. S. Census of Manufactures* casts suspicion on this presumably official source. It would help much to assemble the publishers' working definitions of such terms as "new title," "new edition," "reprint," and "copies printed" (whether counted in sheets, as bound, or as sold), and many more. We should then require inventories of such other books produced (e.g., textbooks) as may not appear in the totals, and of such newspapers and magazines as carry advertising but are given away, and others which are sold but not reported by the Audit Bureau of Circulation because they carry no advertising. Without such inventories, in good years and bad, one cannot tell by how much to correct the published data to estimate changes in the gross annual production of print[12] or in specified categories.

---

[12] See Appendix C for data needed to compare the three standard sources for annual production of print.

One might suppose the trades themselves would find it profitable to inventory the print of all sorts supplied to different markets, if only to appraise more accurately the competition to be met by publications of each type.

2. *Annual changes in production of book titles show the effects of the depression upon publishers' "hunches."*

The hunches consist of several different elements. They vary with the publisher and respond to changes in economic conditions at different rates of speed. The least responsive to economic changes, and the basic element in most publishers' decisions for or against a new title, is the publisher's confidence in his own ability to recognize the successful book by the sheer pleasure he finds in reading the manuscript. His decision to publish thus involves the assumption that he himself, or the associate on whom he relies, reacts to all aspects of the manuscript as the most numerous type of book purchaser will react to the published book. It is also assumed that the book can appear on the market before public interest in it will have been displaced by a competing interest, or by a competing book issued by a rival publisher. Both assumptions are dubious and yet nearly impossible to check in advance of the book's actual adventures on the market.

Aside from publishers' memoranda, memoirs, manuscript critiques, office journals, and the like (cf. Stanley Unwin, *The Truth about Publishing,* Frank Swinnerton, *Authors and Publishers,* and publications listed in *Books about Books,* issued by the [London] National Council of Book Publishers), there are no recorded studies to check these assumptions. But there is a wealth of data on manuscripts, accepted and rejected, in the publishers' files. The collection and analysis of such commentaries in relation to the recorded sales of the manuscripts eventually published can be recommended as a highly useful research.

Considering the important financial rewards that await any tangible findings, the deficiency of such research is best explained by the murderous competition among American publishers, which withholds the sales records of important publishers from students well qualified to define criteria fundamental to the intelligent selection of manuscripts in certain fields. No matter how cleverly the student analyzes the other data obtainable, he has no means of checking his conclusions without the sales records. Hence the research student cannot show what he can do to help the publisher until the publisher is willing to take the slight risk involved in supplying sales records to someone outside his organization. Only the publishers can start the ball rolling. An alternative might be for a group of publishers to train one or more trusted editors in the statistical and other techniques required to make the analyses.

But the publisher's acceptance of a manuscript is, of course, not capricious. He usually tries to compare the proposed volume with others which have sold variously and which resemble it in subject, style (if not authorship), format, price, and other essential features. Fashions in certain lines change so fast as to rule out any mechanical prediction of a new book's success by means of such resemblances. But there is wide room for the analysis of book sales to discover *within what limits* such predictions are valid. In lines where book fashions are less dependent upon current whims, it should be possible to reduce the mortality of bad guesses by extrapolating the trends of former sales, with due imagination and attention to other conditions. To know by how much publishers are actually guided at present by their previous sales would help to indicate social factors of annual changes in book production.

A third type of influence upon book production involves the whole complex of conditions within the industry, of which some doubtless respond more promptly to depression than does the book market as a whole. The conditions are both favorable and unfavorable to the production of new books—as when depression tends both to reduce manufacturing costs and to increase selling costs. To identify and evaluate such of these conditions as have most effect upon the production of different sorts of books during depression, would explain annual changes in book publication by distinguishing the more strictly economic factors from the more general social factors we have hypothesized.

Of research in this area to date there is one study which dwarfs all others, namely, O. H. Cheney's *Economic Survey of the Book Industry, 1930-1931,* conducted for and published by the National Association of Book Publishers. The auspices of the survey and the intelligence of the authorship were such that the findings constitute the first road into the jungle which the publishing industry is for most laymen and apparently for many publishers. The unique importance of the findings is due to the fact that the authors were allowed to consult the records of several publishers far more freely than any other students have consulted them. It would be a piece of good fortune if Mr. Cheney and his associates in the 1931 study could be induced to make a parallel study of postdepression conditions.

Investigation of the several factors affecting publishers' decisions regarding annual lists during depression is needed to determine the relative value of personal hunches concerning the market, actual changes in the market, an changes within the industry. Only in so far as successful analysis permits separate attention to each group of factors can we interpret changes in book production in terms of *social* as distinguished from *industrial* changes.

3. *Annual changes in the production of magazines reflect similar changes in the editorial policies of magazine editors, but more particularly changes in the advertising market and in readers' interests.*

This hypothesis invites much the same type of study as the previous hypothesis concerning book production. One may assume for lack of evidence that the annual changes in magazines imply changes in editorial estimates of reader interest, in sales records, and in manufacturing and selling costs, as with books. But the new element is advertising. To know for the magazines of different types to what extent the changes in content were

due to readers' failure to buy or to industry's failure to advertise,[18] would greatly clarify the social implications of changes in
magazine production. Analysis of annual changes in content
should undertake comparisons with magazines and pamphlets
which carry no advertising and of which annual circulation is
therefore not recorded by the Audit Bureau of Circulations.

4. *Annual changes in newspaper content reflect the publisher's*
efforts to maintain sales and hence advertising volume. The
changes show tendencies to invade the former magazine and
book markets by increasing the proportion of magazine and book
copy, and to attract the less literate readers by expanding comic
strips, sensational pictures, and other graphic material.

That the primary motivation for whatever changes occurred
in the content of newspapers since 1929 was a desire to keep
the papers solvent, is entirely obvious. To describe the nature
and the extent of such changes in content and then to relate
them to changes in circulation, preferably changes in circulation
among different social groups, is the essential research. In planning the analysis of newspaper files to describe changes in content throughout the depression, the student may use the two
hypotheses stated above, but should invent many others which
specifically designate the changes suspected in the particular
papers examined. Local events should suggest many such hypotheses. The student might then relate the changes recorded to
the available data on newspaper reading (Appendix C) to discover how the readers responded whom the changes in content
were designed to attract. Responses of this character should indicate social effects of the changes in newspaper content. No
doubt many such effects are trivial. Others, like the adaptation
of controversial issues to the "tabloid mind," are clearly important and far reaching.

---

[18] Best illustrated by analysis of Hart, Hornell. *Recent Social Trends in the*
United States. New York and London: McGraw-Hill Book Co. 1933. Vol. I.
Chapter VIII

Chapter IV

Distributing Agencies

CHANGES in reading plainly result from changes in the number, the stock, and the administration of the major distributing agencies as they also result from changes in publications or in the readers themselves. As middleman, the distributor's influence naturally works both ways. His prosperity largely determines the publishers' market but is itself determined by the general reader. For this reason one perhaps learns more from the effects of depression upon distributors, than from its effects upon publishers or upon the attitudes of readers. Chapter II has urged the importance of interrelating all three. But when research facilities are limited, the fact that changes in the distributing agencies are so relevant to changes in reading, coupled with the fact that changes in the distributing agencies are so inadequately recorded, should offer a major challenge to students of the central problems.

The number and complexity of conditions affecting the distributing agencies since 1929 may justify an escape to analogy for better perspective. Our figure is a round mill pond, to represent the reading public. A new publication drops into the center of the pond. The immediate effect is a circular ripple, which represents the publishers' stimulus. This, in turn, makes another ripple—a change in the publications carried by the agencies. The second ripple produces a third—a change in what is actually read. The third ripple expands until it reaches the shore line— the limits of reading interest. The limits depend upon the lie of the land—a complex of social compulsions, inhibitions, and group variations in reading interest. Occasionally, of course, a contagious popular response turns the ripple into a wave, which travels farther inland. But all waves die on the shore, just as all reading stops at the limits of social tolerance for reading of any sort.

What happens next is a succession of weaker and conflicting ripples, back from the shore to the center of the pond, the delayed effects of the market upon the supply of current publications. Depression changes people more or less from what they were. Changes in emotional and intellectual emphasis naturally affect the relative demand for different publications. The agencies buy what best meets the demand as felt, thus determining what the publishers publish on the strength of previous sales. Though this stimulus of the publisher by the reader was strong enough during the last depression to "trouble the waters," the contrary stimulus from the publisher, via the distributor, to the reader was and remains much stronger.[1]

To understand the social meaning of the cross currents between reading matter and reading interests, one may well concentrate upon the middleman, the distributor. Students whose facilities discourage·the study of reading problems at large may well study the local distributors of a given type, preferably retail book stores, rental libraries, and magazine agencies. The commercial rivalry which conceals essential facts about these agencies from students seeking to analyze their markets is plainly the most serious obstacle to research in the entire field.

---

[1] For evidence regarding the preponderance of accessibility over subject interest as factors in the selection of actual reading see Waples, Douglas. "The Relation of Subject Interests to Actual Reading." *Library Quarterly.* 2:42-70. No. 1. January 1932; also Carnovsky, Leon. "A Study of the Relationship Between Reading Interest and Actual Reading" *Library Quarterly.* 4:76-110. No. 1. January 1934. The second reference shows that book readers tend to read most on the subjects in which they have previously expressed most interest, when books on such subjects are as accessible, as well advertised, and as readable as other books. Unless the last three factors are held constant, subject-interest is not the most determining factor.

The first step is, logically, to state the major annual changes since 1929 in the status of each important agency and, so far as possible, to relate them to the long time trends. What we know about such changes naturally depends upon the records kept and obtainable. Generally speaking, the only agencies with public records are those supported by taxation, like the public library, and those supported by advertising, viz., all newspapers and most magazines. But even the agencies maintaining public records usually record only the facts about circulation which can be publicized to increase revenues. Changes in the other agencies must at present be inferred largely from changes in their mere numbers and from changes in the proportion of reading matter obtained from each local agency by samples of the readers of selected communities.

Though man may not live by bread alone, Americans normally buy "bread" and many luxuries before they buy print. Group differences in income correspond very closely both to differences in the publications available[2] and in the publications sold.[3] The more money, the more reading matter—is a safe generalization upon the many American communities wherein wealth and purchase of reading matter have been compared.

It is the force of this tendency, of course, which attaches peculiar importance to the study of reading in time of depression. If one could imagine a depression which reduced incomes without affecting either the cost of publications or the general reading interest, there is no reason to doubt that we should buy fewer publications. But the actual depression affects the amount and character of publication, as we have seen. It also affects distribution, as we shall see, by reducing the capital of most

[2] For convincing evidence in terms of several hundred counties, see Purdy, George F. *Public Library Service in the Middle West.* University of Chicago. Unpublished Ph.D. thesis. 1936

[3] See Miller, Robert A. "The Relation of Reading Characteristics to Social Indexes." *American Journal of Sociology.* 12:738ff. No. 6. May 1936

agencies, by changing the size and variety of their stock, and by increasing public demand for the cheaper publications. Again, depression clearly breeds new varieties of popular curiosities and class interests, to which some publications appeal so strongly that reading displaces other diversions formerly preferred.

When all such changes are reconciled as fairly as possible, the prevailing trend during early depression appears to have been an increase in reading, which varies inversely with expenditure for reading matter. How long it might have taken for reading to fall enough below its 1929 level to overtake steadily falling incomes, we cannot tell from the events since 1929 in the United States, because recovery commenced before that point was reached. Several European studies (and especially Lazarsfeld's admirable account of conditions in Marienthal, Austria, where depression probably surpassed the all-time low of any American community since the War[4]) show that continued depression produces an apathy toward ideas as such and the virtual cessation of reading. If the years 1932 and 1933, which (with the help of a presidential year) marked the crest of our reading consumption and the trough of our depression, had been followed by two worse years, the amount of reading might have declined to meet the falling curve of incomes.

In short, poverty as such tends to inhibit reading. Conditions assumed to have increased reading since 1929 were mainly temporary (as when readers turned to public libraries for distraction) or emotional (as when suddenly reduced income sharpened attention to current ideas and events). They were largely (if not only) economic to the extent that other diversions which compete with reading became too expensive. Without any intention to exploit this thesis, the writer finds it more consistent

---

[4] Lazarsfeld, Paul F. *The Unemployed of Marienthal.* Leipzig: Austrian Institute for Psychological Fieldwork. 1935. Also reviewed in an article by McMurry, Robert N. "When Men Eat Dogs." *The Nation.* 136:15-18. January 4 1933

with the entire evidence than any other he can state in as few words as this volume goes to press. Since the descriptions of reading behavior supporting the thesis are too extensive for presentation,[5] the bare statement may furnish a point of departure for supplementary studies.

An important preliminary step is to select the facts about each distributing agency which we need for the social interpretation of their activities. The selection should serve two purposes: to outline the discussion of each agency as a social institution; to indicate, by omissions, the data most needed to show how the changes undergone by each institution during depression affected their distribution of reading matter.

DESIRED DATA CONCERNING EACH TYPICAL DISTRIBUTING AGENCY

Data	*Use*
A. Number of agencies, both independent and chain.	To show trends in relative scope of each agency and the trend toward monopoly as reflected by growth of chains in newspaper, magazine, rental libraries, bookstores, etc.
B. Stock or holdings—Number and variety of publications carried by the agency with annual additions.	To compare changes in scope with changes in character of publications distributed.
C. Income from advertising, sales, rentals, tax appropriation, or other sources.	To show effects of changes in purchasing power upon the stock of publications and promotion policies, for each agency.
D. *Budget,* e.g., ratios of expenditures for new stock to salary, maintenance, promotion, and overhead.	To show effects of administration upon changes in the relative scope of each agency.
E. *Circulation,* of publications (classed by socially meaningful categories) to groups of readers (classed at least by income, sex, education, and occupation).	To indicate and evaluate the social influence of each agency; to explain the effects upon circulation of annual changes in income, stock carried, personnel, and other factors.

Table XI shows, in perspective, which of the five sorts of data

---

[5] Index to Tables reporting results of community studies appears in Appendix B.

TABLE XI

AVAILABLE DATA CONCERNING TYPICAL DISTRIBUTORS

DATA	DISTRIBUTING AGENCIES								
	NEWS AGENTS	RENTAL LIBRARIES	BOOK JOBBERS	BOOK PUBLISHERS	BOOK STORES	PUBLIC LIBRARIES	UNIVERSITY AND ENDOWED LIBRARIES	NEWSPAPERS	MAGAZINES
A. Number . .	1	3	1	7	3	10	13	14	15
B. Annual additions to stock or holdings .	2	4	2	7, 8	6	11	11	—	—
C. Income . .	18	5	18	9	6	12	13	16	16
D. Budget . . .	18	6	18	18	18	11	11	18	18
E. Circulation .	18	6	6	9	—	13	13	17	17 or 16 (b)

Sources:

1. The number of *national* agents—e.g., American News Company—is small. For number of *local* agents see classified telephone directories.
2. See periodical house organs issued by national news agents, e.g., *American News Trade Journal.*
3. *American Book Trade Directory* (1928, 1932, 1935). Appears every three or four years.
4. The home offices of the important national chains; catalogues of selected local chains, if special permission is obtained.
5. Certain chains have supplied on request, when assured that firm name will not be identified with any figures published.
6. Possibly obtainable by interviewing local branches. No regional data have been compiled, but jobbers like A. C. McClurg (333 E. Ontario Street, Chicago) could supply valuable testimony. Doubtless most important jobbers could estimate annual fluctuations in sales to rental library chains or other types of dealers if the considerable expense were covered.
7. *Publishers' Trade List Annual, Cumulative Book Index.* New York: R. R. Bowker Co. office of the *Publishers' Weekly,*
8. *Biennial Census of Manufactures,* U. S. Department of Commerce, Bureau of the Census.
9. No figures on annual changes but much helpful information in Cheney, O. H. *Economic Survey of the Book Industry, 1930-1931.*
10. *American Library Directory,* 1930. Published by American Library Association, 820 N. Michigan Avenue, Chicago.
11. By personal examination of records in selected libraries.
12. American Library Association *Bulletin,* statistics published annually. Must write libraries for data on years.
13. U. S. Office of Education, Biennial Survey. American Library Association *Bulletin*
14. *Editor and Publisher (International Year Book Number).* Annual.
15. *N. W. Ayer and Son's Directory of Newspapers and Periodicals* (annual); also *Editor and Publisher.*
16. Not available as such but see (a) Media records for changes in volume of advertising in representative newspapers in fifty-two selected cities; also (b) *Standard Rate and Data Service, Inc.* (333 North Michigan Avenue, Chicago) for circulation and advertising rates of newspapers and magazines.
17. Audit Bureau of Circulations (165 West Wacker Drive, Chicago) annual reports, some data available in 16 (b)
18. No compilation, but possibly obtainable from officials.

(A-E) concerning each of the more important distributors of print, are to some extent available. The numbers in the table refer to the sources in the list which follows the table.

Table XII presents certain facts which suggest that reading tended to increase when incomes began to decline. The volume of advertising may be accepted as a good index of the economic health of the newspaper and magazine publishing business and perhaps of all printing ventures. There is a steady decline in advertising volume from 1929 to a low in 1933, and then a rise to 1935. During the period studied, 1930 to 1935, public library

TABLE XII
VOLUME OF READING MATTER DISTRIBUTED, BY TYPES OF AGENCIES:
1928–1935

	DISTRIBUTING AGENCY					
YEAR	VOLUME OF NEWSPAPER ADVERTISING (IN BILLIONS OF AGATE LINES)[a]	PUBLIC LIBRARY CIRCULATION (IN THOUSANDS OF LOANS)[b]	SELECTED MAGAZINE CIRCULATION (IN MILLIONS OF COPIES)[c]	CHAIN NEWSPAPER CIRCULATION (IN MILLIONS OF COPIES)[d]	NUMBER OF BOOK STORES[e]	
					TOTAL	RENTAL LIBRARIES
1928	1.80	—	—	—	839	39
1929	1.89	—	57.9	16.5	—	—
1930	1.65	5,116	60.9	17.1	—	—
1931	1.46	5,836	63.6	16.1	—	—
1932	1.49	6,422	58.7	14.9	916	69
1933	1.06	6,611	57.8	13.8	—	—
1934	1.17	6,108	59.0	14.0	—	—
1935	1.24	5,841	60.3	15.8	995	113

[a] Data from *Audit Bureau of Circulations*
[b] Data for 53 selected libraries, obtained through correspondence. (See Table XVI)
[c] Data from *Standard Rate and Data Service, Inc.*, Chicago
[d] Data from *International Year Book Number* of *Editor and Publisher*
[e] Data from *American Book Trade Directory*. For selected cities (see Table XX)

circulation, in contrast, increased to its high point in 1933 and then receded. Magazine circulation and chain newspaper circulation, however, closely follow the volume of newspaper advertising; both decline to their low points in 1933 and increase thereafter. For the years for which data are available on the number of bookstores and rental libraries, 1928, 1932, and 1935, there is a continuous increase.

To isolate the effects of the depression on these distributing agencies the series should be extended as far back as possible and up through the recovery period to show deviations from the trend lines. However, we may well state certain questions suggested by Tables X and XII.

What are we to understand from the increase in the number of book stores and rental libraries, the latter apparently having multiplied faster after 1932 when public library circulation declined? Does the annual establishment of new book shops imply that those of the previous year were unable to meet the demand, or does it mean that many shops for sale or rental of books were opened as side lines, to "bait" customers for other merchandise? It is entirely possible that the shops may have increased in number without any increase in the total volume of books sold or rented.

Is the table correct in the indication that the sales of newspapers declined sooner and further than the *circulation* of books? One might expect the contrary, if readers did read more during depression. One must ask, therefore, to what extent amount of reading is reflected by number of sales. Did enough more people read the same copy of a newspaper or magazine after 1930 to produce an increase in reading even when sales decreased? What increase occurred in the reading of newspapers and magazines found in public libraries, barber shops, beauty parlors, lunch rooms, and the like? Was the decrease in sales normally distributed among those who used to buy one, two, three, four or more newspapers daily? If not, a decrease in sales might represent an actual increase in the number of people who bought, read, and gave away one paper daily and an overcompensating decrease in the number who bought more than one paper in 1930, or more than one magazine in 1931.

If smaller sales do mean that fewer people read newspapers and magazines, was the decline in their reading due to poverty or to changes in the character of the reading matter? Since the volume of advertising seems to have fallen sooner than circulation, it may be that the decrease in revenue forced the omission of certain features and so made the publications less attractive.

Why did public library circulation fall in 1933 and why did it fall so far? Did the causes lie within the institution itself—for example, a decision to balance reduced budgets by discontinuing the purchase of new books; a reduction in the number of local branches and in the number of hours the libraries were open per week; or in failure to meet the increased competition by bookshops and rental libraries which supplied current sensational fiction?

Or did the causes lie outside the institution—for example, reemployment of patrons whose unemployment since 1929 partly explained the library's gains until 1933; or improvement of school[6] and college libraries sufficient to reduce the loans to students, which normally account for over half of public library circulation; or declining interest in book-reading as such—due partly to an abatement of interest in the new deal issues, partly to the discovery that "self-improvement by reading" is no shortcut to prosperity, and partly to a large number of other social factors?

Answers to the foregoing questions are important to the social scientist who would understand the normal social consequences of depression. They are far to seek in the data available. They are not to be found without the additional data needed to interpret the facts we have. It is thus in order to indicate what we know about (1) the relative importance of each agency in the distribution of print, (2) changes within the agency (industry, institution) itself, and (3) changes in the agencies' clienteles, which affect the scope and character of its social influence.

RELATIVE SCOPE OF AGENCIES

About 90 per cent of the literate population reads newspapers with some regularity. The papers are obtained mostly from news-

---

[6] The best source of information concerning school library development is the occasional reporting by the U. S. Office of Education, which prior to 1934-1935 is far from complete.

stands and by subscription. The scope of news agencies causes them to overlap the agencies which distribute books and magazines. In comparing the percentages of publications obtained by all readers from each agency, there is little to be gained by including newspapers, and the proportional supply of other print becomes plainer when they are omitted.

Table XIII shows the relative distribution of magazines and

TABLE XIII

PERCENTAGE DISTRIBUTION OF BOOKS AND MAGAZINES BY AGENCY FROM
WHICH SECURED: SAMPLE FROM SOUTH CHICAGO, 1933[a]

AGENCY	PERCENTAGE DISTRIBUTION		
	MAGAZINES	BOOKS	TOTAL
Public library	.4	28.6	7.2
Friend	18.5	21.0	19.1
Drug store	12.8	—	9.7
Newsstand	13.1	—	9.9
Rental library	—	5.5	1.3
Book store	—	10.3	2.5
Subscription	20.7	—	15.7
All other	34.6	34.6	34.6
Total per cent	100	100	100
Number	8,031	2,548	10,579

[a] Unpublished study of South Chicago by Douglas Waples and others. Some 6,850 persons were interviewed during the winter of 1933–34, and their reading for the two weeks previous to the date of interview recorded.

books to urban readers in one community, South Chicago, in the winter of 1933-34. It consists of a sample of 6,850 residents of South Chicago who were selected proportionally (according to traits like sex, age, education, occupation—which are known to condition reading) and examined individually. The community is highly industrialized. The questioning was mostly by interview. Schedules were substituted for interviews in the case of professional people and other groups who find it easier to write than to talk. The sample is trustworthy for the given data.

To show changes in the relative scope of typical distributors, we need consecutive samples of the same populations at different and equal periods of time. In this respect our sample is lamentably weak. We have no two time samples of any one community taken from readers at large, without bias in favor of any one agency, to show the distribution of all publications obtained from the various local sources of supply. Thus, the best we can do is to describe conditions existing in 1933-34, near the depth of the depression, and then await the collection of comparable data in the same or similar communities and under the more favorable economic conditions of recovery. It should be noted that this "best we can do" would have been far worse if numerous grants for the study of community reading had not produced an abundance of well selected data relevant to the most acute stage of the depression. Though it is now too late to secure more such data for those years, the data are better interpreted now than formerly because of the many relevant depression surveys that are now appearing.

Returning to Table XIII, we note that the distribution of sources of magazines and books combined is heavily weighted in favor of the subscription and "other sources" by the fact that magazines and books are combined. Since the average book reader reads several magazines to one book and obtains most of his magazines by subscription, it is not surprising that "subscriptions" is the largest single source.

But the fact of most interest in the table is that "all other sources" is first in rank and supplies almost one-third of the publications supplied by all sources. "All other sources," when analyzed, shows a wide variety, ranging from books and magazines found in shelters for the unemployed to complimentary copies received by professional men from the publishers. Most of the "other sources," however, are barber shops, beauty parlors, waiting rooms, neighborhood clubs, cafes, and amusement places. Since the "other sources" (supplying 35 per cent) are almost entirely free, we have merely to add the 7 per cent representing public library distribution and the 19 per cent representing what was obtained from friends to learn that *61 per cent of the publications read were secured without cost.*

It would add conspicuously to our knowledge of depression reading to know by how much this proportion of print obtained gratis in 1932 and 1933 was reduced in the following years, when the sales of books and magazines apparently revived. One might readily find out by repeating the same surveys during the present year. Comparison of percentages of free material read should test our basic hypothesis—that the depression actually increased the amount of material read even though it seriously reduced the amount of printed matter sold.

By examining the free distribution of books and magazines separately we see that 84 per cent of the books were obtained without cost as compared with 54 per cent of the magazines. Again we need to know how these percentages changed in the following years of recovery. In 1933 the public library supplied almost one-third of all the books read. How far did this proportion decline thereafter when library circulations fell? Book stores supplied more books than rental libraries and less than half as many as were borrowed from friends, in 1933. Did this percentage decrease in the following years? If so, was this due to the peculiarities of rental library stock, to the weakened competition of the public library, to the multiplication of rental library units, or to the increase in incomes?

"All other sources" in Table XIII obscures two sources that should be specified, because they are likely to increase in importance, namely, school libraries and the federal government. The *Biennial Survey of Education* (1928-1930) reports 6,013 high school libraries of over 3,000 volumes as against 6,675 in 1933-1934, an increase of about 11 per cent. Since the increase resulting from pressure by regional accrediting associations and other authorities was undoubtedly greater in the case of the smaller libraries, the rate of increase from 1930 to 1936 is probably not less than 20 per cent and perhaps much larger. Increases in the school library will probably reduce present public library services to school children more than they add to the total number of books distributed. The federal government publications go mainly to organizations, libraries, students, and since 1934 to the many groups and individuals involved in the activities of the new federal agencies. The increase in these publications as reported by the superintendent of documents appears

TABLE XIV

PUBLICATIONS, INCLUDING ANNUAL REPORTS AND DOCUMENTS PRINTED ON REQUISITION, FOR CONGRESS AND GOVERNMENT DEPARTMENTS AND INDEPENDENT ESTABLISHMENTS: 1926-1935[a]

FISCAL YEAR ENDING JUNE 30	NUMBER OF COPIES (IN THOUSANDS)
1926	59,252
1927	66,629
1928	64,697
1929	60,274
1930	88,098
1931	88,525
1932	80,197
1933	60,564
1934	113,542
1935	129,597

[a] *Annual Reports of the Public Printer.* Washington, D. C : United States Government Printing Office

in Table XIV. To what extent federal publications compete with commercial publications for the attention of different social groups is an important question for study.

CHANGES WITHIN THE AGENCIES

It is hopefully assumed that data for comparison with the facts shown in Table XIII will be assembled for postdepression years. The comparisons will show which agencies expanded and which contracted. Shifts in the relative scope of each agency should be explainable in part by administrative changes within the agencies. Meantime it will be helpful to suggest the types of data needed to make the explanation more nearly adequate.

TABLE XV

TOTAL BUDGET AND BOOK EXPENDITURES AND INDEX NUMBERS OF EACH, FOR SELECTED LIBRARIES: 1930–1935[a]

Year	Budget		Book Expenditures		Book Expenditures as a Per Cent of Total Budget
	Hundreds of Dollars	Index Numbers (1930=100)	Hundreds of Dollars	Index Numbers (1930=100)	
1930	6,805	100	1,384	100	20.3
1931	6,931	102	1,320	95	19.0
1932	6,052	89	1,034	75	17.1
1933	5,306	78	807	58	15.2
1934	5,365	79	892	64	16.8
1935	5,711	84	1,031	74	18.1

[a] Fifty-three libraries ranging from ten thousand to fifty thousand volumes. Data obtained by correspondence from each library, by courtesy of Margaret M. Herdman.

TABLE XVI

PUBLIC LIBRARY CIRCULATION, TOTAL VOLUMES AND TOTAL BORROWERS, AND INDEX NUMBERS OF EACH, FOR SELECTED LIBRARIES: 1930–1935[a]

Year	Total Circulation								Circulation per		Total Volumes		Total Borrowers	
	Number (in Thousands)	Index Numbers (1930=100)	Percentage Distribution						Volume	Borrower	Number (in Thousands)	Index Numbers (1930=100)	Number (in Thousands)	Index Numbers (1930=100)
			Fiction			Non-Fiction								
			Adult	Juvenile	Total	Adult	Juvenile	Total	Total						
1930	5,116	100	49.3	23.3	72.6	14.3	13.2	27.5	100	4.65	18.3	2,072	100	527	100
1931	5,836	114	50.0	23.2	73.2	14.4	12.4	26.8	100	5.06	19.6	2,174	105	561	106
1932	6,422	126	51.4	21.6	73.0	15.5	11.6	27.1	100	5.38	20.1	2,252	109	603	114
1933	6,611	129	51.4	21.0	72.4	16.1	11.4	27.5	100	5.39	20.4	2,312	112	610	116
1934	6,108	119	50.0	21.4	71.4	17.0	11.7	28.7	100	4.87	18.3	2,367	114	630	120
1935	5,841	114	48.6	21.5	70.1	17.7	12.3	30.0	100	4.54	16.8	2,426	117	655	124

[a] Fifty-three libraries ranging from ten thousand to fifty thousand volumes. Data obtained by correspondence from each library, by courtesy of Margaret M. Herdman.

Public Library

One can carry the analysis of annual changes in budgets, purchases, personnel, circulation, and patronage much farther with typical public libraries than with other important agencies. The methods of such analysis are plain enough when the problems are clearly formulated. The best analysis to date of the public library in depression is without much doubt the current work of Margaret M. Herdman[7] from which this monograph has borrowed. Another useful analysis of public library changes is found in an article, "The Public Library in the Depression."[8] Published in October 1932, the article covers the early depression period (1930-1932) for a fair sample of libraries with respect to percentage changes in the following particulars: appropriations, circulation, amounts spent for 13 classes of books and for 11 budget items involving newspapers, periodicals, and binding. It includes 10 methods of making salary reductions, 11 methods of reducing cost of building maintenance, 5 methods of saving on special services, and 5 methods of saving on routine labor. The present discussion of the public library is limited to aspects which the detailed studies have found most important.

First we may notice changes in the public library budgets in relation to annual income. Table XV shows that public library authorities met reductions in income largely by reducing expenditures for books. Book funds suffered much more proportionally than other budgetary items. In 1931 (when income rose 2 per cent over 1930, the book item was decreased by 5 per cent. In 1932 an income reduction of 11 per cent below the 1930 level reduced the book item 25 per cent below the 1930 index. The next year, the income was 78 per cent of the 1930 income, but the book fund was only 58 per cent of the 1930

---

[7] *The Public Library in Depression.* University of Chicago. Ph.D. thesis. 1937

[8] The *Library Quarterly.* 2:321-343. No. 4. October 1932

TABLE XVII

CIRCULATION OF ADULT FICTION AND NON-FICTION BOOKS, PUBLIC
LIBRARIES IN SELECTED CITIES: 1930, 1935[a]

CITY	CIRCULATION (IN THOUSANDS)					
	1930			1935		
	ADULT FICTION	ADULT NON-FICTION	TOTAL[b]	ADULT FICTION	ADULT NON-FICTION	TOTAL[b]
Akron, Ohio	335	106	858	422	218	1,035
Atlanta, Ga.	494	138	989	439	191	1,003
Baltimore, Md.	1,000	420	2,510	1,029	704	2,705
Birmingham, Ala.	535	166	1,008	401	154	803
Buffalo, N. Y.	1,244	516	3,546	1,682	720	4,154
Chicago, Ill.	5,104	2,627	11,196	4,069	2,002	10,193
Dallas, Tex.	257	118	524	449	229	955
Dayton, Ohio	545	226	1,408	711	366	1,644
Detroit, Mich.	2,347	1,216	6,029	1,759	1,233	4,836
Houston, Tex.	260	133	686	259	163	769
Indianapolis, Ind.	1,136	399	2,665	1,393	517	3,277
Jersey City, N. J.	570	312	1,703	697	361	1,895
Kansas City, Mo.	672	281	1,886	827	416	2,381
Los Angeles, Cal.	4,647	2,320	9,682	5,630	3,387	11,799
Louisville, Ky.	522	536	1,794	707	407	1,829
Memphis, Tenn.	564	137	1,114	778	194	1,873
New Orleans, La.	488	129	862	450	110	764
New York public library[c]	4,275	3,034	11,684	4,109	3,697	11,211
Brooklyn, N. Y.[d]	3,637	1,377	7,438	3,368	1,605	6,639
Newark, N. J.	682	433	2,202	589	598	2,454
Oakland, Cal.	686	342	1,563	967	548	2,160
Omaha, Neb.	357	150	818	325	155	689
Philadelphia, Pa.	2,649	766	5,208	1,944	783	3,889
Portland, Ore.	1,014	911	2,892	1,025	1,064	2,897
St. Louis, Mo.	1,123	626	3,474	1,444	712	3,835
Seattle, Wash.	1,236	663	3,304	1,146	758	3,163
Syracuse, N. Y.	543	219	1,193	620	286	1,409
Toledo, Ohio	860	314	2,059	714	422	1,934
Vancouver, B. C.	504	253	954	306	276	720
Washington, D. C.	478	345	1,680	757	649	2,724
Youngstown, Ohio	457	111	858	373	141	717
Total	39,221	19,324	93,787	39,389	23,066	96,356

[a] Book circulation for 1930 and 1935 as reported by libraries serving a population of 200,000 and more. Public libraries in these 31 cities have increased their loans of adult non-fiction 19 per cent during the last five years. Adult fiction loans increased .4 per cent, loans to children below twelve years decreased 4 per cent, and total circulation increased 3 per cent in these cities. Data from *Bulletin of the American Library Association*, December 1936. Pp. 1008 ff.

[b] Includes juvenile circulation

[c] Circulation department only (New York includes Manhattan, Bronx, and Richmond boroughs)

[d] Brooklyn includes Kings borough

book fund. During 1934 and 1935, however, the book-funds were replaced somewhat more rapidly than the total income—rising 16 per cent in terms of the 1930 level as against the 6 per cent increase in the total budget.

The primary causes for the changing allocations of library budgets involve many technical considerations of interest mainly to librarians. But the indications are clear that book funds were cut first—partly in order to maintain salaries, and partly for the moral effect upon the book reading public, whose inability to secure the books they want might raise protests to city councils to the end of more money for the library. This administrative attitude seems to have prevailed until 1933 when, despite the fact that the libraries had been living on their fat for three years, their total circulation reached its peak and their combined budgets touched bottom. (See Table XVI.) The impressive drop in circulation of almost 8 per cent in 1934 seems thereafter to have inspired greater deference to the book item as a means of retaining public patronage and support. In 1935 with a total budget 16 per cent under 1930 (see Table XV) the public libraries spent 26 per cent less for books.

Turning to circulation (Table XVI) we find the largest proportional decline with respect to books for children—which account normally for from one-quarter to one-third of the total annual loans. Loans to children above the eighth grade are usually counted as loans to adults, since from the age of thirteen they increasingly read books which the libraries class as "adult." Loans to students in high school and college, somewhat stabilized by academic assignment, normally constitute from half to two-thirds of the total. Because of the academic influence, annual changes in library loans to students tell us less about the depression's effects upon the library than we can learn from changes in the character of loans to other groups.

Table XVII may reflect administrative changes since 1930 which encouraged the reading of adult non-fiction at the expense of current adult fiction.[9] In the 31 cities reported, 49 adult non-fiction books were read in 1930 for every 100 adult fiction books; in 1935 this ratio increased to 59. This raises a number of interesting questions concerning the depression's effects on the total distribution of print. Did the fiction loans fall off because the libraries bought less current fiction? Or did they buy less because the public substituted "human interest" stories in newspapers and magazines? Or because the rental libraries became more convenient and more numerous? Or because stern realities, intensified by various adult education programs and much else, tended to make non-fiction more interesting to the particular groups (mainly students and housewives) who borrow library books? Some of these questions will be noticed later on, in connection with the comparison of clientèles. Each of them is a fruitful problem for study by local comparisons and by subsequent data on related national trends.

Table XVIII, for example, suggests that rental libraries and bookstores in Chicago may have taken up some of the public library's losses in current fiction readers. While library circulation decreased below its 1930 level after 1932, the number of booksellers remained above the 1930 level and the number of rental libraries increased.

College and University Libraries.—By courtesy of the Secretary, Commission on Institutions of Higher Education, North Central Association of Colleges and Secondary Schools, we quote a summary[10] of depression changes in the library expenditures of 280 higher institutions (110 public and 170 endowed institutions). Similar data, collected and interpreted with the same

---

[9] For reasons which have always impressed the writer as insufficient, librarians classify poetry and drama as non-fiction, thus obscuring the distinction implied in the ratios between informational and recreational literature. It is also probable that the selection of other cities would raise the fiction ratio considerably.

[10] The quotation is from a mimeographed report by Haggerty, William J. and Works, George A. "An Analysis of the Library Data of the Higher Institutions of the North Central Association for the Years 1929-1934"

care, are not available for other regional groups of institutions, and no data of equal scope yet exist for regional groups of elementary or secondary school libraries.[11] Important facts concerning some 40 university libraries have been annually compiled for many years by Dr. James T. Gerould, librarian of Princeton University, who will furnish them on request. Recent years are well reported by the American Library Association. Depression changes in the holdings and expenditures of four American university libraries as compared with several European libraries are discussed by Waples and Lasswell.[12]

The following quotation is restricted to facts on expenditures because they show the effects of depression upon the libraries more clearly than do facts concerning books bought and books borrowed by students. Changes in holdings and in student loans reflect academic policies and instructors' assignments rather than cultural changes related to depression.

The five-year period from 1929-30 to 1933-34 inclusive was a period of curtailment of expenditures on the part of higher institutions. The library expenditures for books were collected for the entire period and it is, therefore, possible to furnish some idea of the extent to which book purchases were reduced as a part of the program of economy.

The data covering total average expenditures are shown in Table XIX. It will be seen from Table XIX that the year 1930-31 was for the institutions as a whole a period of increased expenditures for books as contrasted with the preceding year, when the expenditures are computed on the basis of type of institution. Exceptions to this general statement are endowed junior colleges, public technological institutions, and public liberal arts colleges and professional schools. Beginning with 1931-32, decreases are shown for the institutions as a group and for all types except public liberal arts colleges.

Table XIX also shows the percentage of change in expenditure for books when the first and last years of the five-year period are com-

---

[11] The U. S. Office of Education will however publish a report for 1934-35 and thereafter on all school libraries as obtained from each state superintendent of schools. Reports by state officers show trends in all school libraries for several states.

[12] Waples, Douglas and Lasswell, Harold D. *National Libraries and Foreign Scholarship*. Chicago: University of Chicago Press. 1936. Chapter V

TABLE XVIII

NUMBER AND INDEX NUMBERS OF SELECTED TYPES OF DISTRIBUTING AGENCIES IN CHICAGO: 1929–1936

	DISTRIBUTING AGENCY								
YEAR	PUBLIC LIBRARY[a]		BOOKSELLERS[b]		RENTAL LIBRARIES[b]			NEWS DEALERS, NEWS DELIVERIES[b]	
					INDEPENDENT		CHAIN		
	CIRCULATION (IN THOUSANDS)	INDEX NUMBERS (1930=100)	NUMBER	INDEX NUMBERS (1930=100)	NUMBER	INDEX NUMBERS (1930=100)	NUMBER[c]	NUMBER	INDEX NUMBERS (1930=100)
1929	—	—	152	94	15	71	—	85	96
1930	13,900	100	161	100	21	100	—	89	100
1931	15,800	114	177	110	25	119	4	87	98
1932	15,500	112	177	110	29	138	5	109	122
1933	13,100	94	209	130	32	152	5	81	91
1934	10,900	78	192	119	32	152	5	80	90
1935	10,100	73	177	110	32	152	7	86	97
1936	—	—	167	104	45	214	10	87	98

[a] *Annual Report* of the Chicago Public Library
[b] Classified telephone directory
[c] Index numbers not computed because of lack of 1930 data and small number of cases in subsequent years

TABLE XIX

AVERAGE EXPENDITURES IN DOLLARS FOR BOOKS BY TYPE OF LIBRARY, FOR SELECTED LIBRARIES: 1929-1930 TO 1933-1934 [a]

Type of Library	Number of Institutions	1929–1930	1930–1931	1931–1932	1932–1933	1933–1934	Percentage Decline in 1933–1934 from 1929–1930
All institutions	280	3,959	4,171	3,589	3,171	2,747	30.6
All public institutions	110	6,507	6,624	5,362	5,141	4,225	35.1
All endowed institutions	170	2,348	2,614	2,470	1,901	1,784	24.0
Junior colleges, public	28	1,666	1,734	160	676	668	59.9
Junior colleges, endowed	18	746	703	583	665	764	2.4 [b]
Junior colleges, total	46	1,298	1,322	329	672	706	45.6
Teachers colleges, all public	37	4,080	4,550	3,475	3,150	2,793	31.5
Technological institutions, public	8	2,675	2,100	1,942	1,714	2,061	23.0
Technological institutions, endowed	3	2,507	2,598	2,224	1,859	2,300	8.3
Technological institutions, total	11	2,629	2,236	2,019	1,754	2,126	19.1
Liberal arts colleges, public	3	2,422	5,102	6,672	6,117	1,647	32.0
Liberal arts colleges, endowed	87	1,858	1,977	1,968	1,341	1,302	29.9
Liberal arts colleges, total	90	1,880	2,106	2,126	1,501	1,314	30.1
Liberal arts colleges and professional schools, public	16	5,919	4,521	2,914	2,910	3,047	48.5
Liberal arts colleges and professional schools, endowed	55	2,282	2,741	2,348	1,843	1,754	23.1
Liberal arts colleges and professional schools, total	71	3,039	3,123	2,470	2,072	2,046	32.7
Universities, public	18	21,993	24,189	22,261	19,401	15,143	31.1
Universities, endowed	7	14,980	15,901	16,574	14,272	11,847	20.9
Universities, total	25	21,080	21,929	20,710	18,119	14,319	32.1

[a] Haggerty, William J., and Works, George A. "An Analysis of the Library Data of the Higher Institutions of the North Central Association for the Years 1929–1934." Mimeo. (See p. 108, this monograph)
[b] Increase

pared. The institutions as a group show a decrease of approximately 30 per cent with an average of 35 per cent decrease for public institutions contrasted with 24 per cent for the endowed group. The endowed junior colleges are the only ones showing an increase in expenditures.

There is no doubt but that the expenditure for books is a point at which reductions may properly be made during such a period as is under consideration. The wisdom of these reductions for a given institution can be determined only in the light of its library conditions. From the data that have been presented it is evident that in some institutions the book and periodical resources are so limited that any reduction must of necessity affect materially the effectiveness of instruction. In other institutions the resources are ample enough so that decreases could be effected with little or no effect on the instructional work.

The depression's effects on college libraries should, as the quotation suggests, be studied in terms of effects on college instruction and on uses of the students' leisure time. They have not been so studied. Since college students compose the largest single group of book readers, and since the facts concerning their reading are relatively easy to secure, it is highly desirable to investigate relations between changes in college library status and changes in college reading.

Rental Libraries and Book Stores

Table XX shows changes for the cities named in the number of book stores in the *Directory* listings of 1928, 1932, and 1935. The data are perhaps more interesting than helpful. Until some competent student can, by dint of personality or other pressure, impel the booktrades to tell us who buys which books and how many per store, so that such customers can be "developed" to the bookstores' advantage, there is small sociology to be gleaned from the number of book stores in existence each year. We simply do not know whether more book stores mean more readers and more books sold or fewer readers and smaller sales. The writer has talked and corresponded with several important booksellers and rental librarians. Most have shown an opportunistic interest in the next month's sales and a variously concealed indifference

TABLE XX
NUMBER OF DIFFERENT CLASSES OF BOOK STORES IN SELECTED CITIES: 1928, 1932, 1935[a]

| CITY | CLASSES OF BOOK STORES | | | | | | | | | | | |
| | GENERAL SALES | | | RENTAL LIBRARY | | | DEPARTMENT STORES | | | DRUG STORES | | |
	1928	1932	1935	1928	1932	1935	1928	1932	1935	1928	1932	1935
Brooklyn[b]	37	51	33	3	4	14	7	7	5	2	3	2
Chicago	65	94	103	4	23	33	12	9	6	—	—	—
Cincinnati	7	11	6	1	1	1	4	3	4	—	—	—
Denver	12	14	19	—	—	—	4	4	5	6	1	1
Minneapolis	7	12	13	1	3	7	5	3	3	1	2	2
Newark	4	4	6	2	2	3	5	5	4	—	—	—
New Haven	5	8	8	—	1	2	4	3	2	—	—	—
New York[c]	162	202	199	23	21	25	14	14	12	5	5	5
Philadelphia	34	43	43	1	9	13	6	7	4	3	4	2
Pittsburgh	9	11	12	1	2	3	4	6	5	—	—	—
Rochester	4	5	4	3	2	3	3	3	4	—	—	—
St. Louis	15	14	20	—	1	9	4	5	4	—	—	—
Total	361	469	466	39	69	113	72	69	58	17	15	12

| CITY | SCHOOL SUPPLIES | | | SECOND HAND | | | JUVENILE | | | LAW | | |
	1928	1932	1935	1928	1932	1935	1928	1932	1935	1928	1932	1935
Brooklyn[b]	—	—	—	7	6	9	—	—	—	—	—	1
Chicago	9	6	6	11	9	18	—	—	1	3	3	5
Cincinnati	1	—	1	2	3	3	—	—	—	1	1	1
Denver	—	—	—	3	—	—	—	1	—	2	2	1
Minneapolis	4	3	2	—	—	—	—	—	—	—	—	—
Newark	—	—	—	—	—	2	—	—	—	1	—	—
New Haven	1	—	1	—	—	—	1	1	1	—	—	—
New York[c]	13	6	8	59	25	39	5	3	3	11	—	1
Philadelphia	3	2	2	7	3	4	—	—	1	4	4	3
Pittsburgh	2	—	—	3	3	1	—	—	—	—	—	—
Rochester	1	—	1	1	—	1	—	—	—	2	—	—
St. Louis	1	1	1	3	2	3	—	—	—	—	1	1
Total	35	18	22	96	51	80	6	5	6	24	11	13

| CITY | MEDICAL | | | OLD AND RARE | | | RELIGIOUS | | | TOTAL | | |
	1928	1932	1935	1928	1932	1935	1928	1932	1935	1928	1932	1935
Brooklyn[b]	1	2	1	3	5	8	2	1	3	62	79	76
Chicago	2	2	2	10	21	16	20	12	10	136	179	200
Cincinnati	—	—	—	2	1	1	4	3	5	22	23	22
Denver	—	—	—	2	1	1	1	2	2	30	25	29
Minneapolis	—	1	1	—	1.	2	4	3	2	22	28	31
Newark	—	—	—	1	3	2	1	—	—	14	14	17
New Haven	—	1	1	2	1	—	—	—	—	13	15	15
New York[c]	7	4	3	67	82	91	21	18	24	387	380	410
Philadelphia	1	2	1	12	14	16	14	14	13	85	102	102
Pittsburgh	—	—	—	—	—	2	4	3	4	23	25	27
Rochester	—	—	—	—	1	3	1	1	2	15	12	18
St. Louis	1	2	1	2	2	3	4	6	6	30	34	48
Total	12	14	10	101	132	144	76	63	71	839	916	995

[a] *American Book Trade Directory*
[b] Brooklyn includes Kings borough
[c] New York here includes Manhattan, Bronx, and Richmond boroughs

to the question—who buys the books you have to sell and why?

If forced to an opinion, one could guess that rental library patronage was motivated somewhat like the public library fiction patronage, which declined as the libraries grew worse and times grew better. This would fit reports by some chains to the effect that their sales grew until 1935 and declined thereafter, despite the efforts to increase them by adding new units. Several large chains, which reported both the number of their operating units and their annual receipts from all units, show regular annual increases both in units and receipts until 1932-33. From 1933 to date their units continued to increase at the same rate but their gross receipts fell off. The annual declines in receipts since 1932-33 were much smaller than the annual increases prior to that year, suggesting, perhaps, that the rental library market has just about returned to normal. We need information to check each of these suggestions.

Table XX raises the same questions as to the relation between the number and the receipts of book stores. If the national jobbers like American News or Baker and Taylor, and local book stores in selected communities could be convinced that they stand to gain more than they could lose by making their sales data available to students, then the *Booktrade Directory* might be analyzed to excellent advantage. Reading the bottom row of the table we see that only two types of agency—rental libraries and shops selling old and rare books—increased in number from 1928 to 1932 and from 1932 to 1935. Two types of agency—the drug and department store booksellers—declined in number each year. Of the remaining seven agencies, all but the shops specializing in general sales and juvenile books, which are few, had more outlets in 1928 than in 1935.

Distrust of such "totals" is caused by the wide variations among cities. The general book stores west of the Alleghenies appear to have increased more from 1932 to 1935. Of the twelve cities (reading the right hand column) only four had more book stores in 1932 than in 1928 and more in 1935 than in 1932. Such analysis might be carried far to determine and compare the influences of mere geography, relative wealth and size of

communities, public library status in each community, unemployment ratios, and other factors upon the number of agencies of
each type in each city per year. The analysis would be important
if the results could be interpreted. The results could be interpreted if we knew the relation of books read to books sold, and
of books sold to the number of stores selling books of each type.
The available data on changes in number of stores selling different sorts of books could then be used to interpret changes in
book consumption in relation to possible social changes.

Another line of research should examine the book trade from
the inside, in somewhat the same fashion as we have considered
the public library, i.e., as a social institution, with changing
problems and policies of its own. While somewhat overdrawn,
considering the ever present possibility of a best seller (*Gone
With the Wind,* the author's first novel, having probably established an all-time record sale in its first year of publication), the
following gloomy forecast[13] by an eminent book publisher suggests the variety of internal problems to be studied by competent
members of the craft. His forecast is so prophetic of imminent
changes in the book industry—particularly in respect to cheaper
books—that close analysis of the quotation will suggest several
hypotheses on which students can work to advantage.

In regard to the book business it may be summed up about as follows.
The proletariat has suffered most in the crisis, but it was not as a class
an important factor in our business even in the best of times. The upper
classes have been hurt, too, but neither were they the really significant
elements in the book business. Moreover, the proletariat was already so
close to the mere subsistence level that its drop in the crisis was not
enormous, while the upper classes could afford to lose a great deal and
yet maintain a practically unaltered standard of living. On the other
hand, the middle classes of the cities—the white-collar groups, small
business men, professionals, intellectual workers, etc.—who form the
basis of our market, suffered disastrously in every conceivable way. Their
standards of living were very sharply cut. A large portion of them

[13] Anonymous. "A Few Sour Notes on the Book Business." *The Publishers'
Weekly.* 128:425-430. No. 7 August 17 1935

merged with the proletariat; the rest were reduced to insecurity, fear, and often to a pretty grubby livelihood.

The best economic thought of our times—Soule, Laski, Strachey, and Corey on the left and a host of government investigators on the right —believe that the middle classes are doomed. They believe that a *permanent* expropriation has been effected.

The conclusions to be drawn are obvious. Our public cannot afford to buy our books in anything like the quantity we are now producing them, and it is unlikely that there will be any real change for the better. Suppose you had an income of, say, forty or fifty dollars a week on which to support a family of three or four. How many $2.00 or $2.50 books could you afford to buy? Maybe two a year.

Price is the crux. I say this dogmatically: there aren't more than a hundred books a year that are worth the price at which they are published. I am here using the term 'worth' in a purely psychological sense. In an economic sense they are worth their price, for as the industry is now constructed it is impossible to publish them for much less. But I don't think there is a great deal of consolation in the thought that although you can't sell an article you can justify its selling price.

It does no good to think of petty reforms. The solution lies in a complete overhauling of the structure and functioning of the business —a rebuilding of the methods of production and distribution to make feasible the publication of all new books at drastically lowered prices. This is not the sort of thing that can be done in a day—nor in seven. It must be a gradual and considered process. But it must eventually be done if the business is to survive as a national force and a socially useful entity.

This represents about the best combination of professional experience and intelligent observation so neatly expressed. Since the commercial success of the book trade is a basic element in the effective distribution of reading, the statement should suggest several avenues of productive research.

Newspapers

Changes in the newspaper industry should be described both in terms of its performance—i.e., changes in content and changes in circulation—and in terms of its internal problems. So little is recorded to show changes in content that the rich acres of newspaper files are virgin fields for the student to cultivate. Discussion is thus confined to circulation and to changes in industrial policies.

Table IX in Chapter III presents facts obtainable from *Editor and Publisher*. The figures do not show whether more people read more space per paper as they became poorer and bought fewer newspapers. We know, however, what sorts of newspapers were sold in largest numbers each year. Hence the relation between changes in sales and changes in content can be determined by any student willing to describe the changes in content by analyzing back files. Accordingly newspaper circulation was discussed with magazines and books in Chapter III. What follows concerns changes in the newspaper as a social institution.

The effects of depression on the newspaper have much in common with its effects upon other social institutions, and upon society at large. The newspaper is primarily a business. It exists to make a profit for the publishers and stockholders, by selling advertising space to other businesses. It baits the public to read the advertisements by spreading them with much more interesting print—comic strips, news, and human interest stories. Hence the newspaper serves the dual function of advertising salesman and reporter. It serves two groups of customers, the advertisers and the general public, groups whose interests differ widely and frequently conflict. To this extent the newspaper is a house divided against itself. It would be useful for students to determine how wide the division is.

But both as a commercial enterprise and as a social institution, the newspaper thrives by its news, a commodity more expensive to produce because no single plant can produce it. To meet the costs of news gathering and printing, the paper must choose between a selling price to cover production costs in a small market and a selling price low enough to secure mass sales. If mass sales are secured, the advertiser will produce the additional revenue to cover production costs and show a profit. With a few negligible exceptions, newspapers have made the latter choice.

Approximately 66 to 80 per cent of the American newspaper's revenue comes from the advertiser and only about 20 to 33 per cent from the purchaser.[14] The advertiser's importance is further increased by the fact that "manufacturing costs have mounted until a variation of 15 per cent in the volume of advertising means the difference between profit and loss for most of the newspapers of the country."[15] Hence the newspaper is particularly vulnerable to a depression which reduces the volume of newspaper advertising to the extent shown in the first column of Table XII. Hence also the publisher and members of his executive, editorial, and business staffs do their best to insure the paper's economic stability. One might easily suppose that continued depression would persuade newspaper executives to share the interests of their advertisers. The publisher hesitates to offend his advertisers. What we need very much to know is the extent to which this natural impulse to please the advertiser produced changes in newspaper content. The facts should be exciting though not easy to establish.

In general, the reportorial staffs mediate between the publisher and the public. Did the depression widen the gap between reporters and executives? If the fact were established, it would have important implications for the general reader and for the student of social change. The larger of such implications would involve trends toward monopoly, as represented by the growth

[14] Bleyer, Willard Grosvenor. "Does Press Merit Privileged Place?" *Editor and Publisher*. 67:214. *Golden Jubilee Number*. July 21 1934 (here Bleyer says "2/3 to 5/6") ; Bleyer, Willard Grosvenor. "Freedom of the Press and the New Deal." *Journalism Quarterly*. 11:22-35. March 1934 (here Bleyer says "2/3 to 6/7," p. 26) ; Flynn, John T. "News by Courtesy." *Forum*. 83:139-143. March 1930 ("about 4/5," p. 139) ; Bent, Silas. *Ballyhoo: The Voice of the Press*. New York: Boni and Liveright. 1927. Pp. xviii+398. P. 262 ("Bent gives 3/4")

[15] Beazell, William Preston. "The Party Flag Comes Down." *Atlantic Monthly*. 147:366-372 (p. 367). March 1931. In an earlier article Beazell put the critical margin even lower—at 10 per cent. "Tomorrow's Newspaper." *Atlantic Monthly*. 146:24-30. July 1930

of newspaper chains, the influences upon the selection and presentation of news, and the changing employer-employee relationships within the industry itself. Each of these topics suggests much needed research.

Chains.—Newspapers in the United States have tended toward monopolies. The trend is indicated by five pieces of evidence, namely, the decline in the number of different newspapers despite the growth in circulation, the expansion of daily[16] and weekly[17] newspaper chains, the increasing number of one-newspaper cities,[18] the increasing number of one-city monopolies,[19] and the increasing number of "associated" newspapers[20] (newspapers owned in groups of two or more in the same city).

We much need to investigate the effects of depression upon this trend. The requisite data are reported in *Ayer's Directory.* In doubtful cases the *International Year Book* will help.

Records for chain dailies cover the period from 1923 to 1935. Table XXI shows the increase of chain daily circulation to 1930. From 1930-34 chain circulation lost more than non-chain circulation. In 1935 the chains seem to have recovered so promptly as to give the depression the appearance of a momentary obstacle. Students should ask why.

Ten chains control one-third of all the daily newspaper circulation and almost one-half of all the Sunday circulation in the United States. The ten groups receive all the important news

---

[16] See Weinfeld, William. "The Growth of Daily Newspaper Chains in the United States, 1923, 1926-1935." *Journalism Quarterly.* 13:357-380. December 1936

[17] See Wenninger, William C. "Conclusions Based on Study of 79 Weekly Newspaper Chains." *Inland Printer.* 88:41-43. November 1931

[18] Masche, W. Carl. *Factors Involved in the Consolidation and Suspension of Daily and Sunday Newspapers in the United States Since 1900: A Statistical Study in Social Change.* University of Minnesota. Unpublished M.A. thesis. 1932. Pp. 190

[19] Bleyer, Willard Grosvenor. "Freedom of the Press and the New Deal." *Journalism Quarterly.* 11:22-35 (p. 28). March 1934

[20] Hall, Bob. "Trend to Associated Newspapers Found to Be All-round Benefit." *Editor and Publisher.* 64:30. December 26 1931

TABLE XXI

NUMBER AND TOTAL AND PER CAPITA CIRCULATION OF ENGLISH LANGUAGE CHAIN AND NON-CHAIN NEWSPAPERS, DAILY AND SUNDAY: UNITED STATES, 1923, 1926–1935[a]

YEAR	GENERAL CHAIN NEWSPAPERS						GENERAL NON-CHAIN NEWSPAPERS						PER CENT WHICH CHAINS ARE OF TOTAL			
	DAILY			SUNDAY			DAILY			SUNDAY			DAILY		SUNDAY	
	NUMBER	CIRCULATION (IN THOUSANDS)	CIRCULATION PER 100 POPULATION[b]	NUMBER	CIRCULATION (IN THOUSANDS)	CIRCULATION PER 100 POPULATION[b]	NUMBER	CIRCULATION (IN THOUSANDS)	CIRCULATION PER 100 POPULATION[b]	NUMBER	CIRCULATION (IN THOUSANDS)	CIRCULATION PER 100 POPULATION[b]	NUMBER	CIRCULATION	NUMBER	CIRCULATION
1923	158	9,767	8.8	65	9,129	8.2	1,878	21,687	19.4	482	12,334	11.1	7.8	31.1	11.9	42.5
1924	—	—	—	—	—	—	—	—	—	—	—	—	—	—	—	—
1925	—	—	—	—	—	—	—	—	—	—	—	—	—	—	—	—
1926	223	12,361	10.6	91	11,144	9.6	1,778	23,641	20.3	454	13,291	11.4	11.1	34.3	16.7	45.6
1927	232	14,399	12.2	95	12,275	10.4	1,717	23,567	19.9	431	13,194	11.2	11.9	37.9	18.1	48.2
1928	269	15,539	13.0	114	12,832	10.7	1,670	22,434	18.7	408	12,939	10.8	13.8	40.9	21.8	49.8
1929	318	16,574	13.6	133	14,053	11.6	1,626	22,851	18.8	395	12,827	10.6	16.4	42.0	25.2	52.3
1930	328	17,166	13.9	138	14,277	11.6	1,614	22,423	18.2	383	12,136	9.9	16.9	43.4	26.5	54.1
1931	334	16,099	13.0	138	13,183	10.6	1,589	22,662	18.3	375	12,518	10.1	17.3	41.5	26.9	51.3
1932	346	14,900	11.9	143	12,822	10.3	1,567	21,507	17.2	375	12,038	9.6	18.0	40.9	27.4	51.6
1933	340	13,833	11.0	140	11,931	9.5	1,571	21,342	17.0	366	12,110	9.6	17.7	39.3	27.5	49.6
1934	331	14,020	11.1	132	13,069	10.3	1,598	22,689	17.9	373	13,475	10.7	17.1	38.2	25.9	49.2
1935	328	15,859	12.5	131	14,759	11.6	1,622	22,296	17.5	387	13,389	10.5	16.8	41.6	25.3	52.4

[a] Weinfeld, William. (1) A Statistical Analysis of the Growth of Chain Daily Newspapers in the United States; 1923 to 1934. Unpublished M.A. thesis. University of Minnesota. 1936. Pp. 75, 152. (2) "The Growth of Daily Newspaper Chains in the United States: 1923, 1926–1935." Journalism Quarterly. 13:357–380; (pp. 363, 365, 368). December 1936

[b] Population estimates as of July 1. Data from Statistical Abstract of the United States, United States Department of Commerce, 1935. For a more refined analysis of per capita circulation the population 10 years of age and over, or the literate population 10 years of age and over, can be substituted for the total population.

services—the Associated Press, United Press, and International News Service. The possible extent of monopoly raises many questions of vivid sociological interest which invite careful research. Monopoly affects the presentation of news to the extent that publishers exploit their personal views of what is socially desirable. Extreme instances of such exploitation are found in Chicago.

Another suggestion of newspaper monopoly is the tendency, especially since 1934, for newspapers to control radio stations. In 1935 the number of newspapers' radio stations doubled. Data describing this trend are available in certain issues of *Editor and Publisher*.[21] Newspapers and radio stations naturally compete for advertising, and newspapers try to prevent the stations from broadcasting news before they can print it. The newspapers best able to outbid the stations may be the wealthiest—whether chains or independents. If they are, we may suppose that the two most important sources of news, the newspaper and the radio, are controlled by an ever diminishing number of individuals, whose primary purpose is to make money. If the hypothesis is sound, the effects of such control upon the dissemination and coloring of news would naturally favor propaganda in the interests of important advertisers. The hypothesis should be carefully studied.

Selection and presentation of news.—Most readers of George Seldes' *Freedom of the Press*, Silas Bent's *Ballyhoo*, or certain of the recent biographies of William Randolph Hearst will doubtless admit that newspaper publishers have tended to color news according to their personal sympathies. Oswald Garrison Villard's *Some Newspapers and Newspaper Men* suggests that even the *New York Times* has suppressed or distorted important news unfavorable to its supporting interests. Of course many sorts of bias existed before the depression. How did the depression

---

[21] See also Carskadon, T. R. "The Press-Radio War." *New Republic*. 86:132-135. March 11 1936

change them? Did the depression make it harder to present news impartially? Did the advertisers exert pressure directly or indirectly, and how? Did financiers exert pressure on publishers and editors to print news favorable to them? How do such pressures work, if they exist? To what extent did publishers and editors anticipate the direction of such pressures and so prevent them from being applied? We need the answers.

The answers are not found in available records. They may have to wait for publishers' and editors' autobiographies, written with that fine detachment of the retired executive which at times inspires revelations. Or certain reporters in close contact with executive offices might be persuaded to report on the state of reporting in depression. Or again the student might compare the same news items in several papers, of different political complexion, from year to year, and draw what inferences he can regarding changes in the nature and strength of the "coloring" applied to each. He might seek, for example, to define changes in the attitude of publishers and editors as reflected by news and editorials on such subjects as unemployment, taxes, and the depression itself. It would be helpful to analyze the presentation of depression news separately in the news pages, the editorial columns, and in the financial pages; then to compare the three versions as appearing annually in several selected papers. One might well find a sharp discrepancy between the financial facts as published and the news items reporting such facts, or between different versions of the extent of unemployment, in the same papers. It would make for a much needed social appraisal of the newspaper, first to establish such discrepancies and then to explain them in terms of conflicting policies.

Publisher vs. reporter.—The recent history of the press in this country suggests another basis on which to examine the degree of difference between the interests of publishers and reporters. William Preston Beazell, Silas Bent, Willard Grosvenor Bleyer, Bruce Bliven, John T. Flynn, Ernest Gruening, George

Seldes, Oswald Garrison Villard, and William Allen White have described the newspaper as a major business, in many cases "big business," well before the last depression. By way of presenting an hypothesis for students of American journalism to check, the following paragraphs suggest some possible effects of the big business motive during depression. If the account is somewhat overdrawn, it should define the issues all the more sharply.

From October 1929 to about June 1933 the press along with the country at large was bewildered by the sudden shrinkage of capital and tried to find and to give reassurance wherever it could. To quiet the public's nerves, the press naturally toned down the facts of unemployment, bank failures, and other events while it drew pictures of prosperity around the corner.[22] Following Roosevelt's inauguration in March 1933 the extent to which the American press supported the President surprised even foreign observers.

The support lasted until the National Industrial Recovery Act confronted newspaper publishers with a code covering hours of work, wages, and fair practices in common with other business and industry. Thereupon the American Newspaper Publishers' Association (ANPA) telegraphed its members to disapprove the code and so preserve the freedom of the press. Some of the larger publishers held that the newspaper's social services were such as to exempt it from regulations applied to other businesses. At this point opposition developed. Some daily newspapers denied that the code would endanger the freedom of the press.[23] The same interpretation was given the "free press" issue by some liberal weekly magazines.

---

[22] Anonymous. "Press Underestimated the Slump, Journalism Students Are Told." *Editor and Publisher*. 65:26. April 8 1933; Brant, Irving. "After 'Contagious Magic' Had Failed." *Editor and Publisher*. 65:7. March 25 1933

[23] Bleyer, Willard Grosvenor. "Journalism in the United States, 1933." *Journalism Quarterly*. 10:296-301 (p. 297). December 1933

Certain groups of reporters then sought to improve their status by invoking Section 7a of the code, which guarantees the right of workers to organize for collective bargaining. By December 1933 the American Newspaper Guild had been established as a national organization. Its formation was encouraged by the labor clause (Section 7a) in the NRA Code and by the (10 to 50 per cent) salary cuts and dismissals from 1929 to 1933. During its first three years the Guild has won certain concessions affecting wages, hours, and conditions of work, and recognition of the union.

Despite such concessions, the Guild has probably tended to alienate publishers from their reportorial employees. Some publishers have argued that newswriters cannot be union members and impartial reporters at the same time. Others have replied that reporters are seldom impartial anyway. Charles P. Howard, president of the International Typographical Union, went farther by suggesting that the class consciousness of unionized reporters would benefit the papers by coloring the news in the interests of the larger public. In either case, the depression appears to have produced a wider division of interests between publishers and their editorial employees than has existed before in American publishing history. If the division becomes still wider it may have visible effects upon the presentation of news. It is highly desirable for some student to look for the effects to date. Seldes' book, *Freedom of the Press,* suggests a useful procedure.

To hypothesize: one effect of depression upon the newspaper is the reporters' greater sympathy with organized labor. Another effect is the increased class consciousness of publishers, disposing them to stress the strictly business function as against the quasi-social or quasi-public function of the newspaper. If the latter hypothesis is examined, the student would ask whether publishers in general since 1933 have become more antagonistic toward organized labor; have increasingly defended big business and fought government regulation; and have opposed liberal parties, liberal legislation, and liberal movements, both here and abroad.[24] To define the term "liberal" in this connection is not easy. It might be defined by patient analysis of representative daily newspapers, year by year, with reference to changes in relevant editorial policy. Sir Willmott Lewis, Washington correspondent of the London *Times,* characterized the class consciousness of newspaper publishers as "the millionaire philosophy."[25] He saw it a growing threat to freedom of the press because of the public resentment its excesses would cause. Is it true, as George Seldes points out in *Freedom of the Press* (page ix), that the public is growing more and more suspicious of newspapers? Is it true that "the prestige of the daily press is lower today than at any time since the country was founded"?[26] What exactly are the newspaper's social responsibilities which entitle it to low mail rates and other privileges? Which of such responsibilities has it met and failed to meet, and to what extent since 1929? Answers can be approached by analysis and comparison of representative newspapers.

CLIENTELES

There remain at least two more questions about distributing agencies during depression. The first is, how did their clienteles change? The question is important because changes in patronage with a uniform circulation and changes in circulation to the same clientele may both reflect the influence of depression equally. When both circulation and clientele vary from year to year,

---

[24] Such points are documented in Seldes, George. *Freedom of the Press.* New York: The Bobbs-Merrill Co. 1935; "The Press," *The Fight.* Pp. 5-6. December 1936; in various articles by Bliven, Bruce. *New Republic.* 1933-1936; and in various articles by Broun, Heywood and Villard, Oswald Garrison. *The Nation.* 1930-1936

[25] Anonymous. "Millionaire Philosophy Is Called Greatest Threat to Free Press." *Editor and Publisher.* 67:10. November 1934

[26] T.R.B. "Washington Notes." *New Republic.* 89:16-17 (p. 16). November 4 1936

one may seek relationships between them which help to explain one variable by the other or to suggest a common cause.

The second question asks how the publications obtained by each group from each agency changed during the depression and recovery periods. If the same agencies were patronized by the same groups to the same extent in depression as at other times, we should want to know whether each group obtained the same reading matter. Changes in the publications obtained from each agency by each group suggest social aspects of changes in the distributing agencies.

Data to meet both questions are not available for each agency and each year. For the winter of 1933-34 in Chicago and the fall of 1934 in St. Louis we have data to show at least *how* the questions can be met. The data can be used in two ways. We can describe the facts available[27] and invite all interested students to use them for comparison with facts which they can still secure to describe the postdepression situation. An abundance of highly trustworthy evidence covering 1933-34, which it is no longer possible to obtain for these years, has been tabulated, indexed, and filed for the benefit of all readers of the present volume. Access to the data can be arranged by correspondence with the writer.

Another possibility is that by use of appropriate economic indexes one might use the available records to sample two groups of the same social composition, in the same or different cities during 1933-34, of whom one was mainly employed and the other mainly unemployed. If so, it might be found that the agencies patronized by the two groups differed more during 1933-34 than those used by either group changed from those years to, say 1937. Such comparisons are much needed.[28]

---

[27] At the Graduate Library School, University of Chicago.

[28] A suggestive illustration is Miller, Robert A. "The Relation of Reading Characteristics to Social Indexes." *American Journal of Sociology.* 41:738-756. No. 6. May 1936

The remaining tables of this chapter supply examples of evidence relevant to the questions just raised about the changes in distributing agencies and in their clienteles during depression. The tables show what publications were supplied by each agency in South Chicago to their respective clienteles during the winter of 1933-34. The data were obtained in the course of a study directed by the writer under the joint auspices of the Graduate Library School and the Social Science Research Committee of the University of Chicago.[29] Approximately 6,850 residents responded by interviews and schedules in six census tracts. The tracts were chosen to cover the range throughout the South Chicago area in per capita wealth, average years of schooling, percentage of unskilled labor, and other conditions known to influence the supply and consumption of reading.

A number of different social problems had previously been studied by social science faculties of the University, the Chicago Institute of Juvenile Research, and other groups in the same and other tracts; hence an abundance of data was already available for the sociological interpretation of reading. As reflecting the influence of the depression upon reading, the South Chicago industrial area well represents the social effects of depression at their worst, since steel, the dominant industry, was hard hit. Yet as a source of information concerning the central tendencies of reading during depression, South Chicago was not well chosen. It has the disadvantage that the community reads about as little as any urban community of comparable size, and the local supply of publications is therefore much below normal. Probably each of these two conditions is partly the cause and partly the

---

[29] The only reports on the study which have appeared to date are the article by Robert A. Miller, noted in the preceding footnote, and the following three theses by students of the Graduate Library School. University of Chicago: Ellsworth, Ralph E. *The Distribution of Books and Magazines in Selected Communities.* Ph.D. 1937; Fair, Ethel M. *The Public Library versus Other Sources of Books.* M.A. 1935; Foster, Jeannette Howard. *An Experiment in Classifying Fiction Based on the Characteristics of Its Readers.* Ph.D. 1935

TABLE XXII

PERCENTAGE DISTRIBUTION OF MAGAZINES AND BOOKS FOR SELECTED CATE-
GORIES, BY TYPE OF AGENCY FROM WHICH SECURED, AND SEX OF READERS:
SAMPLE FROM SOUTH CHICAGO, 1933[a]

SELECTED CATEGORIES	PUBLIC LIBRARY			FRIEND			DRUG STORE		
	MALE	FE-MALE	TOTAL	MALE	FE-MALE	TOTAL	MALE	FE-MALE	TOTAL
Magazines									
Detective, adventure	.6	.8	.7	30.9	7.5	19.0	34.4	4.9	18.9
Weekly news	.3	—	.1	1.6	1.4	1.5	3.9	2.1	2.9
Movie, radio, love	.6	1.3	.9	10.1	30.6	20.6	5.7	41.1	24.2
5¢ weeklies	.3	—	.1	5.1	7.8	6.5	25.6	12.0	18.5
Monthly story	—	.3	.1	5.7	5.8	5.7	7.2	10.1	8.7
Religious	—	—	—	—	.8	.4	.4	—	.2
Parents', women's, home. . .	.6	.5	.5	2.2	13.9	8.2	4.3	26.9	16.1
All others	2.5	.3	1.3	16.5	6.9	11.6	18.6	3.0	10.4
Total	5	3	4	72	75	74	100	100	100
Books									
Good fiction	18.1	27.7	23.1	5.5	6.3	5.9	—	—	—
Other fiction	33.3	30.7	32.0	10.9	7.6	9.2	—	—	—
Juvenile	12.8	19.6	16.4	2.8	4.3	3.6	—	—	—
Psychology	3.6	2.5	3.0	.8	1.4	1.1	—	—	—
Biography, travel	5.6	4.8	5.2	1.8	1.1	1.4	—	—	—
Social problems.	.8	.8	.8	.6	.3	.4	—	—	—
Literature	1.4	2.0	1.7	.6	1.0	.8	—	—	—
All others	19.7	8.8	14.0	4.8	3.3	4.0	—	—	—
Total	95	97	96	28	25	26	—	—	—
Total per cent books and maga-zines	100	100	100	100	100	100	100	100	100
Total number books and maga-zines	360	397	757	986	1,035	2,021	489	535	1,024

	NEWSSTAND			BOOK STORE			RENTAL LIBRARY		
Magazines									
Detective, adventure	23.8	5.2	14.7	—	—	—	—	—	—
Weekly news	4.5	3.5	4.0	—	—	—	—	—	—
Movie, radio, love	8.4	30.6	19.3	—	—	—	—	—	—
5¢ weeklies.	28.7	17.6	23.2	—	—	—	—	—	—
Monthly story	9.0	8.7	8.8	—	—	—	—	—	—
Religious	.4	.2	.3	—	—	—	—	—	—
Parent's, women's, home . . .	3.7	28.0	15.7	—	—	—	—	—	—
All others	21.5	6.2	14.0	—	—	—	—	—	—
Total	100	100	100	—	—	—	—	—	—
Books									
Good fiction	—	—	—	5.8	32.5	18.6	32.5	56.4	49.6
Other fiction	—	—	—	22.6	19.8	21.3	47.5	29.7	34.8
Juvenile	—	—	—	13.9	15.1	14.4	2.5	1.0	1.4
Psychology	—	—	—	10.2	7.1	8.7	—	5.0	3.5
Biography, travel	—	—	—	6.6	7.1	6.8	12.5	4.0	6.4
Social problems	—	—	—	.7	.8	.8	2.5	—	.7
Literature	—	—	—	2.2	1.6	1.9	—	2.0	1.4
All others	—	—	—	38.0	15.9	27.4	2.5	2.0	2.1
Total	—	—	—	100	100	100	100	100	100
Total per cent books and maga-zines	100	100	100	100	100	100	100	100	100
Total number books and maga-zines	534	517	1,051	137	126	263	40	101	141

[a] Unpublished study of South Chicago by Douglas Waples and others. Some 6,850 persons were
interviewed during the winter of 1933–34, and their reading for the two weeks previous to the date of
interview recorded.

TABLE XXII (Continued)

Magazines	Magazine Subscription			All Others			Total		
Detective, adventure	1.8	.3	.9	11.0	2.0	6.5	16.2	3.2	9.3
Weekly news	8.2	5.1	6.4	3.1	3.9	3.5	3.4	3.0	3.2
Movie, radio, love.	.4	2.4	1.6	5.4	14.5	10.0	5.5	17.9	12.0
5¢ weeklies.	11.7	10.3	10.9	18.9	17.4	18.1	14.9	11.9	13.3
Monthly story	7.9	13.9	11.5	8.5	7.7	8.1	6.9	7.9	7.4
Religious	5.9	7.9	7.1	2.3	3.0	2.6	1.7	2.6	2.1
Parent's, women's, home. . .	8.9	44.6	30.0	7.6	19.8	13.8	5.2	22.3	14.2
All others	55.1	15.5	31.7	17.4	9.4	13.3	21.2	8.0	14.3
Total	100	100	100	74	78	76	75	77	76
Books									
Good fiction	—	—	—	3.9	5.4	4.7	4.2	6.7	5.5
Other fiction	—	—	—	4.4	3.6	4.0	7.1	5.8	6.4
Juvenile	—	—	—	4.6	5.0	4.8	3.5	4.2	3.9
Psychology	—	—	—	3.1	3.2	3.1	1.8	1.8	1.8
Biography, travel	—	—	—	1.8	1.3	1.6	1.7	1.2	1.4
Social problems.	—	—	—	.4	.2	.3	.4	.2	.3
Literature	—	—	—	1.1	.7	.9	.7	.6	.6
All others	—	—	—	6.5	3.0	4.7	5.7	2.6	4.1
Total	—	—	—	26	22	24	25	23	24
Total per cent books and magazines	100	100	100	100	100	100	100	100	100
Total number books and magazines	681	984	1,665	1,799	1,858	3,657	5,026	5,553	10,579

effect of the other. To offset this bias of the South Chicago sample, Appendix A presents somewhat comparable data, based on 3,543 cases, from residential districts of St. Louis in the fall of 1934, where the effects of depression were relatively slight. The districts enjoy unusually good public library service and perhaps read as much above the national average as South Chicago reads below it. When both the South Chicago data and the St. Louis data are examined with reference to questions about the status of distributing agencies in depression, the student is more likely to get at central tendencies in reading distribution.

Table XXII shows the relative extent to which the different agencies in South Chicago supplied different sorts of publications in 1933-34. It is clear that the agencies differ in the kinds of reading matter they supply, and hence that they differ in the nature of their social influence, in so far as reading has a social influence, and in the nature of their social functions. The public library supplies more books of fiction than anything else, and supplies more of it to women than to men; 55 per cent of its supply is adult fiction, and 72 per cent is fiction if the juveniles are added. Friends supply mostly magazines, especially detective, adventure, movie, radio, and love magazines which together amount to 40 per cent of the publications obtained from friends. "All other sources," next to the right-hand column of the table, also yield three times as many magazines as books, of which movie, radio, love, 5¢ weeklies, and women's magazines constitute 42 per cent.

These three agencies—public library, friends, and all other sources, constitute the *free* agencies which were most heavily patronized and supplied most reading matter in South Chicago during middepression. From the bottom row of the table we see that the largest number of magazines and books obtained from any of the sources listed were secured from "all other sources," next most from friends, next came magazine subscriptions, next the newsstands (excluding newspapers), next the drug stores, next the public library, next the bookstore, and last the rental library. Presumably the same was true of other poverty stricken communities. If so, it would not be hard to find out how the relative importance of the free agencies changed during years of recovery and whether there was any appreciable change in the proportion of publications which each supplied to the community.

Turning to the commercial agencies as shown in the same table (XXII), we see that the drug stores and newsstands supplied mostly the same types of magazines. Subscriptions differed in that detective, adventure, movie, radio, and love magazines are rarely subscribed for whereas women's magazines are 30 per cent of those so obtained. The bookstore and the rental library provide largely fiction, the former selling a larger percentage of "good" fiction to women and the latter renting a larger percentage of "other" fiction to men. If we like to impute more social benefits to the reading of "good" fiction books than

TABLE XXIII

PERCENTAGE DISTRIBUTION OF BOOKS AND MAGAZINES BY AGE AND SEX OF
READERS, BY TYPE OF AGENCY FROM WHICH SECURED:
SAMPLE FROM SOUTH CHICAGO, 1933[a]

AGE	PUBLIC LIBRARY			FRIEND			DRUG STORE		
	MALE	FEMALE	TOTAL	MALE	FEMALE	TOTAL	MALE	FEMALE	TOTAL
10–19	50.0	63.7	57.2	36.4	31.9	34.1	24.7	21.7	23.1
20–29	23.6	16.1	19.7	32.7	32.9	32.8	30.5	32.5	31.5
30–44	19.7	13.6	16.5	21.0	21.8	21.4	32.7	34.0	33.4
45 and over	6.7	6.6	6.6	9.9	13.3	11.7	12.1	11.8	11.9
Total	100	100	100	100	100	100	100	100	100
Number books and magazines	360	397	757	986	1,035	2,021	489	535	1,024

	NEWSSTAND			RENTAL LIBRARY			SUBSCRIPTION		
10–19	23.4	18.0	20.7	12.5	9.9	10.6	11.5	5.6	8.0
20–29	30.0	31.5	30.7	37.5	47.5	44.7	14.1	16.4	15.4
30–44	29.0	36.0	32.4	35.0	31.7	32.6	42.7	48.1	45.9
45 and over	17.6	14.5	16.1	15.0	10.9	12.1	31.7	30.0	30.7
Total	100	100	100	100	100	100	100	100	100
Number books and magazines	534	517	1,051	40	101	141	681	984	1,665

	BOOK STORE			ALL OTHERS			TOTAL		
10–19	28.5	24.6	26.6	31.1	30.7	30.9	29.2	26.3	27.6
20–29	26.3	27.0	26.6	21.3	23.8	22.6	24.8	25.7	25.3
30–44	24.1	35.7	29.7	28.3	29.1	28.7	28.7	31.3	30.0
45 and over	21.2	12.7	17.1	19.3	16.4	17.8	17.2	16.7	17.0
Total	100	100	100	100	100	100	100	100	100
Number books and magazines	137	126	263	1,799	1,858	3,657	5,026	5,553	10,579

[a] Unpublished study of South Chicago by Douglas Waples and others. Some 6,850 persons were interviewed during the winter of 1933–34, and their reading for the two weeks previous to the date of interview recorded.

of fiction books not so good, then rental libraries and book stores probably have a better case than public libraries, during depression in South Chicago. If, however, the case is argued in terms of effortless entertainment, the positions are reversed. To know how the fiction ratios have changed since 1933-34 would help both to describe and to evaluate the agencies' cultural influence.

Or again, we may ask how the agencies compare as distributors of books on social problems. Table XXII shows that a very small proportion of the books supplied by any agency are of this character. Oddly enough, the proportion supplied to men by the rental libraries is the largest of all, 2.5 per cent, and the other proportions are all less than one per cent. Such conditions as these invite further study for comparison with possible changes in postdepression years. They invite comparisons of the extent to which literature on social problems is distributed in book form to any considerable extent as contrasted with magazines. If the magazine is the chief vehicle, it would be well to determine how much of the content of general magazines during this period dealt with social problems. No fair estimate can be made from the titles alone.

The nature of each agency's influence appears not only in differences among the publications it supplies but also in differences among the social groups to whom it supplies them. Table XXIII describes the distribution of books and magazines to the patrons of each agency by sex and age, Table XXIV by sex and education, and Table XXV by sex and occupation. In combination the three tables fairly well describe the modal patron of each agency. Thus the mode for the public library is a girl between ten and nineteen years who has not yet completed the eighth grade and who is still a student. The predominating borrower-from-friend is a boy of the same age, and same schooling. The modal patron of "all other agencies" is a housewife with less than eight grades of schooling. The free agencies are thus more largely patronized by adolescent students and by housewives than by other sorts of readers.

The drug stores and newsstands are used mostly by middle-aged housewives with less than eight years of schooling as a source of magazines, which are doubtless read as well by other

TABLE XXIV

PERCENTAGE DISTRIBUTION OF BOOKS AND MAGAZINES BY EDUCATIONAL
STATUS AND SEX OF READERS, BY TYPE OF AGENCY FROM WHICH
SECURED: SAMPLE FROM SOUTH CHICAGO, 1933[a]

EDUCATION	PUBLIC LIBRARY			FRIEND			DRUG STORE		
	MALE	FEMALE	TOTAL	MALE	FEMALE	TOTAL	MALE	FEMALE	TOTAL
Under 8 years	46.4	51.1	48.9	61.8	59.8	60.8	44.4	52.0	48.3
High School.	40.6	42.3	41.5	30.7	33.0	31.9	43.4	36.8	39.9
College	13.1	6.5	9.6	7.5	7.1	7.3	12.3	11.2	11.7
Total	100	100	100	100	100	100	100	100	100
Number books and magazines	360	397	757	986	1,035	2,021	489	535	1,024

	NEWSSTAND			RENTAL LIBRARY			SUBSCRIPTION		
Under 8 years	42.3	42.4	42.3	20.0	12.9	14.9	30.5	31.9	31.3
High School.	33.7	38.1	35.9	32.5	47.5	43.3	30.8	43.2	38.0
College	24.0	19.5	21.8	47.5	39.6	41.8	38.7	25.0	30.7
Total	100	100	100	100	100	100	100	100	100
Number books and magazines	534	517	1,051	40	101	141	681	984	1,665

	BOOK STORE			ALL OTHERS			TOTAL		
Under 8 years	67.6	46.5	57.4	48.1	50.6	49.4	47.6	47.7	47.6
High School.	16.2	33.1	24.3	32.3	35.3	33.8	33.2	37.3	35.4
College	16.2	20.5	18.3	19.6	14.1	16.8	19.3	15.0	17.0
Total	100	100	100	100	100	100	100	100	100
Number books and magazines	137	126	263	1,799	1,858	3,657	5,026	5,553	10,579

[a] Unpublished study of South Chicago by Douglas Waples and others. Some 6,850 persons were interviewed during the winter of 1933–34, and their reading for the two weeks previous to the date of interview recorded.

members of the family, which they report as having obtained from "other sources." The modal readers of magazines obtained by subscription differ from the drug store and newsstand patrons only in that they have had some high school education.

The rental libraries are mostly patronized by younger house-wives, still in their twenties, who also have had secondary edu-

TABLE XXV

PERCENTAGE DISTRIBUTION OF BOOKS AND MAGAZINES BY OCCUPATION AND
SEX OF READERS, BY TYPE OF AGENCY FROM WHICH SECURED:
SAMPLE FROM SOUTH CHICAGO, 1933[a]

OCCUPATION	PUBLIC LIBRARY			FRIEND			DRUG STORE		
	MALE	FEMALE	TOTAL	MALE	FEMALE	TOTAL	MALE	FEMALE	TOTAL
Unemployed	4.2	6.3	5.3	12.2	1.5	6.7	7.0	3.4	5.1
Unskilled	28.3	3.5	15.3	39.0	16.6	27.8	33.7	17.8	25.4
Skilled trades	9.4	3.0	6.1	12.1	.4	6.1	22.7	3.2	12.5
Housekeepers and housewives	1.9	27.0	15.1	1.6	51.9	27.4	.6	61.5	32.4
Shopkeepers	4.4	1.5	2.9	4.6	1.4	2.9	7.0	.7	3.7
Clerks, stenographers.	2.5	5.5	4.1	3.9	6.1	5.0	5.5	4.1	4.8
Students	43.6	50.4	47.2	23.3	18.7	21.0	16.0	5.8	10.6
Professional	5.6	2.8	4.1	3.3	3.4	3.4	7.6	3.6	5.5
Total	100	100	100	100	100	100	100	100	100
Number books and magazines	360	397	757	986	1,035	2,021	489	535	1,024

	NEWSSTAND			RENTAL LIBRARY			SUBSCRIPTION		
Unemployed	4.7	2.7	3.7	2.5	3.0	2.8	3.7	1.4	2.3
Unskilled	26.8	11.4	19.2	12.5	9.9	10.6	15.8	4.4	9.1
Skilled trades	24.9	3.1	14.2	37.5	1.0	11.3	18.9	4.4	10.3
Housekeepers and housewives	.6	61.3	30.4	—	55.4	39.8	1.9	73.4	44.1
Shopkeepers	12.2	4.8	8.6	15.0	1.0	5.0	15.4	1.6	7.3
Clerks, stenographers.	4.5	7.7	6.1	12.5	10.9	11.3	5.1	4.1	4.5
Students	15.0	6.2	10.7	5.0	10.9	9.2	9.8	3.4	6.0
Professional	11.4	2.7	7.1	15.0	7.9	9.9	29.3	7.3	16.3
Total	100	100	100	100	100	100	100	100	100
Number books and magazines	534	517	1,051	40	101	141	681	984	1,665

	BOOK STORE			ALL OTHERS			TOTAL		
Unemployed	2.2	4.0	3.0	5.5	2.9	4.2	6.4	2.7	4.5
Unskilled	27.7	8.7	18.6	25.6	8.2	16.8	28.0	10.0	18.6
Skilled trades	23.4	4.8	14.4	16.4	1.3	8.8	17.3	2.2	9.4
Housekeepers and housewives	2.9	46.8	24.0	1.2	48.7	25.2	1.3	54.6	29.3
Shopkeepers	5.8	4.8	5.3	10.7	1.9	6.3	9.4	1.9	5.5
Clerks, stenographers.	1.5	4.8	3.0	3.6	7.9	5.8	4.1	6.3	5.2
Students	23.4	16.7	20.2	26.4	24.8	25.6	22.3	17.7	19.9
Professional	13.1	9.5	11.4	10.7	4.2	7.4	11.3	4.5	7.7
Total	100	100	100	100	100	100	100	100	100
Number books and magazines	137	126	263	1,799	1,858	3,657	5,026	5,553	10,579

[a] Unpublished study of South Chicago by Douglas Waples and others. Some 6,850 persons were interviewed during the winter of 1933–34, and their reading for the two weeks previous to the date of interview recorded.

cation. The book stores are used almost equally by housewives in their thirties and early forties, by boy students, and by men who divide themselves between skilled and unskilled laborers. None of these predominating types of book store customers has completed the elementary school. This fact plainly suggests the quality of fiction sold by the bookstores. Was it worse during depression than it was before and after?

The implications of the last three tables are, of course, only glanced at by the foregoing summary and comment. The data can be profitably examined from many different angles. The implications of the three tables most profitably investigated are perhaps best revealed by comparing the South Chicago picture of reading in middepression with the far brighter picture in St. Louis as drawn by the facts in Appendix A. It should clarify the sociological aspects of the data to show, by examples, what sorts of hypotheses best fit the two communities. The best means of finding important hypotheses is probably to ask, first, what generalizations regarding the activities of each agency in the distribution of reading matter do the facts support? When the generalizations have been stated in terms of conditions existing in 1933-34, one should then ask whether the condition has any clear relation to the depression, and if so, he should state it. The statement should constitute a fair hypothesis for investigation. If this formula is applied by individual readers of this volume to the different sorts of data presented, the resulting hypotheses will do more to stimulate energetic research than the hypotheses herein stated for sake of illustration.

The next three tables (XXVI, XXVII, and XXVIII) present the same facts as the last three tables but so organized as to permit direct comparison of the agencies in terms of differences in their clientèles. Read in sequence, Table XXVI shows, for example, that friends and "all others" are the most abundant sources of magazines and books (which we have just learned means mostly "low-brow" magazines) for South Chicagoans

TABLE XXVI

PERCENTAGE DISTRIBUTION OF BOOKS AND MAGAZINES BY TYPE OF AGENCY FROM WHICH SECURED, FOR MALE AND FEMALE READERS BY AGE: SAMPLE FROM SOUTH CHICAGO, 1933[a]

Age and Sex		Public Library	Friend	Drug Store	News-stand	Rental Library	Subscrip-tion	Book Store	All Others	Total	Number Books and Magazines
10–19	Male	12.3	24.5	8.3	8.5	.3	5.3	2.7	38.1	100	1,466
	Female	17.3	22.6	8.0	6.4	.7	3.8	2.1	39.1	100	1,459
	Total	14.8	23.6	8.1	7.5	.5	4.5	2.4	38.6	100	2,925
20–29	Male	6.8	25.8	11.9	12.8	1.2	7.7	2.9	30.8	100	1,247
	Female	4.5	23.9	12.2	11.4	3.4	11.3	2.4	31.0	100	1,427
	Total	5.6	24.8	12.1	12.1	2.4	9.6	2.6	30.9	100	2,674
30–44	Male	4.9	14.4	11.1	10.8	1.0	20.2	2.3	35.3	100	1,440
	Female	3.1	13.0	10.5	10.7	1.8	27.2	2.6	31.1	100	1,738
	Total	3.9	13.6	10.8	10.7	1.4	24.0	2.5	33.0	100	3,178
45 and over	Male	2.7	11.2	6.8	10.8	.7	24.7	3.3	39.7	100	873
	Female	2.8	14.9	6.8	8.1	1.2	31.8	1.7	32.8	100	929
	Total	2.8	13.1	6.8	9.4	.9	28.4	2.5	36.2	100	1,802
All ages	Male	7.2	19.6	9.7	10.6	.8	13.5	2.7	35.8	100	5,026
	Female	7.1	18.6	9.6	9.3	1.8	17.7	2.3	33.5	100	5,553
	Total	7.2	19.1	9.7	9.9	1.3	15.7	2.5	34.6	100	10,579

[a] Unpublished study of South Chicago by Douglas Waples and others. Some 6,850 persons were interviewed during the winter of 1933–34, and their reading for the two weeks previous to the date of interview recorded.

TABLE XXVII

PERCENTAGE DISTRIBUTION OF BOOKS AND MAGAZINES BY TYPE OF AGENCY FROM WHICH SECURED, FOR MALE AND FEMALE READERS BY EDUCATIONAL STATUS: SAMPLE FROM SOUTH CHICAGO, 1933[a]

Education and Sex		Public Library	Friend	Drug Store	News Stand	Rental Library	Subscription	Book Store	All Others	Total	Number Books and Magazines
Under 8 years	Male	7.0	25.4	9.1	9.4	.3	8.8	3.8	36.2	100	2,389
	Female	7.7	23.5	10.5	8.3	.5	11.7	2.2	35.5	100	2,647
	Total	7.3	24.4	9.8	8.8	.4	10.3	3.0	35.9	100	5,036
High School	Male	8.7	18.1	12.7	10.8	.8	12.7	1.3	34.9	100	1,668
	Female	8.1	16.5	9.5	9.5	2.3	20.3	2.0	31.7	100	2,072
	Total	8.4	17.2	10.9	10.1	1.6	16.9	1.7	33.1	100	3,740
College	Male	4.8	7.6	6.2	13.2	2.0	27.6	2.3	36.4	100	969
	Female	3.1	8.9	7.2	12.2	4.8	29.2	3.1	31.4	100	834
	Total	4.0	8.2	6.7	12.7	3.3	28.3	2.7	34.1	100	1,803
Total	Male	7.2	19.6	9.7	10.6	.8	13.5	2.7	35.8	100	5,026
	Female	7.1	18.6	9.6	9.3	1.8	17.7	2.3	33.5	100	5,553
	Total	7.2	19.1	9.7	9.9	1.3	15.7	2.5	34.6	100	10,579

[a] Unpublished study of South Chicago by Douglas Waples and others. Some 6,850 persons were interviewed during the winter of 1933-34, and their reading for the two weeks previous to the date of interview recorded.

TABLE XXVIII

PERCENTAGE DISTRIBUTION OF BOOKS AND MAGAZINES BY TYPE OF AGENCY FROM WHICH SECURED, FOR MALE AND FEMALE READERS BY OCCUPATION: SAMPLE FROM SOUTH CHICAGO, 1933[a]

Occupation and Sex		Agency								Total	Number Books and Magazines
		Public Library	Friend	Drug Store	News-stand	Rental Library	Subscription	Book Store	All Others		
Unemployed	Male	4.6	37.2	10.5	7.7	.3	7.7	.9	31.0	100	323
	Female	16.8	10.7	12.1	9.4	2.0	9.4	3.4	36.2	100	149
	Total	8.5	28.8	11.0	8.3	.8	8.3	1.7	32.6	100	472
Unskilled	Male	7.2	27.4	11.7	10.2	.4	7.7	2.7	32.8	100	1,404
	Female	2.5	30.9	17.1	10.6	1.8	7.7	2.0	27.5	100	559
	Total	5.9	28.4	13.2	10.3	.8	7.7	2.5	31.3	100	1,963
Skilled trades	Male	3.9	13.7	12.8	15.3	1.7	14.8	3.7	34.1	100	868
	Female	9.7	3.2	13.7	12.9	.8	34.7	4.8	20.2	100	125
	Total	4.6	12.4	12.9	15.0	1.6	17.3	3.8	32.3	100	993
Housekeepers and housewives	Male	10.4	23.9	4.5	4.5	—	19.4	6.0	31.3	100	68
	Female	3.5	17.7	10.9	10.5	1.8	23.8	1.9	29.8	100	3,029
	Total	3.7	17.9	10.7	10.3	1.8	23.7	2.0	29.8	100	3,097
Shopkeepers	Male	3.4	9.5	7.2	13.8	1.3	22.2	1.7	40.9	100	472
	Female	5.6	13.0	3.7	23.1	.9	14.8	5.6	33.3	100	108
	Total	3.8	10.2	6.6	15.5	1.2	20.9	2.4	39.5	100	580
Clerks and stenographers	Male	4.4	18.6	13.2	11.8	2.5	17.2	1.0	31.4	100	204
	Female	6.3	17.9	6.3	11.4	3.1	11.4	1.7	41.9	100	351
	Total	5.6	18.2	8.8	11.5	2.9	13.5	1.4	38.0	100	555
Students	Male	14.0	20.5	7.0	7.1	.2	6.0	2.9	42.4	100	1,120
	Female	20.4	19.8	3.2	3.3	1.1	3.4	2.1	46.8	100	983
	Total	17.0	20.2	5.2	5.3	.6	4.8	2.5	44.5	100	2,103
Professional	Male	3.5	5.8	6.5	10.8	1.1	35.3	3.2	33.9	100	567
	Female	4.4	14.1	7.6	5.6	3.2	28.9	4.8	31.3	100	249
	Total	3.8	8.3	6.9	9.2	1.7	33.3	3.7	33.1	100	816
Total	Male	7.2	19.6	9.7	10.6	.8	13.5	2.7	35.8	100	5,026
	Female	7.1	18.6	9.6	9.3	1.8	17.7	2.3	33.5	100	5,553
	Total	7.2	19.1	9.7	9.9	1.3	15.7	2.5	34.6	100	10,579

[a] Unpublished study of South Chicago by Douglas Waoles and others. Some 6,850 persons were interviewed during the winter of 1933–34, and their

under thirty years of age. Beyond thirty, friends yield to subscriptions. The sex differences are small. Table XXVII continues the story by showing that friends and "all others" supply more (near pulp) magazines than any other agency to readers whose education has not reached the college level. To those who have had some exposure to college, most publications are supplied by "all others," subscription, and newsstand, in this order.

Table XXVIII is the most interesting of the three because it shows which agencies supply most reading matter to the different occupational groups. From the bottom row we learn what we expect, that to the entire sample publications are supplied in rapidly diminishing amounts by "all others," friends, subscriptions, newsstands, drug stores, public library, book stores, and rental library, and about equally to each sex. The same distribution pattern applies only to the clerical occupation, with the order of the book stores and rental libraries reversed.

Taking the other groups in order, we see that "other sources" are by far the most important for most groups. This collection of agencies would have been broken down farther but for the fact that the constituent agencies supply so little, that, taken singly, their importance is negligible. The only groups to whom "other sources" do not supply more reading matter than any other agency are unemployed men and unskilled females, who obtain most from friends, and professional men and skilled tradeswomen, who obtain most from subscriptions.

The gist of the last six tables is, obviously, that South Chicago in middepression read mainly the pulp magazines, presumably for what thrills they may have afforded. But the tables have not been shown to say merely that. They have been presented to demonstrate methods of differentiating the social and cultural influences of typical agencies for the distribution of print. To describe each agency fairly in terms of the publications it supplies in different amounts to different types of readers, as compared with other agencies, is a highly important task that has seldom been attempted. The more of such descriptions we have for different agencies, different types of communities, and different periods of time, the more possible it becomes to evaluate the publishing and distributing agencies in terms of contemporary cultures.

If the reader has followed the last discussion with a *method of deriving hypotheses* in mind rather than the content of the examples used for illustration, the discussion has served its purpose. Hypotheses relating differences among the agencies to the assumed influences of depression are limited only by the supply of facts concerning "who got what" from each agency, during and after depression; and by the fertility of mind required to find plausible social explanations for the changes that occurred. Research in this area at present probably needs scholarly inventiveness even more than it needs additional facts.

By disregarding considerations of space, one might produce an impressive list of hypotheses by mechanical extraction from the data contained in this monograph. The hypotheses would range from the vaguely general to the most specific hypotheses which the existing and obtainable evidence offers any fair chance of testing. At the outset one would state the hypothesis to which the present chapter is addressed: that the depression changed the agencies in various ways which, in turn, changed the character of the print to which the population was exposed. One might next break this into its two plain implications: first, that depression affected the agencies directly, through changes in annual publication, shrinkage in capital, higher selling costs, higher taxes, etc.; and second, that the agencies were affected indirectly and via the consumer. The latter hypothesis gives direction to the next chapter on readers.

The meaning of all this for social science may be obscure unless the data are approached from the standpoint of social changes as such. The approach will be more effective if the student attends separately to different population groups who were differently affected by depression. One may assume, for example, that hard times tended to confine the reading of skilled and unskilled labor to what the newsstands offered in magazines. Pressing this further, we should ask what the heavier patronage of newsstands did to direct the workingman's attention toward or away from serious social issues—as suggested by the newsstand column of Table XXII and by more intensive analyses of other such rough indications.

Similar questions involving other groups, other localities, each agency, and each year can be asked and answered to the limits of the evidence, *with reference always to changes in the aspects of the social environment about which the reader reads.* The aspects can be described coarsely, as by the sixteen broad types of publications in Table XXII, or they can be carried to the refined analysis of individual publications. In so far as social science is concerned with changes in the range, the degree of uniformity, the intellectual maturity, the partisanship, or any other socially important aspect of the ideas circulated by print, it is concerned with the effects of depression upon the circulating agencies.

For example, one may approach the public library with questions like the following: How did the public library's influence (as inferred from the publications it supplied) differ as between male and female patrons? What had the more feminine taste for motion picture, radio, and love magazines to do with the library's purchases of such during middepression? How is the sex, age, schooling, and occupational distribution of the few readers of library books on social problems explained by comparison with the patronage of other book agencies? Why does the proportion of "good" fiction loaned by the public library to the unemployed differ from the proportion loaned to unskilled labor, to skilled labor, to students, and to professionals? Is it because the latter groups obtain their "good" fiction elsewhere?

For further example, one might ask what the depression did

to particular concepts as shown by changes in the distribution of the literature expressing them, e.g., the concept of Americans as God's elect, a concept which implies international pre-eminence, resulting from the virtues of the pioneer—glorified in *Drums Along the Mohawk, Ramona,* and many other popular novels sold and rented by the commercial agencies. The answer is suggested by changes during depression in the number of such novels supplied by all agencies. Or, the student might check in the same way the effects of depression upon "the hope of economic security achieved by technical invention"—a hope much magnified by the writers of each nation who tend to impute the decisive inventions in each field to their own nationals, e.g., C. C. Furnas, *The Next Hundred Years.* Or, one might discover how "the chance of escaping plain duties" fared during depression—a notion perhaps born of the movie and fostered by sensational biographies of royal courtesans and other darlings of fortune by Emil Ludwig, E. Barrington, and others. Or, as a last illustration, one might examine popular expressions of fear at the many present threats to personal income, security, and social prestige—well exemplified by the large, prompt, and continuing response to Sinclair Lewis's *It Can't Happen Here.*

Many more such ideologies stimulated by depression can well be studied in terms of the social distribution of the publications which express them and which, for reasons easily hypothesized, have caught the public eye at a particular stage of depression. It should be possible to learn how much the depression had to do with their vogue.

In conclusion, we may infer that the public library circulation increased from 1929 to 1933 partly because of its more stable finances as against other book agencies, and partly because of several incentives toward increased reading. The decline in library loans and book store sales after 1933 may have been partly due to the rôle of the school library, and partly to the smaller popular consumption of "better" books. The latter is probably partly explained by an increased supply of "worse" books of the rental store variety and of cheap magazines. The rise of magazine reading is suggested by the number of new magazines issued (Table II). It is also likely that the 1932-33 peak in print distribution was due in large part to the event of a presidential year, with the many extraordinary incentives to reading which the last one supplied; and that the steady growth in distribution of the more sensational books, magazines, and newspapers since 1929 served both to support the peak and to explain the following decline in library circulation and book store sales.

Problems

Investigations needed to round out the foregoing sketch of the distributing agencies during the depression conform to about five types.

1. Inventing and checking hypotheses for the depression curves of income and circulation for each agency, in terms of its changing relations with other agencies serving a similar clientele, and with other relevant contemporary changes of any sort. The records of leading jobbers—Baker and Taylor, American News Company, A. C. McClurg, and others—could be usefully analyzed in this connection.

2. Comparisons to show the annual economic status of one or more commercial agencies in several one-industry communities, ranging from prosperous to bankrupt.

3. Postdepression studies, in selected communities, of the patronage of each agency; to show mean age, occupation, schooling, and income of patrons in relation to publications obtained from each agency for comparison with depression data.

4. Studies to determine changes in the number, holdings, expenditures, and use of school libraries. Such facts are not now available. The predominance of students in the patronage of

the public library and other agencies, makes the facts necessary to explain changes in public library clienteles.

5. Analyses of the sources by which ideas reach isolated relatively self-sustaining communities—e.g., Versailles, Illinois, or Georgetown, Delaware—to learn how local opinion is affected by differences in the nature and amount of print imported, as against ideas received by radio, movies, correspondence, conversations with visitors, and other sources. Such simultaneous analyses of all means of communication of ideas would help greatly to define the social importance of print and, consequently, of the typical agencies for the distribution of print.

Chapter V

Readers

THE plan of this chapter differs somewhat from that of the last two chapters. Too little is known about changes in the attitudes and status of readers since 1929 to show how such changes affected their reading, independently of changes in publication and distribution. So we must hypothesize certain effects of depression on readers of different sorts, then examine the evidence to see how far it goes. Shortages in the evidence as applied to the hypotheses should show the directions in which further study is most necessary.

Several factors in combination have added much to the evidence since 1929. They include the federal relief money supplied to universities for local research, numerous local surveys which have included reading behavior, systematic records of newspaper and magazine circulation by advertisers, partial recognition of adult education as a state and federal responsibility, and generous grants by the larger foundations. Without any doubt, more time and money have been more efficiently spent upon studies of community reading since 1929 than during any previous seven-year period. Despite this fact, the net results are not sufficiently coherent to relate economic conditions and reading behavior satisfactorily, nor are they so spaced in time as to establish trends. Fundamental research on readers most needs facts to differentiate the changes in reading behavior produced by changes in the publication and distribution of print from those caused by changes in the social status and attitudes of readers as people. Lacking such facts, we can best use the

145

facts we have by describing reading behavior during the trough of the depression. When comparable data are obtained for post-depression years, the comparisons should bear upon the hy-- potheses of Chapter I.

READING IN MIDDEPRESSION

Subjects of Interest to Readers. To explain any reading behavior one should distinguish intrinsic from extrinsic motives. Intrinsic motives are personal compulsions to know more about some particular subject or to experience a quality of emotion expected from a particular author or title. Extrinsic motives are incentives supplied by the mere accessibility, or advertising, or other impersonal facts about the publication read. The distinction is useful because of the common tendency to disregard or to underestimate the rôle of extrinsic motives.[1] We do disregard them when we assume that readers, in general, read most about the topics which seem to them most important or most interesting at the time. The full weight of evidence contradicts this emphasis. When the four factors—accessibility, advertising, simplicity of text, subject interest—have been compared under test conditions, subject interest is found to rank last for the large majority of readers.[2] What most of us read, in other words, is determined mainly by what lies within easy reach, next by what can be read with the least effort, and then by what the writer is writing about.

We are here concerned with an interpretation of reading behavior that will describe social attitudes during depression. Considerable work to this end was accomplished during the three

[1] The distinction between extrinsic and intrinsic motives is identical with the distinction between supply and demand, as made in Chapter I. The restatement in terms of motives is required by the present chapter's attention to readers.

[2] For an overview of the studies mentioned see Carnovsky, Leon. "A Study of the Relationship Between Reading Interest and Actual Reading." *Library Quarterly.* 4:76-110. No. 1. January 1934; Waples, Douglas. "The Relation of Subject Interests to Actual Reading." *Library Quarterly.* 2:42-70. No. 1. January 1932. The original studies are cited in both articles.

years of middepression, much more than can be adequately reported here. The results possibly were conclusive on certain
points. They showed in general that most of us no more read
what we like than we wear the clothes we like best to wear, or
spend our time as we like best to spend it, or live where we like
best to live. In each case we make the best of limiting conditions.
For the average reader of high school education, a normal relationship between the non-fiction subjects of most interest and
the subjects most read about is represented by a Pearson coefficient of correlation approximating .25 ± .02.[3] This offers a
strong caution against using different intrinsic motives to explain differences in reading behavior unless there is good reason
to suppose that at least the factors of supply and advertising
are nearly constant—as they are, for example, in the circulation of books from the same college library to different groups
of students in the college.

Second, the results show that the influence of intrinsic motives depends largely upon amount of schooling—those with
most schooling tending to read more nearly what they like than
those with least schooling. Third, we find book reading a better
indication of subject interest than magazine reading, and magazine reading a better indication than newspaper reading. This
is partly because those with most schooling tend to read more
books per magazine and more magazines per newspaper. It is
also due, of course, to the fact that the contents of books stick
far more closely to a given subject than do the contents of magazines and newspapers.

These results of recent studies imply that changes in the reading of well educated readers disclose personal preferences and
attitudes more plainly than changes in the reading of less educated readers. Hence shifts in social attitudes are more apparent
in what is read by the more cultivated minorities than in the

[3] For supporting evidence see Waples, Douglas. "The Relation of Subject
Interests to Actual Reading." *Library Quarterly.* 2:57-66. No. 1. January 1932

reading of the less cultivated masses. Students of public opinion, who infer group opinions from the reading of groups with no more than eight years of schooling, are thus more likely to learn what opinions were formed by the publications read than they are to learn what opinions are expressed by the readers' choice of publications.

It is probably safe to conclude that whatever source yields most data on changes in the books read by the various book reading minorities will contribute most to a sociology of readers.

TABLE XXIX

PERCENTAGE DISTRIBUTION OF READING MATTER, BY TYPE OF PUBLICATION READ: SAMPLE FROM SOUTH CHICAGO, 1933[a]

Type of Publication Read	Percentage of Adults Interviewed
Nothing	8.2
Books	17.4
Magazines	50.2
Newspapers	90.0

[a] Fair, Ethel M. *The Public Library versus Other Sources of Books.* University of Chicago. Unpublished M.A. thesis. 1935

As we shall presently show, this source is for several groups the public library. For others it is the rental library or book club, and for a few highly specialized groups it is the publisher of technical books. Considering the far greater ease of securing data from non-commercial sources like libraries, the fact that libraries can contribute so much to the purpose is all to the good.

Newspaper readers.—Table XXIX shows the distribution of an industrial population (South Chicago) among non-readers, and readers of papers, magazines, and books. Apparently almost everyone reads newspapers. Hence the questions of most social importance are, what changes if any in social attitudes does newspaper reading produce and what changes does it reflect? As suggested in Chapter III, the first question is best met by relating facts concerning annual changes in newspaper content to facts concerning the attitudes of readers as reflected by other evidence—such as election returns, group familiarity with current events as measured by such instruments as the Minnesota Contemporary Affairs test, or surveys to determine the opinions of different publics on specific issues of which the press has championed one side.

The second question—what social changes does newspaper reading reflect?—cannot be answered satisfactorily by data short of records to show the particular items read by different groups in all papers for a reliable time sample and independent evidence of previous social change—for example, changes from dislike to approval of the NRA codes in small communities where the local press may later have followed the local opinion.[4]

The titles of newspapers read by different groups, through time, do not bear on the question. There is so much material common to all metropolitan dailies that differences in the papers read by different groups are very hard to interpret. There is evidence to show that most newspaper readers read headlines, news summaries, comics, sports or women's features, and very little else. The proportion reading any one of the other conventional features may well be less than ten per cent of all newspaper readers. Readers' testimony as to the features they sometimes read does not go far enough and is seldom reliable. The very difficulty of learning what newspaper features are read by any one like-minded group over a period of years offers a severe challenge to all who recognize the many values such group patterns would serve. Moreover, the research to obtain such facts is expensive, so expensive that it is more likely to be made by the newspapers themselves than by independent students. Students of journalism have shown little interest to date in the develop-

---

[4] See Gallup, George. *An Objective Method for Determining Reader Interest in the Content of a Newspaper.* University of Iowa. Unpublished Ph.D. thesis. 1928; also see files of the American Institute of Public Opinion for description of a promising technique

ment of simpler techniques for the accurate description of newspaper reading by groups. Gallup[5] and Nafziger[6] are two conspicuous exceptions.

Magazine readers.—Changes in readers' attention to magazines have similar implications: they may signify changes in group preferences for titles restricted to particular subjects, or they may imply changes in the groups' response to the wide variety of emotional and intellectual stimuli contained in the same general magazines.

Excepting factory workers and high school and college students, we have insufficient evidence concerning the particular items (stories, articles, advertisements, special features, and columns) read by particular groups in the general (the most widely read) magazines. To collect such evidence now would be useful, because it might show group variations in selection. The amount of variation is large. High school students, who are heavy magazine readers, read less than half of each issue of the magazines they say they read "regularly." Testimony concerning changes in their selection both of magazines and of magazine features since 1932 might be obtained with satisfactory reliability by interviewing samples of certain groups. The comparisons should help to interpret the marked preference of widely different groups for the same magazine titles—e.g., the *Saturday Evening Post* and other low priced miscellanies.

Concerning group preferences for different classes of magazines we have somewhat conclusive data for two communities for the years 1933-34. Table XXX supplies a gross comparison of these communities. South Chicago (1933-34) is primarily a steel mill community in which relatively few books of any sort are read. The St. Louis sample (1934) is a normal middle class residential population.

[5] Gallup, George. *Op. cit.*

[6] Nafziger, Ralph O. "A Reader-Interest Survey of Madison, Wisconsin." *Journalism Quarterly.* 7:128-141. No. 2. June 1930

TABLE XXX

PERCENTAGE DISTRIBUTION OF MAGAZINES READ BY SUBJECT CATEGORY OF
MAGAZINE: SAMPLES FROM SOUTH CHICAGO (1933) AND ST. LOUIS (1934)

SUBJECT CATEGORY OF MAGAZINES	SOUTH CHICAGO[a]	ST. LOUIS[b]
Detective and adventure	12.4	1.3
True story and love	13.2	1.4
Radio and movie	4.1	3.1
5¢ Weekly	18.1	21.2
Humorous	.2	.4
Sensational fiction	9.9	15.5
Readers Digest	.8	1.5
Weekly news	4.0	6.6
Religious	3.1	2.3
Fine arts	.2	.5
Juvenile	1.4	2.2
Parents', women's, and home	17.9	31.2
Liberal and radical	.4	.4
Quality	.8	1.0
Elite	.4	.5
Monthly review	.3	1.1
Popular science	4.4	2.8
Sports and outdoor	1.0	.9
Trade	1.1	1.0
Fraternal	1.0	.4
Farm	.5	.5
Professional	.9	1.0
Travel and foreign lands	1.6	2.6
Business, commerce, and finance	.6	.3
Foreign language	.8	.1
Foreign (in English)	.4	.1
Health	.5	.2
Belles lettres	—	—
Total	100	100
Number	8,031	6,901

[a] Unpublished study of reading in South Chicago by Douglas Waples and others. Some 6,850 persons were interviewed during the winter of 1933–34, and their reading for the two weeks previous to the date of interview recorded.

[b] Unpublished study of St. Louis by Douglas Waples and others. Some 3,500 persons were interviewed during the fall of 1934, and their reading for the two weeks prior to the date of interview recorded.

Without analyzing the social traits of the various groups
represented in the two populations, one cannot go far beyond
the superficial differences shown in Table XXX. The table is

152 READING IN THE DEPRESSION

TABLE
PERCENTAGE DISTRIBUTION OF MAGAZINES AND
AND FEMALE READERS BY OCCUPATION:

OCCUPATION AND SEX		DETECTIVE ADVENTURE	WEEKLY NEWS	MOVIE, LOVE, RADIO	5c WEEKLIES	FICTION MONTHLIES	RELIGIOUS	PARENTS', WOMEN'S, ETC.	ALL OTHERS	TOTAL
Unemployed	Male	33.5	1.9	9.9	8.0	6.2	1.5	6.5	13.0	80.5
	Female	2.0	2.7	18.8	13.4	5.4	2.0	18.8	7.4	70.5
	Total	23.5	2.1	12.7	9.7	5.9	1.7	10.4	11.2	77.2
Unskilled labor	Male	24.4	1.9	9.3	11.4	7.1	1.7	3.8	17.9	77.5
	Female	8.3	1.4	44.0	6.5	5.7	1.1	11.1	6.1	84.2
	Total	19.8	1.8	19.2	10.0	6.7	1.5	5.9	14.5	79.4
Skilled trades	Male	8.9	5.4	4.0	22.0	8.5	2.3	6.3	22.6	80.0
	Female	2.4	4.0	7.3	18.5	13.7	1.6	29.1	5.6	82.2
	Total	8.1	5.2	4.4	21.6	9.2	2.2	9.2	20.4	80.3
Housekeepers and house- wives	Male	4.4	5.9	14.7	1.5	1.5	8.8	19.1	11.8	67.7
	Female	2.8	3.2	16.5	13.1	8.9	3.8	26.9	8.5	83.7
	Total	2.9	3.3	16.4	12.8	8.8	3.9	26.7	8.5	83.3
Shopkeepers, Salesmen	Male	6.6	6.1	3.4	25.0	9.1	.8	7.4	23.5	81.9
	Female	2.8	5.6	13.0	13.0	6.5	2.8	25.0	11.0	79.7
	Total	5.9	6.0	5.2	22.8	8.6	1.2	10.7	21.2	81.6
Stenographers, Clerks	Male	8.8	5.9	7.4	23.5	9.3	1.0	5.9	20.0	81.8
	Female	1.4	1.7	14.8	17.4	11.1	1.4	23.9	7.7	79.4
	Total	4.1	3.2	12.1	19.6	10.5	1.3	17.3	12.3	80.4
Students	Male	20.2	1.3	2.9	8.2	4.0	.5	3.1	20.4	60.6
	Female	2.3	2.2	14.4	8.4	4.0	.4	13.1	6.6	51.4
	Total	11.8	1.8	8.2	8.3	4.0	.5	7.8	14.0	56.4
Professional	Male	1.2	5.5	.7	19.9	8.1	3.2	6.9	33.3	78.8
	Female	2.4	7.2	2.0	11.2	10.0	1.2	24.2	13.7	71.9
	Total	1.6	6.0	1.1	17.3	8.7	2.6	12.2	27.3	76.8
Total	Male	16.2	3.4	5.5	14.9	6.9	1.7	5.2	21.2	75.0
	Female	3.2	3.0	17.9	11.9	7.9	2.6	22.4	8.0	76.9
	Total	9.3	3.2	12.0	13.3	7.4	2.1	14.2	14.4	75.9

TYPE OF

MAGAZINES

[a] Unpublished study of reading in South Chicago by Douglas Waples and others. Some 6,850 persons were interviewed during the winter of 1933–34, and their reading for the two weeks previous to the date of interview recorded.

XXXI
BOOKS BY TYPE OF LITERATURE FOR MALE
SAMPLE FROM SOUTH CHICAGO, 1933[a]

	Books									Number Books and Magazines
Good Fiction	Other Fiction	Juvenile	Psychology	Biography, Travel	Social Problems	Literature	All Others	Total	Total Books and Magazines	
3.4	8.0	.6	1.5	1.2	—	.6	4.1	19.4	100	323
11.4	11.4	3.4	1.3	.7	.7	—	.7	29.6	100	149
5.9	9.1	1.5	1.5	1.1	.2	.4	3.0	22.7	100	472
2.9	8.0	.6	2.1	.7	.1	.6	7.5	22.5	100	1,404
3.4	4.3	2.5	2.0	1.4	—	.4	1.8	15.8	100	559
3.1	6.9	1.2	2.1	.9	.1	.5	5.9	20.7	100	1,963
3.2	5.6	.2	1.5	2.6	.5	.6	5.8	20.0	100	868
4.8	8.1	1.6	.8	2.4	—	—	—	17.7	100	125
3.4	5.9	.4	1.4	2.6	.4	.5	5.0	19.6	100	993
4.4	10.3	4.4	4.4	1.5	—	—	7.4	32.4	100	68
4.9	4.2	1.0	2.0	.8	.2	.5	2.7	16.3	100	3,029
4.9	4.3	1.0	2.1	.8	.2	.5	2.8	16.6	100	3,097
3.8	5.5	.6	2.1	1.3	.2	1.3	3.2	18.0	100	472
9.3	7.4	—	—	—	—	.9	2.8	20.4	100	108
4.8	5.9	.5	1.7	1.0	.2	1.2	3.1	18.4	100	580
6.9	5.9	.5	1.0	1.5	—	1.0	1.5	18.3	100	204
9.4	6.0	1.1	.9	1.7	.6	—	.9	20.6	100	351
8.5	5.9	.9	.9	1.6	.4	.4	1.1	19.7	100	555
7.1	10.1	14.7	.9	2.0	.1	.4	4.1	39.4	100	1,120
12.1	10.8	18.4	.1	1.9	.1	1.2	3.9	48.5	100	983
9.5	10.4	16.5	.5	1.9	.1	.8	4.0	43.7	100	2,103
2.8	1.9	.4	3.2	2.8	1.8	.9	7.4	21.2	100	567
8.4	3.6	—	7.2	2.8	—	2.4	3.6	28.0	100	249
4.5	2.5	.2	4.4	2.8	1.2	1.3	6.2	23.1	100	816
4.2	7.1	3.5	1.8	1.7	.4	.7	5.7	25.1	100	5,026
6.7	5.8	4.2	1.8	1.2	.2	.6	2.6	23.1	100	5,553
5.5	6.4	3.9	1.8	1.4	.3	.6	4.1	24.0	100	10,579

useful as a rough indication of questions for further study—questions suggested by variations in the reading by the two populations of the same types of magazines. It would clearly be desirable to obtain postdepression samples of Chicago and St. Louis to match the depression samples, for new comparisons in which time is a major variable. The indicated changes in readers' attitudes might then be examined in the light of other local evidence regarding each group.

Book Readers.—Table XXXI gives a fair indication of the relative amount of reading in magazines and books by each group and the types of magazines and books read. The sample represents the South Chicago population, which was described and used in the foregoing chapter to distinguish the clienteles of the distributing agencies during the winter of 1933-34. The obvious facts are that most readers read more magazines than books; that most men are divided in their allegiance to "all other" magazines, for the most part technical, local, fraternal, or "high-brow," as against detective and adventure stories; and that women prefer parents' and women's magazines and movie, love, and radio. Interesting differences in patterns of reading can be discerned for the various sex and occupational groups as well. Duplication of Table XXXI for the same sample in 1937 would doubtless show many interesting changes.

If we had a comparable picture for 1937, we might expect some points of difference to signify changes in reading since the winter of 1933-1934. One such might be a change in the attention to weekly news and to fiction magazines—of the adventure and love story type. Another might be an increase in books of biography among the book reading groups. A third might be an increase in the proportion of good fiction books to "other" fiction books. It would be interesting to note the group changes, if any, in the extent of book reading on "social problems," of which there was less in South Chicago in the period studied than reading in any other category.

Book readers in general read more books of fiction (and some

groups more of current fiction) than of all other books combined. The simplest and, in some respects, the most meaningful
classification of fiction books is by authorship. It would therefore economize the sociological interpretation of fiction reading,
if fiction authors could be classed or graded according to the
educational, occupational, and hence economic status of their
readers. Foster's work, to identify fiction writers with the particular culture group by which each writer is somewhat exclusively read,[7] has demonstrated the practicability and value of
such classification. The study was undertaken mainly on be-
half of public librarians, who have not yet evolved entirely satisfactory methods of classifying fiction. Her findings, however,
should benefit the social scientist far more, since they show,
more clearly than any previous research has shown, what cultural
differences can be readily and objectively described by facts obtainable from public library records, or any better record of the
novels read in a given community.

Table XXXII shows Foster's classification of the fiction writers most widely read by some 15,000 readers in five communities. The writers are classed according to fifteen subject categories and six cultural levels. The relation between a fiction
writer's classification and the cultural status of the large majority[8] of his readers is stated by Foster as follows:

Very briefly, the two hundred and fifty-odd, most-read authors of
fiction were selected, and the average age, occupation level, and general
reading habits of their readers were determined. At the same time, these
authors were divided into six definite quality levels on the basis of
reviews and first-hand acquaintance with their work. They were also
assigned places in a subject classification made up of the fifteen subject
divisions most universally used in library tools and bibliographies.
The average reader's characteristics were then carefully studied for each
individual author and for the groups comprising each quality level and
class.

More significant, however, in testing subjectively defined quality levels

[7] Foster, Jeannette Howard. *An Approach to Fiction through the Characteristics of Its Readers.* University of Chicago. Unpublished Ph.D. thesis. 1935
[8] See *ibid.* for statistical validation of the criterion employed

TABLE XXXII

FOSTER'S CLASSIFICATION OF FICTION WRITERS ACCORDING TO SIX
CULTURE LEVELS AND FIFTEEN SUBJECT CATEGORIES[a]

	1 (Lowest)	2	3	4	5	6 (Highest)
1. Detective	Adams Eberhart Freeman Keeler Lincoln, N. S. Packard Rohmer Vance Wells, C. Wentworth	Biggers Christie Fletcher Oppenheim Plum Wallace, E. Austin, A.	Collins Doyle Le Blanc Rinehart Stewart Van Dine Webster, H. K. Phillpotts			
2. Adventure	Bower Beach Burroughs Connor Cullum Hendryx Knibbs Raine Seltzer	Ames Bindloss Gregory Grey Haggard Marshall Morrow Mulford Spearman Kyne	Davis Dumas Garstin Komroff London Nason Verne White	Buchan Kipling McFee Nordhoff and Hall	Defoe Masefield Stevenson	Melville
3. Romance	Chambers Curwood McCutcheon McGrath Hope-Hawkins Wright Fox	Farnol McCarthy Parrish, R. Wren Burnett, F. H. Sabatini	Ford Locke Major	Allen Blackmore Byrne		
4. Love	Barclay Dell Reed Porter, G. S. Hill-Lutz Prouty Pedler Loring Oemler	Norris, K. Bailey Baldwin Richmond Ruck Widdemer	King Deeping Hurst Ferber	Barrie	Brontë	
5. Cheerful	Porter, E. H. Hueston Montgomery Rice	Webster, J. Miller, A. D. Wiggin Train	Lincoln, J. C. Hannay Rosman Alcott Arnim	Aldrich, T. B. Priestley Henry, O. Tarkington		
6. Humorous	Cohen, O. R.	Smith, T.	Stockton Wodehouse		Clemens	
7. Satiric	Kelland Roche Chamberlain	Thayer Arlen	De la Pasture	Erskine Parrish, A. Morley Nathan	Macaulay Carroll, L.	France

TABLE XXXII (*Continued*)

FOSTER'S CLASSIFICATION OF FICTION WRITERS ACCORDING TO SIX
CULTURE LEVELS AND FIFTEEN SUBJECT CATEGORIES[a]

	1 (Lowest)	2	3	3	5	6 (Highest)
8. Character		Brush Fairbank Corbett Burnett, W. R.	Stone Ashton Baum Thompson Young, F. B. Carroll, G. H. Deland	Bromfield Dickens Dreiser Balzac Lewis Glasgow Beith Gale	Bennett Eliot Hugo Hemingway Remarque Maugham	Maupassant Thackeray Austen, J.
9. Family		Aldrich, B. S.	Barnes Bentley Kennedy Suckow Jameson	Stern De la Roche Dane Walpole	Galsworthy Undset Lagerlöf	
10. Psychological		Glaspell Wilson	Hull Ostenso Bottome Young, E. H.	Milne, A. A. Swinnerton Hergesheimer Poole Sinclair, M. Ertz	Sedgwick Rogers Wharton Lehmann Sackville-West	Joyce Conrad Woolf
11. Philosophical problems	Burnham Martin	Douglas Benson	Gibbs, P.	Fisher, D. C. Hilton	Morgan Hawthorne Blasco-Ibanez	Tolstoi Hardy
12. Social and political problems	Dixon	Stowe	Norris, C. Sinclair, U.	Gibbs, A. H. Wells, H. G. Norris, F.	Fallada Feuchtwanger	
13. Special groups	Terhune	Jackson, H. H.		Peterkin La Farge Asch	Reymont Buck	
14. Setting		James Eggleston	Burke Stribling Miln, L. J. Crawford	Hobart Kaye-Smith Heyward	Cather Hudson Young, S. Rolvaag	
15. Historical	Hough Wallace, L.	Wister Page Bacheller	Atherton Beck Johnston Roberts Churchill	Miller, C. Boyd Cooper	Wilder Sienkiewicz Scott	

[a] Foster, Jeannette Howard. *An Approach to Fiction through the Characteristics of Its Readers.* Unpublished Ph.D. thesis. University of Chicago. 1935

are the average age, education, and occupational levels of readers in each level. The general conclusion is that a consensus of critical rating is upheld by objective evidence.

When one approaches subject classes, the problem is less simple. Fifteen classes of fiction were chosen. The questions here to be answered were, first, to prove whether these divisions would prove artificial or sound units on the basis of their readers; second, whether they would bear as definite relation to quality as one hears imputed to many of them; and then, of course, what kind of people read them?

At the outset, there was no obvious order in which to arrange the classes as there had been for quality levels. When readers' characteristics were averaged, however, certain classes scored much higher than others in what we may call our readers' maturity index—age, education, occupation, and amount of non-fiction read. There were a number of factors uncontrolled in arriving at this maturity index, such as young students being required to read many of the authors in the "character" and "social problem" classes, and clubwomen all devouring books of the moment, several of which two seasons ago were in the "family chronicle" class. So the quality sequence of subject classes must not be taken as finally established.

Besides the comparative quality of the various subject classes, our second major interest was whether these classes are sound; that is, whether they represent true units of subject interest. One of the tests was homogeneity of readers' characteristics within the class. Another was the extent to which readers choose more than one author or title per fortnight from the same class; for it seemed that genuine subject interest would lead to concentration. One conclusion from these tests is that the readers of good fiction are more apt to choose their reading for its quality than for its subject type, that is, they choose good authors from different classes oftener than several from the same class. The tendency in the lower level classes is strongly the opposite.

The fundamental factors separating good from inferior fiction are these: first, true to human experience; second, a degree of universality or human importance in the experience presented; third, an emotional detachment which keeps the author reasonably impartial about his chief characters; and, fourth, some beauty and distinction in manner of presentation.

It is the immature, whether they be fourteen or forty, who will shun the better and crave the more wish-fulfilling fiction. Moreover, they will seek those stories in which they can most creditably identify themselves with the successful character. Hence, the clear definition of subject classes in the lower level where each represents a distinct pattern of personality. Hence, too, the improbability that even with further data the upper subject classes will ever become as sharply distinguished. On the basis of present findings it seems likely that four or five subject classes will be the number distinguishable.

There is one fairly objective class including stories of "settings" and the more externally presented "character study"; another psychologically, including all subjective treatment of human relationships; a third embracing all stories tinged with propaganda; and a fourth taking in all novels with philosophical implications, including critical satire.

All this last comes dangerously near to encroaching on the question of why people read what they do, a province where no scientific foot has yet been set. The excursion was deliberate, however, because there seems no reason why that province should not fairly soon be entered.[9]

The next steps for research in this important area are well defined by Foster in reporting her study. Essentially they consist in checking and extending the classification by means of other available records of individual fiction readers and of the fiction authors they read. There are many such records now available which Foster was unable to include. Any public library can supply similar records for current years, except for the important item of the readers' schooling, which can be obtained without much trouble. Hence comparisons between depression and post-depression readers of fiction, to discover which groups moved from less "mature" to more "mature" authors, and vice versa, are entirely practicable. Considering the plainer visibility of cultural differences among book readers as against magazine and newspaper readers, and considering also the predominance of fiction readers among book readers, one may predict important results from such comparisons. At the least they should suggest possible effects of depression upon the "mental age" of different social groups. The implications would be yet more interesting if the data were analyzed geographically for the same years. The "possible effects" of depression as suggested would naturally serve as hypotheses for study in relation to other evidence concerning each group's resistance to depression.

[9] Foster, Jeannette Howard. "More Definite Terms to Describe Types of Reading" (abridged). *Bulletin of the American Library Association.* 30:683-684. No. 8. August 1936

The public library reader.—Since public library readers have been studied more intensively than other readers and since there are many similarities between library readers and book readers in general, it is in order to present typical findings on the former. The following sections therefore describe library readers and reading—both to illustrate the sorts of data available and to suggest the other sorts needed to increase their meaning and value for social science.

Before proceeding with the exhibits, however, it is necessary to emphasize the fact that much work remains to be done before we shall know to what extent and under what conditions the reader of library books does resemble the reader of books as such and the reader of books from other sources. To make a start, the student may assume that book readers who do not use public libraries are of three sorts: professional and technical readers, who demand more highly specialized books than those found in public libraries; readers in the middle and higher income brackets, who prefer to buy currently popular titles than to wait their turn at the libraries; and the consumers of rental library and newsstand fiction, which falls below the library's limits of mediocrity. It would thus be expedient to sample each of these three classes, in communities of widely differing type. A more ambitious research would examine the non-library reader at large, to sharpen contrasts with the library readers.[10] The resulting evidence should point to much needed economies in sampling the book reading population. It should furnish a shortcut to what we want to know, namely, the nature of the social þrocesses and culture patterns which are efficiently described in terms of book reading. The evidence should make for a sociology of the more intelligent, and hence more literate and influential minorities, which certainly contain the largest number of readers of substantial books.

---

[10] For one such sample see Ridgway, Helen A. "Community Studies in Reading. III. Reading Habits of Adult Non-Users of the Public Library." *Library Quarterly.* 6:1-33. No. 1. January 1936

To illustrate the sorts of information we have concerning the public library reader, the New York Public Library is a good choice for several reasons: its fifty-nine branches are centrally administered with admirable efficiency; they represent the wide social differences of neighborhoods in the Bronx, Manhattan, and Richmond; analyses of the 1932-33 circulation in terms of borrowers have been carried to a point of statistical reliability not reached by other such analyses known to the writer; somewhat comparable data were secured in 1936; and the tempo of life in New York, as compared with other communities sampled to date, apparently shortens the lag between social changes and their expression in reading. This assumption, however, should by all means be confirmed by studies in the geography of reading.

In 1932-33 the New York Public Library ciientele was sampled by selection of five branches: the East 58th Street branch, where the music collections are concentrated to benefit suburban residents; the Fordham (West Bronx) branch in an upper middle class community; the Woodstock (East Bronx) branch, serving a poorer and more largely foreign population; the Seward Park (lower East Side) branch, serving perhaps the poorest district; and the Bruce Branch, West 125th Street, near Columbia University, but not monopolized by students. While it would be premature to regard the social conditions common to these branches as representing a national norm, the data are a demonstrably fair sample of New York Public Library readers and the best available base for comparison of depression and postdepression tendencies among library readers.[11]

Before attempting to show who read what sorts of library books during the heart of the depression, for comparison with similar data for postdepression years, it should be useful to sketch the public library population as such. To understand its

[11] The technical procedure used to analyze the circulation in terms of borrowers has been recorded in detail with statistical checks and is available by correspondence with the writer.

TABLE XXXIII

PERCENTAGE DISTRIBUTION OF LIBRARY PATRONS AND ADULT POPULATION, BY SEX AND OCCUPATION: FORDHAM (N. Y.), 1932[a]

Sex and Occupation	Per Cent of Adult Population[b]	Per Cent of Registration[c]
MALE		
Professional	1.8	2.5
Students	8.1	29.4
Clerks, shopkeepers, salesmen	7.8	5.3
Skilled tradesmen	14.1	4.1
Unskilled labor	6.8	1.6
Unknown	10.6	1.4
Total male	49.2	44.3
FEMALE		
Professional	1.6	5.0
Students	8.4	27.6
Clerks and stenographers	4.7	5.9
Skilled trades	3.1	1.9
Housewives	27.0	13.8
Unknown	6.0	1.5
Total female	50.8	55.7
Total	100	100
Number	194,601	2,100

[a] Waples, Douglas, and Others "Analysis of Circulation in Five Selected Branches of the New York Public Library, 1932." Chicago: Graduate Library School, University of Chicago

[b] Percentage distribution of gainful workers 10 years of age and over, for approximate area served by library. Based on census tract data

[c] Percentage distribution of a 20 per cent sample of the adult registration

relation to the total community, one may compare the percentages which certain groups are of the borough populations and of the public library registration. Tables XXXIII and XXXIV show the comparisons for two typical neighborhoods—one urban and one suburban. In both, the student and the professional groups are conspicuously better represented in the library registration than in the population at large.

We may next note the relation of registration to circulation. As shown in Table XXXV, which combines two branches, the borrowing by each sex is nearly proportional to registration, but the borrowing by the different school and age groups is not. The two younger groups borrow proportionately more, for school assignments and for other reasons which need to be explored. It is desirable to make similar comparisons in other communities because how evenly the library is serving the community appears in such data. How have they changed since 1933? Table

TABLE XXXIV

PERCENTAGE DISTRIBUTION OF ADULT POPULATION AND LIBRARY
PATRONS, BY OCCUPATION: HINSDALE, ILLINOIS, 1933[a]

OCCUPATION	PER CENT OF ADULT POPULATION	PER CENT OF REGISTRATION
Housewives	31.4	37.8
Students.	13.5	24.9
Agriculture, fishing, and forestry	2.1	1.0
Manufacturing, mechanical industries	14.0	3.1
Transportation and communication	6.4	1.4
Trade.	12.4	6.6
Public service	1.0	.1
Professional service	8.8	14.0
Domestic and personal service	9.1	3.4
Clerical occupations	1.2	3.6
Unknown	.1	4.1
Total	100	100
Number	6,923	1,000

[a] Carnovsky, Leon. "Community Studies in Reading. II. Hinsdale, a Suburb of Chicago." *Library Quarterly*. 5:8 No. 1. January 1935

XXXVI shows the occupational distribution of borrowers from the Fordham branch, which is plainly dominated by students. Because of the small number of cases, however, this table is by no means conclusive. Generally speaking, the libraries with a high percentage of circulation to students appear to distinguish the book reading patterns of non-student groups more plainly than libraries with low student percentages. One explanation, perhaps, is that the libraries frequented by students tend to have better book collections; but the observation should be checked.

The social composition of library readers has always been described in terms of persons borrowing one or more books per year, or per other time period, and for no better reason than that

TABLE XXXV

PERCENTAGE DISTRIBUTION OF LIBRARY REGISTRATION AND CIRCULATION, BY
SEX AND AGE GROUPS: SEWARD PARK AND WOODSTOCK (N. Y.) 1932[a]

SEX	PER CENT REGISTRATION	PER CENT CIRCULATION
Male	57.4	55.8
Female	42.6	44.2
Total	100	100
AGE		
Junior high	13.0	18.9
Senior high	21.1	26.9
Post high	17.3	16.1
Adult	48.6	38.1
Total	100	100
Number Persons	3,016	2,566

[a] Waples, Douglas, and Others "Analysis of Circulation in Five Selected Branches of the New York
Public Library, 1932." Chicago: Graduate Library School, University of Chicago

TABLE XXXVI

OCCUPATIONAL DISTRIBUTION OF FORDHAM (N. Y.) LIBRARY PATRONS: 1932[a]

OCCUPATION AND SEX	PER CENT OF BORROWERS
MALE	
Students	29.0
Clerks	6.0
Skilled tradesmen	2.5
Shopkeepers and salesmen	2.0
Professional	2.0
Unskilled labor	1.5
Unknown	2.0
Total male	45.0
FEMALE	
Students	31.0
Housewives	12.5
Clerks and stenographers	6.5
Professional	4.0
Skilled trades	.5
Unknown	.5
Total female	55.0
Total	100
Number persons	200

[a] Waples, Douglas, and Others "Analysis of Circulation in Five Selected Branches of the New York
Public Library, 1932." Chicago: Graduate Library School, University of Chicago

serviceable data are always at hand in the registration file. It is altogether plain, however, that the reader of one book per year and the reader of fifty books per year should not have the same weight in comparisons to show differences in the number and character of books loaned to each group.

The gross misconceptions of group differences in attention to library books which result from Table XXXIV are implied by the data in Tables XXXVII and XXXVIII. Table XXXVII reveals striking differences in the rate of borrowing of all books and, furthermore, portrays differences, as well, among the five library branches studied. The differences in range, as between 58th Street and Woodstock, for example, make clear that the individuals composing the fastest borrowing tenth in the more exclusive 58th Street neighborhood determine the size and the character of the total branch circulation far more than the other nine-tenths at 58th Street, and considerably more than the most rapid tenth at Woodstock determines its total circulation. It thus becomes a matter of real importance to the social policy of public library administration, and one of lively interest to students of urban culture, to know what books are read by the small percentage of borrowers who tend thus to monopolize the library's services.

It would be highly desirable to analyze the characteristics of, and the books read by each class interval of borrowers grouped by rate of withdrawal of books (Table XXXVII). Such studies should be undertaken for both the depression and recovery periods if possible.[12] In the absence of such materials the data in Table XXXVIII permit a somewhat similar but much rougher differentiation of readers by rate of borrowing. This table identifies the occupational groups by sex who have the highest borrowing rates and shows occupational and sex differences in fiction and non-fiction borrowing as well. The

---

[12] They can be based on "used up" book cards matched to registration records.

data are based on average borrowings in four New York City library branches in 1932 and can be easily duplicated for post-depression years. The summary presented obscures branch library differences, which can be studied where desired, and is not necessarily representative of urban communities. It would

TABLE XXXVII

PER CENT OF CIRCULATION WHICH IS WITHDRAWN BY REGISTRANTS WHO BORROW AT VARIOUS RATES: FIVE PUBLIC LIBRARY BRANCHES, NEW YORK CITY, 1932[a]

THE TENTH OF REGISTRANTS ARRANGED IN ORDER OF BORROWING RATE	PER CENT OF CIRCULATION					
	FORD-HAM	BRUCE	58th ST.	WOOD-STOCK	SEWARD PARK	AVERAGE
Most rapid tenth	62.5	73.6	75.4	52.0	73.0	67.3
Second most rapid tenth	19.1	10.5	11.4	23.4	14.9	15.9
Third most rapid tenth	7.6	6.0	5.7	9.1	6.1	6.9
Fourth most rapid tenth	4.6	3.4	2.7	6.2	2.9	3.9
Fifth most rapid tenth	2.5	2.0	1.8	3.7	1.4	2.3
Sixth most rapid tenth	1.4	1.5	1.2	2.1	.7	1.4
Seventh most rapid tenth	.9	1.1	.8	1.4	.4	.9
Eighth most rapid tenth	.6	.8	.5	.9	.3	.6
Ninth most rapid tenth	.5	.6	.3	.7	.2	.5
Slowest tenth	.3	.5	.2	.5	.1	.3
Total	100	100	100	100	100	100
Number	10,000	10,000	10,000	10,000	10,000	10,000

[a] Waples, Douglas, and Others "Analysis of Circulation in Five Selected Branches of the New York Public Library, 1932." Chicago: Graduate Library School, University of Chicago

be highly desirable to have broader and more representative studies of this type made in a number of communities for the depression and recovery periods. Changes in reading habits may, under adequate control conditions, indicate the effects of the depression upon the relative group interest in library books and should, if possible, be related to changes in the economic status of each group of borrowers.

If we examine total reading first, it is apparent that the "unknown" (i.e., largely unemployed) among the males, and the housewives among the females are the most heavily represented in the fastest borrowing groups. The former borrows an average of almost 20 books per year in each library branch studied, of which approximately 8 are fiction and 12 non-fiction. The latter borrows approximately 21 books on the average, nearly 15 fiction and 5 non-fiction. Other interesting comparisons can be made between comparable categories of the sexes. The figures may show group variations in the strength of the "escape motive" as reflected by heavy fiction reading during the depression. Again the interpretation demands comparable pictures for pre-depression and recovery years.

The type of non-fiction read (by Dewey classification groups) is indicated in the table. A clean cut problem for research would be the discovery of the types of fiction and more specific kinds of non-fiction read during the depression and recovery periods. The current data are available from the same branches. To get a clearer picture of reader differences the averages should be weighted by the number of readers in each branch.

The names for the columns in Table XXXVIII, based on the Dewey classification system, are often misleading, because the particular subjects represented by the figures are not suggested by the general class. We note, for example, that women engaged in unskilled labor read a great deal of "philosophy" relative to their other non-fiction reading. The mystery is somewhat cleared by the fact that the 100 class includes such subheadings as psychoanalysis, alcoholism, telepathy, hypnotism, mental tests, and sex ethics. The tables are useful if for no better reason than that libraries habitually describe circulation in terms of these classes; hence comparable data for later years are easier to obtain. The ambiguities are usually fewer in the "religion," "pure science," and "fine arts" classes than in the others. Hence the major shifts in group demand from 1932 to date can be interpreted with some clarity in these classes. Yet where the group data can be obtained for the entire classes, it is usually possible to break down the class figures into their more specific and hence more meaningful subdivisions.

TABLE XXXVIII

AVERAGE ANNUAL NUMBER OF BOOKS PER BORROWER PER BRANCH IN SELECTED LIBRARY BRANCHES, BY DEWEY CLASSIFICATION OF BOOKS AND BY SEX AND OCCUPATION OF BORROWERS: NEW YORK CITY, 1932[a]

Sex and Occupation of Borrowers	Number Persons in Sample	Fiction	Philosophy (100)	Religion (200)	Social Science (300)	Philology (400)	Pure Science (500)	Useful Arts (600)	Fine Arts (700)	Literature (800)	Biography	Travel and History	Total
Male													
Professional	105	3.8	.6	.2	.6	.1	.3	.2	2.5	1.3	.5	1.1	11.2
Students	513	6.6	.6	.1	1.0	.2	.7	.7	3.4	2.2	.8	1.1	17.4
Salesmen and shopkeepers	127	4.1	.4	.1	.9	.2	.4	.6	1.5	1.2	.7	1.0	11.1
Clerks	280	6.2	.6	.1	.9	.2	.3	.6	.5	1.5	.6	.9	12.4
Skilled trades	320	7.1	.3	.4	.6	.2	.6	.5	2.3	.8	.5	1.0	14.3
Unskilled labor	154	7.4	.4	.4	1.5	.1	.6	.9	.5	1.2	.4	1.3	14.3
Unknown	101	7.9	1.1	.4	1.3	.2	.8	.9	2.3	2.4	1.1	1.5	19.9
Average male	1,600	6.1	.6	.3	1.0	.2	.5	.6	1.9	1.5	.6	1.1	14.4
Female													
Professional	91	4.3	.3	.2	.4	*	.1	.1	1.2	1.3	.7	.7	9.3
Students	552	8.6	.3	.1	.7	.1	.3	.3	1.6	2.6	.6	.7	15.9
Clerks and stenographers	313	8.7	.3	.1	.4	*	.2	.3	.5	2.2	.9	.7	14.1
Skilled trades	102	9.8	.4	.1	.1	.1	.1	.5	.4	.9	.3	.7	13.9
Unskilled labor	86	12.3	.6	.8	.2	.1	—	.4	.1	.8	.7	.7	15.5
Housewives	190	14.6	.3	.1	.3	*	.1	.5	1.3	1.4	.7	.8	20.8
Unknown	120	6.0	.2	.1	.4	*	*	.1	.8	1.9	.6	.8	10.9
Average female	1,454	9.2	.4	.2	.3	.1	.1	.3	.8	1.6	.6	.7	14.3
Average registrant	3,054	7.7	.5	.2	.7	.1	.3	.4	1.3	1.6	.6	.9	14.3

[a] Data are for four branches: Bruce, 58th Street, Seward Park, and Woodstock. Averages are unweighted for number of readers. Waples, Douglas, and Others "Analysis of Circulation in Five Selected Branches of the New York Public Library ,1932." Chicago: Graduate Library School, University of Chicago

* Less than .05 per cent

Despite the limitations indicated it is possible to discern patterns in the reading of the groups reported. For example, male clerks on the average drew approximately the same number of books, per library branch studied, as did male professional persons. But the clerks read 50 per cent more fiction, the same amount of philosophy (of a different character perhaps), half as many books on religion (probably because of clergymen among the professionals), about 50 per cent more in the social sciences, three times as much in the useful arts, and one-fifth as much in the fine arts. Male unskilled laborers, who drew approximately the same number of books as those in the skilled trades, read more than twice as many volumes in the social sciences, approximately one-fourth as many in the fine arts, and 50 per cent more in literature. Further differences in reading patterns among the occupational groups within each sex and between the sexes can be detected. In general it is evident that males and females drew approximately the same number of books; that females drew 50 per cent more fiction than males, approximately two-thirds as many volumes in philosophy, one-third as many in the social sciences, about one-fifth as many in pure science, approximately one-half as many as in the useful arts and fine arts, approximately two-thirds as many in travel and history, and about the same number in literature and biography. Approximately two-thirds of the volumes drawn by females were fiction, in contrast with less than one-half of those drawn by males.

Shifts in the pattern of each group from depression to date are easily shown by repeating the analysis. It would also help in estimating the library's cultural influence to compare the eleven groups shown in the tables with reference to the subjects commonly read and the subjects read only by certain groups like students.

Table XXXIX permits a further analysis of withdrawals by

TABLE XXXIX

PERCENTAGE DISTRIBUTION OF BOOKS WITHDRAWN BY DEWEY CLASSIFICATION OF BOOKS, BY SEX AND OCCUPATION OF BORROWERS IN SELECTED LIBRARY BRANCHES: NEW YORK CITY, 1932[a]

Sex and Occupation of Borrowers	Fiction	Philosophy (100)	Religion (200)	Social Science (300)	Philology (400)	Pure Science (500)	Useful Arts (600)	Fine Arts (700)	Literature (800)	Biography	Travel	History
Male												
Professional	2.9	9.3	13.1	5.2	4.7	4.7	3.6	14.3	5.2	6.1	6.3	6.7
Students	14.3	23.3	12.5	23.9	22.8	31.6	27.1	21.3	18.9	20.7	23.9	30.4
Salesmen and shopkeepers	2.4	2.9	3.1	6.4	6.7	5.5	5.3	4.7	2.9	4.8	5.9	3.9
Clerks	6.1	10.5	1.9	10.2	8.5	6.3	10.2	4.4	5.5	6.9	4.8	9.0
Skilled trades	7.0	5.2	14.5	6.6	9.6	10.1	6.2	9.2	3.5	6.7	11.3	7.1
Unskilled labor	3.1	2.2	8.2	5.7	.9	5.7	3.2	2.3	2.0	2.3	3.7	4.3
Unknown	2.7	6.3	4.0	7.9	4.6	6.1	4.3	4.6	3.7	3.8	3.6	5.1
Total males	38.5	59.7	57.3	65.9	57.8	70.0	59.9	60.8	42.1	51.3	59.5	66.5
Female												
Professional	5.6	5.1	15.9	2.4	7.2	5.3	1.2	7.9	7.7	9.3	5.0	2.9
Students	18.4	10.5	10.7	15.9	16.7	13.0	10.5	14.2	23.1	12.4	14.1	18.8
Clerks and stenographers	14.4	9.7	7.0	8.8	7.6	5.1	10.5	5.9	15.1	11.1	9.2	5.4
Skilled trades	3.9	3.1	.7	.1	.6	.5	3.4	1.5	1.3	3.5	.8	.9
Unskilled labor	4.4	3.7	1.2	.6	5.0	—	2.7		1.1	1.1	3.5	.8
Housewives	11.0	5.1	5.6	3.2	3.8	5.0	9.1	6.5	4.4	6.4	6.1	3.2
Unknown	3.8	3.1	1.6	3.1	1.3	1.1	2.7	3.0	5.2	4.9	1.8	1.5
Total females	61.5	40.3	42.7	34.1	42.2	30.0	40.1	39.2	57.9	48.7	40.5	33.5
Total	100	100	100	100	100	100	100	100	100	100	100	100
Number of books in sample	16,222	488	174	777	85	375	410	1,094	1,524	622	325	555

[a] Data are for four branches: Bruce, 58th Street, Seward Park and Woodstock. Waples, Douglas, and Others "Analysis of Circulation in Five Selected Branches of the New York Public Library, 1932." Chicago: Graduate Library School, University of Chicago

occupation and sex groupings of the population. It is directly apparent, for example, that females read more than three-fifths of the fiction withdrawals, almost three-fifths of the literature and smaller proportions of the volumes in each of the other categories. Male readers get 70 per cent of the pure science withdrawals, two-thirds of the history and almost two-thirds of the social science withdrawals. Variations in the reading patterns of the sexes undoubtedly reflect broader cultural sex differences. Variations in the patterns of occupational groups differently affected by depression are also noteworthy. The study of changes in these reading patterns may therefore reveal significant cultural changes.

The foregoing data support interesting and important generalizations: public library borrowers are not a cross-section of the population of the area served; from half to three-fourths of the library's loans are made to about one-tenth of the total number of borrowers; school and college students alone account for more than half of the loans; the number of loans to housewives is also conspicuous; and each occupational and sex group has a pattern of non-fiction reading which, to some extent, distinguishes it. The public library supplies far more fiction than anything else. How do each of these conditions differ from the predepression period and how far have they changed since 1932?

Social Problems. As one means of describing depression reading on social problems, Table XL distributes the loans of certain titles among professionals and students as against all other groups. The twenty-eight titles listed in the table are those of which at least one copy was loaned from a list of sixty-four recent titles of "social criticism," highly popular in 1932. The percentages at the bottom row of the table show the titles to have been borrowed nearly twice as often by men as by women—63 per cent and 37 per cent, respectively. But they were also borrowed nearly twice as often by professionals and students of each sex as by "all

TABLE XL
CIRCULATION OF SELECTED TITLES IN SELECTED LIBRARY BRANCHES, BY TYPE
AND SEX OF BORROWER: NEW YORK CITY, 1932[a]

AUTHOR AND TITLE	PROFESSIONAL AND STUDENTS		ALL OTHERS		TOTAL
	MALE	FEMALE	MALE	FEMALE	
Beard, Charles A.					
American Leviathan	41	53	11	3	108
America Faces the Future	61	35	25	10	131
Calkins, Clinch					
Some Folks Won't Work	26	17	20	14	77
Chase, Stuart					
Nemesis of American Business	25	17	11	11	64
A New Deal	16	12	10	2	40
Cole, G. D. H.					
A Guide through World Chaos	2	–	7	3	12
Cregg, Alliston					
Understanding the Stock Market	22	11	17	1	51
Dice, C. A.					
New Levels in the Stock Market	7	2	10	1	20
Ely, R. T.					
Hard Times—The Way In and the Way Out	17	10	5	3	35
Fisher, Irving					
The Stock Market Crash and After	13	4	18	3	38
Flynn, John T.					
Investment Trusts Gone Wrong	14	2	5	2	23
Hamlin, Scaville					
Menace of Overproduction	11	9	8	6	34
Hansen, A. H.					
Economic Stabilization in an Unbalanced World	10	8	7	5	30
Hindus, Maurice					
Red Bread	52	52	23	28	155
Hoover, Calvin B.					
Economic Life of Soviet Russia	19	5	3	6	33
Ilin, M.					
New Russia's Primer	49	23	14	9	95
Keynes, J. M.					
A Treatise on Money	18	10	9	2	39
Laidler, H. W.					
Socialist Planning and Socialist Program	26	18	23	14	81
Levine, Isaac Don					
Red Smoke	12	–	12	–	24
Lippmann, Walter					
Interpretations	8	4	13	–	25
Mazur, Paul M.					
New Roads	22	8	7	5	42
Moulton, H. G. and Pasvolsky, L.					
War Debts and World Prosperity	5	1	1	2	9
Rogers, J. H.					
America Weighs Her Gold	9	6	5	2	22
Rugg, H. O.					
Changing Civilizations in the World	21	20	6	3	50
Salter, Arthur					
Recovery	75	22	47	22	166
Simonds, F. H.					
Can America Stay at Home?	10	6	9	2	27
Thomas, Norman					
As I See It	44	36	27	26	133
America's Way Out	34	18	11	8	71
Total	669	409	364	193	1,635
Per cent	41	25	22	12	100

[a] Waples, Douglas, and Others "Analysis of Circulation in Five Selected Branches of the New York Public Library, 1932." Graduate Library School, University of Chicago

others"—66 per cent and 34 per cent, respectively. It is too bad that the total circulation of these "most popular" books on social problems current in 1932 was too small to permit comparison of smaller groups. One may hypothesize that professionals and students who borrowed books from the selected New York libraries during the depression paid twice as much attention to the "whys" of depression as the other groups of library borrowers. The latter may have been more concerned with what to do about the depression or with how to forget it.

The relatively slight attention paid to these widely publicized titles by all groups is consistent with the data previously shown. Current social criticism probably is read in the press and the magazines by most of us in preference to books. The most popular of the twenty-eight titles are clearly the simplest (e.g., *New Russia's Primer*), or those with alluring titles (e.g., *Red Bread,* and *Recovery*), or those by public characters (e.g., Norman Thomas), or by authors appealing directly or assigned to students (e.g., Charles A. Beard). The least read are Moulton and Pasvolsky's *War Debts and World Prosperity,* and G. D. H. Cole's *A Guide through World Chaos,* both of which are among the more scholarly works.

Since these particular titles have lost the pull of novelty, there would be small point in learning how widely they are read today. It would be interesting, however, to compare the library loans in 1937 of a somewhat comparable list of recent and popular books of social criticism, in order to discover shifts in the relative status of the "all others" as against the students and professionals. Do we as a people read more about the *why's* of social change in good times than in bad times?

Although the Dewey classification does not clearly segregate them, the "300" class is intended to cover books on social science. One may accordingly analyze the loans in this class to discover to what groups they were made and to what extent. In

1933 the men borrowed, on the average in each library branch studied, one book on social and economic problems out of each fourteen books; the women borrowed one such out of each forty-eight books; the unskilled laboring man borrowed one out of ten; one out of twenty-three was borrowed by professional women; and one out of sixty-nine by housewives. (See Table XXXVIII.) Such data, of course, could be made directly comparable with postdepression data to show changes in group attention to social science since 1932.

One can profitably examine similar ratios for any other field of interest—for example, travel and history. One out of every thirteen books loaned to men is a book of travel and history; one out of every twenty loaned to women; one out of every eleven to salesmen and shopkeepers; one out of every fourteen to male clerks; one out of twenty to skilled tradeswomen. Similar ratios have been determined for each of the major book classifications. They await only comparison with previous and subsequent ratios to define socially important changes in attitudes of such groups. From this variety of facts concerning readers of public library books in 1932, we turn to certain fragmentary bits of evidence concerning changes that have since occurred.

CHANGES IN GROUP READING

Newspaper readers.—There are virtually no data to show how changes in readers affected newspaper circulation. As described in Chapter III, daily newspapers and their Sunday editions both lost about 10 per cent of their circulation between 1929 and 1933. Foreign language dailies and weeklies lost much more (28.6 and 29.3 per cent, respectively). Weekly newspapers lost both in number (40.4 per cent) and in circulation (36.2 per cent). All categories of newspapers lost circulation, and the number of newspapers in almost all categories decreased from 1929 to 1933.

Why did daily newspaper circulation fall during the depres-

sion years 1929 to 1933? Why did the Sunday editions lose only
slightly more than the daily editions? Why did foreign language
dailies and their Sunday editions lose almost three times as much,
relatively, as the English language dailies?[13]

The questions cannot be answered without facts which would
show how many *and what sorts* of subscribers took no daily
newspaper, how many took one, two, three, four, or more during predepression, depression, and postdepression years. One
might then inquire what kind of subscriber discontinued how
many newspapers and why. No such analyses of the number of
daily and Sunday newspapers taken by typical subscribers at different periods of depression have been found. The R. L. Polk
Company of Detroit has such data in raw form for certain cities,
but they do not show trends.

Negroes constitute one-tenth of the population of the United
States. It is, therefore, important to know what happened to the
Negro press during the depression. Data on the number and
circulation of Negro newspapers are available in the *International Year Book Number* of *Editor and Publisher.*

Lacking any data specifically describing changes in newspaper
readers as such, we must turn for hypotheses to other national
trends during depression that are most relevant .The first of these
is the tendency for the metropolitan daily newspaper, and particularly the chain newspaper, to. take circulation from its rivals.
Four functions of the newspaper which may be listed are: (1)
to supply the news, information, and opinions which make
community life possible in large cities; (2) to supply entertainment and recreation; (3) to facilitate the forming of public
opinion; (4) to play an important rôle in economic organization as an advertising medium.[14] It may be assumed that each

---

[13] See Young, Donald. *Research Memorandum on Minority Peoples in the
Depression.* (monograph in this series)

[14] See unpublished manuscript of the Research Committee on Urbanism of
the National Resources Committee, dealing with communication facilities. The
author is indebted to Dr. Louis Wirth for access to this document.

of these social functions of the press has some equivalent in social satisfactions or demands. If so, one may hypothesize certain effects of depression upon the relative strength of such demands.

We should then guess that the depression tended to magnify the first two functions at the expense of the two others. If it did the fact would check our assumption that reading interest and actual reading increased as sales of printed matter declined. The depression certainly stimulated interest in the news during the early thirties by producing so much news of absorbing interest. For periods of several months' duration the daily paper carried much of the excitement of war bulletins. The entertainment value also increased as more expensive diversions were discontinued. On the other hand, the extent to which the press formed public opinion probably declined, if we may judge from discrepancies between the politics of frankly partisan newspapers and the votes of their subscribers during the last presidential election. As an advertising medium, we have seen (Table XII, p. 97) that the curve of revenue from advertising closely matches the segment of the business cycle studied, as drawn for example by Mitchell and Burns.[15]

Considerable progress toward checking each of these assumptions regarding changes in readers that may explain changes in the press since 1929, can be made by interrelation of the data supplied by this volume and by studies of recent changes in communication facilities.[16] To understand changes in any one medium of communication one must study changes in others as well. The fact that receipts from advertising by the broadcasting stations fall back in the year 1933 only and in 1935 were

---

[15] Mitchell, Wesley C. and Burns, Arthur F. *Production During the American Business Cycle of 1927-1933*. New York: National Bureau of Economic Research. 1937
• [16] National Resources Committee. *Op. cit.*

far above the 1929 receipts, is one example of the need for cross-fertilizing the available facts.

Magazine readers.—The evidence thus far presented to show differences among readers of different magazines during the depression has not yet, to the best knowledge of the writer, been related to comparable data for later years. The research to describe changes in magazine readers is thus suggested about as clearly as is now possible by problems involving the effects of depression on readers of newspapers and books. Books and newspapers together exhibit nearly all the important characteristics of the magazine, which combines many features of both.

Book readers.—Changes in book readers should be most apparent among readers of fiction, which is read over twice as much as non-fiction. Table XLI is based on the two distinctions of most significance in describing book readers, namely, differences in sex and differences between students and members of other occupations. The changes in popularity of authors like Buck, Dickens, Dumas, Tarkington, and Wells are largely explained either by the filming of their novels or by the date of a recent best seller. Other changes during the four-year period cannot be explained offhand. The rank order correlations imply that the reading of students changed most, of women next, of non-students next, and of men least of all; hence women students doubtless varied their fiction authors most and the men other than students remained most loyal to their 1932 favorites. But students' changes in preference are perhaps least likely to express changes in attitudes related to depression. They are more likely explained by current motion pictures, by academic assignments, and by the process of growing up.

The research thus indicated should utilize the available facts to break down the non-student males into smaller groups, groups sufficiently small to show at least the age, schooling, and definite occupation of those who represent sharply differing

TABLE XLI

RANK ORDER OF SELECTED FICTION AUTHORS, BY SEX AND TYPE OF BORROWER:
BRANCH LIBRARY CIRCULATION, NEW YORK CITY, 1932, 1936

AUTHOR	MEN		WOMEN		STUDENTS		ALL OTHERS	
	1932[a]	1936[b]	1932[a]	1936[b]	1932[a]	1936[b]	1932[a]	1936[b]
Bennett	23	19.5	18	14.5	21.5	18	20.5	14
Bojer	22	19.5	23	26	25	26.5	22	20
Buck	24	10	26	5.5	26.5	5	24.5	25
Cather	18	10	11	2	13	3	14.5	4.5
Dickens	10	5	7	8.5	8.5	10	16	2.5
Dreiser	16	26	13.5	11.5	18	23	10.5	8.5
Dumas	4	13	6	5.5	4	7	7	20
Farnol	7	19.5	15	19.5	11	13.5	10.5	25
Ferber	8	13	4	14.5	5	13.5	2	14
France	17	19.5	9.5	19.5	15	23	23	14
Galsworthy	9	7	1	5.5	3	10	1	2.5
Glasgow	27	19.5	22	11.5	26.5	13.5	18.5	14
Grey	6	3	3	5.5	10	3	8	8.5
Lewis	19	1	21	1	19.5	1	18.5	1
Lincoln	11.5	19.5	8	14.5	16.5	23	4	8.5
London	1	7	9.5	23.5	1	18	5	8.5
Maugham	11.5	7	13.5	8.5	12	10	12	4.5
Norris, K.	26	26	19.5	19.5	23.5	18	20.5	25
Richmond	25	26	25	26	23.5	26.5	26.5	25
Rinehart	15	19.5	5	19.5	8.5	18	9	20
Sabatini	13	10	19.5	23.5	16.5	13.5	17	20
Tarkington	5	13	2	3	2	6	6	6
Undset	21	19.5	16	19.5	19.3	18	14.5	20
Van Dine	20	19.5	24	19.5	21.5	23	24.5	14
Verne	14	19.5	27	26	14	23	26.5	25
Wells	2	4	17	14.5	6	8	13	14
Wodehouse	3	2	12	10	7	3	3	14
Rank r	.60 ± .09		.42 ± .11		.38 ± .12		.43 ± .11	

[a] Waples, Douglas, and Others "Analysis of Circulation in Five Selected Branches of the New York Public Library, 1932." Chicago: Graduate Library School, University of Chicago

[b] Unpublished analysis of circulation in all 59 branches of the New York Public Library, by William A. Haygood. This analysis in January 1936 covered two weeks' reading.

responses to such popular and different authors as Cather, Galsworthy, Lewis, London, Rinehart, Tarkington, Wells, and Wodehouse. In any such study as this, where a time difference is involved, the student must be careful to see that the population samples at the two different periods are comparable. Relation to depression conditions could also be interestingly shown in terms of economic differences among the New York neighborhoods which the branches represent. Appendix D shows the evidence supplied for the same year by the New York Market Analysis, compiled and copyrighted 1933 by the *New York Herald Tribune, The News,* and *The New York Times.* Since the library's loans of these authors are so large, the relation of branch loans of each author to the economic facts should give rise to a series of definite, important, and practicable studies to interpret the extensive data shown roughly by the table.

Table XLII shows the number of loans in fiction and the various non-fiction categories for selected groups of Fordham borrowers, for the depression year 1932 and for the recovery year 1936. Although the number of cases is too small to allow for an analysis of changes in types of reading matter between 1932 and 1936, the table, nevertheless, exhibits a technique for measuring possible changes that may have occurred. Given several hundred (or preferably several thousand) books read by each type of person the investigator could compute, for example, the rank order correlations between categories of reading matter in 1932 and 1936 for males and females by occupation. The size of the coefficients would be an index of the degree to which the literature read in 1932 and 1936 was similar. The computation of the percentage distribution of books borrowed in 1932 and 1936 for each type of reader would permit a more detailed analysis.

The interpretation of any changes that might be uncovered between 1932 and 1936 can have significance, of course, only if the persons composing the sample groups in the two periods of

TABLE XLII

NUMBER OF BOOKS BORROWED FOR THIRTY-EIGHT DEWEY CLASSES, BY SEX AND OCCUPATION OF READERS: FORDHAM BRANCH, NEW YORK PUBLIC LIBRARY, 1932, 1936

DEWEY CLASSES		NUMBER OF BOOKS BORROWED									
		MALE				FEMALE					
		PROFES-SIONAL		SKILLED TRADES		HOUSE-WIVES		PROFES-SIONAL		SKILLED TRADES	
		1932[a]	1936[b]	1932[a]	1936[b]	1932[a]	1936[b]	1932[a]	1936[b]	1932[a]	1936[b]
Fiction		21	47	23	16	165	42	43	40	12	9
Biography		2	7	9	—	3	—	2	3	—	1
All	(000)	1	1	—	—	—	—	1	1	—	—
Philosophy	(100)	—	1	—	—	—	1	—	—	—	—
Mind and body	(130)	—	—	—	—	1	—	—	—	—	—
Psychology	(150)	1	—	—	—	—	—	1	—	—	—
Ethics	(170)	—	2	—	—	1	—	1	—	—	—
All other	(100)	1	5	1	—	—	—	—	—	—	—
Religion	(200)	—	2	—	—	1	—	—	—	—	—
Economics	(330)	—	3	—	1	1	1	2	1	—	1
Law	(340)	—	1	1	—	1	—	—	—	—	—
Associations	(360)	2	—	—	—	1	—	—	—	—	—
Education	(370)	—	2	—	—	2	1	1	2	—	—
Customs	(390)	—	—	—	—	—	1	—	—	—	—
All other	(300)	2	5	1	1	3	—	1	—	—	—
Philology	(400)	—	—	—	—	—	1	1	—	—	—
Science	(500)	1	3	—	—	1	—	—	1	—	—
Mathematics	(510)	—	—	—	—	1	—	—	1	—	—
Chemistry	(540)	—	1	—	1	—	1	—	—	—	—
Biology	(570)	—	—	—	—	2	—	—	—	—	—
All other	(500)	—	—	2	—	—	—	—	1	—	—
Medicine	(610)	—	4	—	—	—	—	—	—	—	—
Engineering	(620)	—	1	2	1	1	—	—	—	—	—
Communication	(650)	1	—	2	—	2	—	—	—	—	—
Chem. tech.	(660)	—	—	1	—	—	—	—	—	—	—
All other	(600)	1	1	—	—	1	—	—	—	—	—
Drawing	(700)	1	—	1	—	—	—	—	—	1	—
Music	(780)	—	1	—	—	—	—	1	—	—	—
Amusements	(790)	—	1	—	—	1	1	1	3	—	—
All other	(700)	4	3	1	1	1	—	—	1	—	—
Literature	(800)	—	1	2	—	3	—	5	1	1	—
Am. Literature	(810)	1	6	3	—	5	3	—	2	—	—
Eng. Literature	(820)	1	1	2	—	3	1	2	5	—	—
All other	(800)	—	3	—	1	—	1	1	3	1	—
Travel	(910)	4	—	4	—	6	—	3	1	—	—
History, modern European	(940)	2	6	1	1	1	—	1	3	—	—
History, North American	(970)	—	1	—	—	—	2	—	1	—	—
All other	(900)	2	—	2	1	—	1	—	—	—	—
Number books		48	109	58	24	207	57	67	70	15	11

[a] Waples, Douglas, and Others "Analysis of Circulation in Five Selected Branches of the New York Public Library, 1932." Chicago: Graduate Library School, University of Chicago

[b] Unpublished analysis of circulation in all 59 branches of the New York Public Library, by William A. Haygood. This analysis in January 1936 covered two weeks' reading.

time are similar. If the reading population has changed significantly in its social characteristics between the two periods the
results will be invalidated. If it is too late to obtain the desired
data for a recent depression year such a study could still be made
for the recovery period.

As a final exhibit, largely to illustrate a desirable type of research, we may notice Table XLIII, presenting changes in the

TABLE XLIII

PERCENTAGE DISTRIBUTION OF PUBLIC USE OF REFERENCE DEPARTMENT, BY
TYPE OF BOOK WITHDRAWN BY PURPOSE FOR WHICH INTENDED:
NEW YORK PUBLIC LIBRARY, 1934, 1936[a]

TYPE OF BOOK	PURPOSE FOR WHICH INTENDED							
	INTELLECTUAL		VOCATIONAL		RECREATIONAL		TOTAL	
	1934	1936	1934	1936	1934	1936	1934	1936
Art	40.3	54.6	32.6	39.1	27.1	6.3	100	100
Economics	48.3	49.4	32.1	43.1	19.5	7.5	100	100
Science	37.5	48.0	50.0	44.7	12.5	7.3	100	100
Chemistry	28.9	39.5	65.8	55.5	5.3	5.0	100	100
Technology	44.5	49.2	38.1	44.8	17.4	6.0	100	100
Patents.	21.5	28.2	78.5	71.8	–	–	100	100
Periodicals	29.3	43.0	40.9	31.7	29.8	25.3	100	100

[a] Unpublished analysis of circulation in all 59 branches of the New York Public Library, by William
A. Haygood. This analysis in January 1936 covered two weeks' reading.

proportion of reading, from the reference division of the New
York Public Library, on each of the subjects shown which the
readers designated as "for business reasons," "to answer a question," and "for entertainment" respectively. Since the readers
are with very few exceptions mature persons who consult the
central branch of the library for serious purposes, the responses
have a high degree of credibility.

We may note a general decrease from 1934 to 1936 in vocational reading in general science, chemistry, patents, and scientific periodicals. Art and economics increased. Recreational reading in reference books declined the most in art, economics, and

technology. Changes in the "intellectual" column uniformly show an increase.

The readers here represented are perhaps the best sample obtainable of urban residents who take reading seriously. Further analysis of reading changes in such groups by individual students would be desirable and practicable.

Chapter VI

Overview and Summary

THE preceding pages will be recognized for what they are—
an effort to discuss certain broad questions of theory on
the strength of evidence regarding questions of fact. Collection
of the evidence available was mainly financed, and therefore
inspired, by institutions and foundations concerned with particular administrative problems—problems confronting librarians, publishers, "educators of adults," advertisers, students of
public opinion, teacher-training schools, colleges, high schools,
and many others. Had the data been assembled with sociological
generalizations as the desired product, the results would doubtless have a richer theoretical value than has been extracted from
the somewhat accidental by-products of the original research.

Yet this somewhat overstates the limitations of the data. The
present objective, as defined by the directing committee, is less
to attempt the impossible task of producing all the answers, than
the far more fruitful one of clarifying issues, suggesting sources
and procedures, and stimulating students at large to advance beyond previous findings. Hence the pure optimist might even re-
joice that the evidence is so spotty. Big gaps are easier to see
and usually more exciting to fill than small ones. The wide variety of small samples of evidence should help to show what
kinds of evidence best apply to whatever major problems the
student prefers to attack.

Despite their many serious omissions, what the last three
chapters most need is a synthesis—an overview which transcends
artificial distinctions among publications, distributors, and

readers, and states as plainly as possible what we can learn from reading, about the great depression of the early 1930's. To make such a synthesis, the reader should detach himself from the data about as far as the generalities of Chapter I. Proper distribution of emphasis is easier in retrospect than during the piecemeal discussion of the social problems involved in the production, distribution, and consumption of print.

SOCIAL IMPLICATIONS OF READING BEHAVIOR

Basic to the entire discussion is the question whether analysis of reading behavior promises enough important contributions to social theory to claim the serious attention of social scientists. To provoke as much research as possible, the argument has bolstered the affirmative.

The affirmative position might be supported by several volumes, devoted respectively to: bibliography; the history of literary criticism; the history of books in education; the importance of literary culture to the elite of each age; sociology's dependence upon social distinctions, patterns, processes, and values as recorded in print; and contemporary evidence to show the rôle of print among the many factors which initiate, direct, and record social processes.

The facts which show *who* reads *what* at any given time and place, go far to depict culture patterns to which all social scientists must pay attention, namely, a pattern arranging the various elements of society according to their intellectual interdependence. The pattern appears in the facts which show how far each social group seeks to improve its status by reading, that is, by learning the wisdom of rival groups who have recorded their wisdom in print. In short, reading has an ancient and honorable reputation almost as distinguished as that of literary culture itself, the source of most scholarship. As such, its implications must appear among the sources of a genuine social science.

On the other hand, the contributions, to date, by students of

reading per se to the social sciences come far short of expecta-
tions. The wide discrepancy between what social science wants
to know and what students of community reading have discovered, has many explanations. One reason is the inverse relation
between the social groups of most interest to social science and
the groups who do the most reading. The heavy readers in modern society are those with little else to do—students, teachers,
some housewives, editors, writers, and a few persons of leisure.
As against the population at large, such groups may not amount
to much.

Another reason is the frequently mentioned fact that group
differences in the amount and character of reading today reflect
differences in the production and distribution of print more
clearly than they reflect differences among readers. Hence questions raised by social science regarding differences among people
do not appear in reading records until the differences produced
by the commercial zeal of publishers and distributors are defined and subtracted.

Other reasons for the social scientist's present indifference to
the changing patterns of popular reading have been noticed
throughout the text and are implicit in Chapter II. In the aggregate, they suggest that social scientists will follow the leads
indicated by the data to the extent that those best qualified to
show the leads, namely, publishers, librarians, and others concerned with who-reads-what, will demonstrate their importance
by conducting the prerequisite research.

The field of reading today is in the stage of observation and
description, a stage which normally precedes the identification
and correlation of variable elements and the formulation of
scientific theory regarding their relationships. The preliminary
stage of observation will not be passed until students have extended the scope of their observations to include all readers, all
publications, and all means of distribution in their studies of
each variable factor. Depression (implying reduced sales of pub-

lications) is one factor. To observe particular readers, particular publications, and particular distributors with this one factor in mind (much though such observations contribute to the development of technique) will not produce a social theory which embraces the many important factors involved. There is consequently an urgent need to recruit collectors, analysts, and synthesizers of the obtainable facts.

Major Sources

One might expect some sociological studies of the depression as such, because of its far reaching influences, to help students of reading more than students of reading have helped social science. At least five reports have rendered such help. Each should be searched before attempting studies of independent problems related to the topics. Two, prepared by the Research Committee on Urbanism of The National Resources Committee, are in manuscript form. These manuscripts are concerned with recreation and communication in the urban community.[1] The third is *Rural Social Trends During the Depression*, by Edmund deS. Brunner and Irving Lorge.[2] It is important because of our conspicuous neglect of data concerning reading behavior in rural areas as such. Another manuscript pending publication which should also be searched is closer to the field of reading, viz., Louis R. Wilson, *The Geography of Reading Facilities in the United States*.[3] The fifth is *Middletown in Transition*.[4]

Other sources of quantitative information on aspects of social life during depression are perhaps no less useful to students of

---

[1] The author is indebted to Dr. Louis Wirth for access to these manuscripts.

[2] New York: Columbia University Press. 1937

[3] Especially valuable for data on school libraries, which were insufficiently treated in Chapter IV. Publication pending. University of Chicago Press

[4] Lynd, Robert S. and Helen M. *Middletown in Transition*. New York: Harcourt Brace & Co. 1937

reading, and will be found in the other monographs in the series on the social aspects of the depression. The reason for stressing the five sources just cited is that they enable any interested student to extend and enrich the interpretations supplied in this text, by relating one or more tendencies in reading behavior to other tendencies in the same direction. What, for example, does the relation between the annual sales of playing cards and sales of cheap magazines suggest as to the effect of depression upon domestic recreation?[5] How far do annual changes in the relation of library circulation to the patronage of other forms of public recreation (museums, art galleries, zoos, taverns, parks, etc.) explain the social implications of library patronage? U. S. Commissioner of Education Studebaker reports that of 350 public forums existing in 1936 with audiences estimated at over half a million people, over two-thirds have been organized since 1929. Did attendance at forums affect library circulation? If so, how much and in what directions? What had the development of roads by WPA funds to do with changes in the cultural status (including reading behavior) of the rural areas affected by the new roads? Similar questions should be raised concerning the relation of reading to each type of recreation and each type of communication, as they prospered during depression: railroads, postal service, telephones, radio, movies, and many more.

Such relationships can be traced to the limits of the student's ingenuity. They can be explored to the extent of the evidence in the sources mentioned and in others the student can discover for himself. The more fully the implications and relationships in the present data are interpreted, the more useful they become, and the more one is encouraged to supply further facts that are hard to secure.

---

[5] See also Steiner, Jesse F. *Research Memorandum on Recreation in the Depression.* (monograph in this series)

A conspicuous weakness of the preceding chapters is that they have virtually ignored data concerning differences and changes in the economic fortunes of different population and industrial groups before and since 1929. In general, the discussion has postulated *the* depression curve, represented, probably as well as by any other single index, by the volume of newspaper advertising shown in Table XII. The fact is, of course, that *the* depression is a mere abstraction, at best combining the midpoints of the annual curves for the many industries and social groups that were differently affected. There were naturally many depressions of different groups at different times and in different degrees. We should consider the reading behavior of each group in terms of its own depression curve. We did not do so because the income facts available do not concern the population groups who do the larger amounts and hence distinguishable kinds of reading, nor do they describe occupational groups in terms of traits, like sex and education, which differentiate reading behavior among members of the same occupation. Data on unemployment are of small use unless we know what the unemployed in each occupation actually read—or stopped reading.

It may be too late to make studies of reading that would contain adequate controls on employment and unemployment and on economic status in general during the depression. It may be possible however, and it would be distinctly worth trying, to study reading during the recovery period under such control conditions. Furthermore, it may also be possible to relate quantitative data such as have been reported in this volume, built up into longer series, to the various economic indexes which are available. There is room for exercising an ingenuity that may be amply rewarded.

Publication and Reading

We have seen (Table X, p. 84) that the printing of books, pamphlets, magazines, Sunday and daily newspapers declined from 1929 to 1933 in this order. Production fell at a rate more or less proportional to the price of each type of publication, implying a close relation between production and sales, in depression as also in better times. Since depression increases the dangers of producing more than the market can immediately absorb, it should tend to hold production closer to actual sales. In 1932 several million copies of books in "sheets" were idle in the warehouses of New York publishers who took too much for granted.

Assuming that the curves of production and sales are much alike, three types of relation between production (or sales) and amount of reading during depression are theoretically possible, namely, a positive relation, a negative relation, or no relation. Each of these might be treated as an hypothesis.

A close positive relation implies that readers normally buy so much of what they read that inability to buy means a large decrease in the number of different publications read. It might also imply a decrease in the total amount of reading done, though restriction to fewer publications is usually offset by more reading in each one. From the evidence presented it seems safe to reject this hypothesis on three grounds. First, there is the indication afforded by public library circulation (and to a less extent by the rental library data) that the same economic conditions which reduced the sales of printed matter also increased the general desire to read.[6] Second, it is easier to assume that the cheaper diversions like reading were preferred to the more expensive, than to assume the contrary. If so, one would expect attendance at picture theaters, sporting events, and other amusements to have declined more rapidly than the sales of the cheaper publications. Attendance at movies certainly did. The figures in millions are for 1930, 117; for 1933, 60; and for 1935, 80. The annual changes in patronage of other amusements (especially the radio)[7] can be so related as to sug-

---

[6] See Table XVI, p. 104

[7] From unpublished manuscript on communication. National Resources Committee. *Op. cit.*

gest changes in the relative popularity of reading, which would serve to check the assumption of a marked increase from 1930 to 1933. Third, we know that most reading is normally done by persons of most education and (or) income—persons whose ability to buy at least the newspapers and magazines they wanted was least affected by depression and who (lacking evidence to the contrary) can be assumed to have wanted to read rather more than less.

The three indications, and many more suggested in other chapters, deny a close positive relation between the production and consumption (or reading) of print during early depression. Does it then follow that the relation is consistently negative, i.e., that reading varies inversely with production? This also seems unlikely for reasons given. To argue that the less we buy the more we read, one must show a positive relation between reading interest and poverty as such. Studies to this end, as in Marienthal, Austria,[8] have shown the opposite tendency, the tendency for continued poverty to kill reading interest. During long continued depression, when sales reach the minimum, it seems that readers become too apathetic to read old publications borrowed from friends or other free sources.

Thus, the available evidence indicates neither a close positive nor close negative relationship between publication and reading. It is conceivable, however, that such relationships may exist to a degree that defy detection through available sources and techniques. To explain what this relationship actually is, one must identify as many as possible of the existing conditions tending to increase publication, to decrease publication, to stimulate reading, and to inhibit reading. Furthermore, it is important and often necessary to identify such conditions separately for each major type of publication and for each socio-economic group of readers. From the data supplied in the last chapter, the same environmental conditions (e.g., the 1932 campaign)

[8] Lazarsfeld. *Op. cit.* (See note 4, p. 94)

seem to have increased certain types of publication, decreased others, stimulated some groups to read books on the social issues involved, and encouraged other groups to read on very different subjects.

To examine the hypotheses in terms of particular publications and groups will not merely enrich the interpretation of the available data on reading. It should also greatly economize the conduct of future reading studies. The economy will result from defining tendencies among readers, which are very difficult and expensive to record, in terms of tendencies in publication already recorded in official documents.

Distribution and Reading

The effects of depression upon the distributing agencies are plainer than the depression's effects upon readers. The latter cannot be described without trustworthy samples of reading behavior in predepression, depression, and recovery periods. Ideally such data should permit the isolation of depression deviations from the long time trends. A cross-section of the last two chapters suggests that the tax supported distributors—school and public libraries—made heavy gains at the expense of the commercial distributors, until well into 1934. Important differences between the publications carried by the free as against the commercial agencies should thus help to explain changes in the reading of those who changed from one to the other in early depression.

To the extent that any distinguishable group of readers turned abruptly from the commercial agencies to the public library, the turn probably changed the amount and almost certainly changed the character of their reading. For such readers dependent upon the public library, the amount of magazine reading probably declined and the quality probably improved, since our samples show that libraries supply relatively few but the better sort of magazine. The amount of book reading probably increased for some groups and decreased for others. Those whose book reading decreased were doubtless discouraged by having to wait for new books and by the several other inconveniences of library borrowing.[9] The character of their book reading probably changed from recent to older titles, from popular to less popular titles, and from the more trivial to the more serious reading. Insufficiency of trivial books in public libraries perhaps best explains the sharp rise of the rental libraries in early depression.

Similar hypotheses apply to the commercial agencies. As a group they were probably not much affected by reduced publication. Each could buy far more than it could sell. But their sales declined at different rates, depending upon the economic status of their clienteles and the average price of their wares. Those who suffered least sold the cheaper books and magazines to relatively prosperous customers. Those who suffered most were the agencies catering to middle class intellectuals who formerly bought important new books.

We have no clear evidence to show how reading was affected by changes in the commercial agencies. We know that many agencies were affected, and often disastrously so, by changes in what readers were willing to pay for what they wanted to read. But not even the somewhat spectacular multiplication of rental library units has yet been shown to have increased the net consumption of rental library books.

Technical Problems

There are several technical problems to be solved before the important hypotheses regarding social aspects of reading can be properly examined. Most are problems in sampling.

The first is to determine *what categories of books, magazines, and newspapers most accurately reflect changes in the production of all publications of each type.* Until we have statistical justi-

---

[9] See Waples, Douglas. "Community Studies in Reading. I. Reading in the Lower East Side." *Library Quarterly.* 3:1-20. January 1933

fication for the selection of certain categories to yield an index of production as such, the great variety of publications will discourage students from relating changes in production to changes in other factors of reading behavior. A valid index of production will reflect changes in content or quality no less than changes in quantity.

The second is to determine *in which categories the publications purchased by each of the typical distributing agencies best reflect changes in the number and character of the publications they actually distribute.* The problem may be insoluble for certain agencies, like scholarly libraries, whose purchases need have no direct reference to their probable rates of circulation. Also the problem is meaningless as applied to borrowing from personal friends. But for some agencies, like book stores, rental libraries, and magazine shops, an index of distribution derived from *purchase records* in selected categories of the faster moving publications, instead of from the present inadequate and often inaccessible sales or circulation records, would greatly facilitate research. The interrelation of the indexes for the several agencies of a community should supply the first comprehensive picture of the distributing network, as affected by production at one end and by readers' consumption at the other.

A third problem is *to identify the population groups that best sample the adult reading population.* Such groups will be found among those who have completed high school, who are engaged in occupations which stimulate reading but do not require it, whose incomes are probably above three thousand dollars, and who range in age from twenty-five to forty-five years. That much is fairly clear. But we do not know that each of these traits is needed to identify the modal reader of general publications, nor how to use available social statistics to distinguish groups according to the traits which are known to differentiate the amount and character of reading. School and college students should probably be excluded from the sample. They read so much and so uniformly that variations in their reading are perhaps not important enough to justify the considerable labor of analysis when the purpose is to describe social changes as such.

A fourth problem is *to specify the aspects of publication, distribution, and reading which respond most directly to economic and other social changes.* Several such aspects have been noted in the present sketch. But to know which are most prophetic of social change from among those best covered by the sources, would add much to the value of our present interpretations and would greatly reduce the expense and labor of making them. To know what reading factors best signify social change should be enough to precipitate studies to determine their complicated interrelationships.

Changes in the Social Uses of Reading

To know what social purposes are served by print and how such purposes are affected by depression, is another way of stating the major problem of this entire book. The distinguishable motives for reading, and the corresponding uses for reading, differ but slightly from those of conversation, or of other behavior that reveals the specific and intimate relations of an individual to his changing social environment. Moreover, if the reiteration be pardoned, the same reading behavior which serves to describe social relations serves also to change them. Reading, for some social groups, is both a means of social analysis and a means of changing the conditions analyzed.

To anticipate the analyses required to relate social changes and reading changes, we must resort once more to hypotheses. The frame of reference will be the different uses of print as made by readers of all sorts. There is, of course, some relation between the writer's purpose, which makes the publication what it is, and the reader's purpose in reading it. But the uses to which the more widely read publications are put by different readers are so varied that differences among readers' purposes are more useful than writers' purposes in hypothesizing the social uses of print. Five such uses may be noted.

1. *To follow the news.*—The term "news" is so ambiguous that it scarcely serves to indicate a reading motive.[10] News about what? must be answered before changes in the degree of readers' curiosity about current events become meaningful. One may, however, compare the reading of publications rich in news value (say news magazines) with reading in other publications, and contrast the ratios for periods of social emergency with those for other periods. One would expect the news interest to increase with the state of public anxiety and to decline when the public has become used to the changed conditions or when the emergency has passed. The student would naturally compare the attention to various other sources of news (radio, lectures, news reels, etc.) with the reading of news publications. The relation is probably positive and close, though reading may prove too slow a news vehicle to compete with some of the other sources when excitement runs high.

Somewhat akin is the problem of analyzing reading on current events in order to describe or to forecast public opinion. As a comprehensive bibliography will testify,[11] this problem has been studied, heretofore, largely in terms of the press. Comparisons between the 1936 election returns and the political complexions of the local papers will show that Republican papers almost monopolized many states which voted Democratic. It would seem more efficient to predict public opinion not only from the press but from reading in other publications as well, publications which are easier to rank on any scale of political

[10] For a convincing account of the confusion between the "human interest story" and the news as such, see Hughes, Helen MacGill. "The Lindbergh Case." *American Journal of Sociology.* 42:32-54. No. 1. July 1936

[11] Lasswell, Harold D., Casey, Ralph D., and Smith, Bruce Lannes. *Propaganda and Promotional Activities.* An annotated bibliography, prepared under the direction of the Advisory Committee on Pressure Groups and Propaganda. Social Science Research Council. Minneapolis: University of Minnesota Press. 1935

prejudice because they make less effort to conceal their partisanship in the selection and presentation of pre-election news—e.g., *Wall Street Journal, New Republic, New Masses.* By selecting the states which analyses of returns since 1900 have shown to have voted most consistently with the nation as a whole from election to election, one might sample shifts in the reading of definitely party organs for different population groups from now on, and check the forecast by the 1940 returns.

2. *To find evidence.*—Table XLIII showed changes during depression among the readers who seek information as such. A more interesting question, which we lack the facts to answer, is How did the depression affect fact finding as against the other uses of print? A good guess might be that fact finding or reference reading is a characteristic interest of people who, by temperament, training, and occupation, are disposed to seek facts in good times and bad; also that such readers read factual if not scientific publications much more than they read anything else.

But this begs the sociological question of most importance, namely, how did depression affect popular interest in the truth about current issues, as against interpretations colored to match the desires of important groups? To answer the latter question in terms of reading behavior the student should work upon widely read publications containing both articles of a factual sort and emotional interpretations of the same or similar facts. *The Saturday Evening Post,* for example, is read by millions. It combines articles on foreign policy with stories of foreign wars. How many and what sort of people read the stories only? How many read only the articles? How many read both?

If we had the answers to such questions if not for a longer period, then as of 1929, 1933, and 1936 (which unfortunately we do not have), we could make a better guess than is now possible. The guess is that the story readers normally outnumber the article readers not less than two to one; that this ratio increased from 1929 to 1933 and decreased from 1933 to 1936. The guess might yet be checked by interviewing readers of the *Post,* or other comparable miscellany, to learn what they say about their changing predilections for stories as against articles since 1929.

3. To experience thrills.—Thrills can be found in all sorts of print, from the penny thriller to the work of art. But most thrill seekers want their sensations raw. The tabloid press, the pulp magazines, the bloodthirsty adventure story, and the erotic novel are the best vehicles for thrills delivered wholesale.

How far and in what direction the predepression interest in such literature was changed by depression, we do not know. It is probable that the interest increased. Steady consumers of "Westerns" today have been found largely among men of all ages with less than high school education. Their mental maturity is about that of a normal ten year old boy, who has not yet developed an interest in sex. Steady consumers of pornographic prints are but slightly more advanced. Both groups predominate among those who suffered most during depression.

It would be a simple matter to plot the net paid circulation of the more frankly pornographic magazines since 1929, for comparison with the circulation curve of other magazines at the same price level. It would not be surprising if pornography sold better until 1934, and if the increase in readers were proportionately larger than the increase in sales. For readers of the sort suggested, pornography might compensate the probably severe sex frustrations resulting from depression,[12] and stories of wild adventure might similarly compensate the dreariness of daily living.

But the circulation comparisons may easily exaggerate the search for thrills as against other uses of print during the depression. They should be interpreted with due regard to such changes in the availability of thrillers as the distributing agencies may have made when the sales of other magazines fell off.

4. To improve vocational competence.—From the testimony

---

[12] Cf. Stouffer, Samuel A. and Lazarsfeld, Paul F. *Research Memorandum on the Family in the Depression.* (monograph in this series). Chapter VI

of public librarians, the sales of "success" magazines, the incentives supplied by federal efforts to educate unemployed adults, and many other indications, it is safe to say that much reading during the early depression was prompted by vocational motives. The sudden increase in the leisure of many men and fewer women, between the ages of twenty-five and forty-five, afforded a long sought opportunity to repair their educational deficiencies, especially along vocational lines, in the hope of increasing their incomes. The testimony also indicates, as one might suppose, that the urge toward vocational reading was strongest among the underprivileged, who doubtless expected more help from books than they actually found in them; hence the somewhat abrupt decline in the vocational reading of non-student groups after 1933. The data most needed to check this hypothesis are perhaps those supplied by analyses of public library loans in postdepression years for comparison with the relevant data supplied in Chapter V.

5. *To defend class interests.*—A general depression, as severe as ours, inevitably threatens the security of all classes, and different social groups react to the threat in different ways. In so far as such reactions are discernible in reading behavior, they apparently took three forms, each of which suggests a somewhat different field of research.

The three modes of reading may be distinguished by differences in the clarity with which existing conditions were viewed. For short, they may be labelled "uncritical," "partisan," and "highly critical." Such oversimplification is probably justified if we recognize that different groups of readers passed from one to another of these modes at different times and in a different sequence. If one had the temerity to guess the trend for the country as a whole, he would probably guess that it followed the order stated, from an uncritical stage, through a series of ineffective political and economic nostrums, to a more realistic view of the conditions essential to greater security.

The uncritical phase is best exemplified by "the prosperity around the corner" period from 1929 to 1932. The press persistently poured soothing syrup over the disturbing facts and more disturbing tendencies. It played up the calming voice of Mr. Roosevelt in his first presidential broadcast, and thereafter, until the NRA controversies began, a variety of publications proclaimed that all was increasingly well in the land and we needed merely to wait. After the 1936 election the phase was resumed and featured an easy nationalism as the prevailing political expression; the radio, press, and movies conspiring to fix public attention on interesting trivialities. At least, these are speculations which can be checked. The files of the press are always available. It would be useful to carry out the analytic description of changes in the content of the daily press, as recommended in Chapter III. We have shown that, for the less educated groups, the press during early depression tended to crowd out more expensive publications. A description of the changes in the character of social criticism supplied by the press would at least refine the crude hypotheses and might show how threats to the security of certain economic groups were softened by newspaper reading.

The second mode of reading is more safely attributed to depression than the first. It represents the allegiance of millions of persons to various messiahs—whether the Huey Longs, Coughlins, or Townsends of radio fame or the several prophets of a new political and economic order who confined their presentations to print. The depression doubtless encouraged such loyalties among persons seeking a formula by which to solve their economic perplexities. As reflected in reading, the various loyalties can be found in the increased consumption of party organs of all sorts—but more especially of publications by the small and more radical parties.

To estimate the extent of resistance to depression by means of organizations and formulas, one might profitably investigate annual changes in the reading of "panacea" journals and books, by readers representing different levels of income and schooling. The sales and circulation figures for the journals and books respectively can be obtained from the sources given, but there is no easy means of identifying their readers beyond the community studies described in the last chapter. The data available from such studies should show who read radical and panacea publications clearly enough for comparison with similar post-depression records.

The third or *critical* mode of resisting threats to security is more largely confined to readers of college education and middle age. Such readers we may assume to have done their duty by the annual crop of popular non-fiction and to have found it steadily less convincing as the depression wore on. From his close observation of changes in depression attitudes, Professor Robert S. Lynd generalizes the effects of depression upon such readers as "increasing distrust of the expert." To investigate the changing status of such types as the professional economist, the banker, the newspaper proprietor, the college professor, the prohibition agent, and members of the national congress might be to learn that each one lost appreciably in popular esteem. Enough authorities in many fields generalized beyond their wisdom and were accordingly discredited to induce deep skepticism among critical readers. The facts to estimate the growth of the skepticism may consist in postdepression records to show the virtual absence of such reading, as compared with 1933 and 1929. Today such readers are probably more disposed to read books of genuine artistic and scholarly excellence than arguments defending particular programs like technocracy.

A Sociology of Reading

To conclude the overview of problems, one may suppose that a sociology of reading will develop in so far as we learn *who reads what and why, over consecutive periods of time.* The supposition rests on two assumptions: that what people read can be used to describe their attitudes, and that the people whose attitudes are of most interest to sociology in the study of public opinion actually read enough to reveal their attitudes.

On the strength of such assumptions, the development of the field involves three major tasks: (1) to determine the most significant facts concerning the reading of any population group, i.e., facts that best describe their total reading behavior and which also bear most directly upon important hypotheses of social science; (2) to devise valid indexes of the facts that reflect central tendencies, indexes which will enable social scientists to apply reading data to their own problems; (3) to arrange for the continuous recording of such facts for adequate samples of the reading population in relation to social changes in the population at large.

The mere suggestion of cooperative studies in the field of reading is enough to inflame the student's imagination. He pictures first a common interest among several departments sufficient to produce conclusive data upon the more fundamental of the theoretical problems of reading in its social aspects. But his dreams do not stop there. They go forward to an institute (which should be spelled in capitals) wherein the social aspects of *all* the present arts of communication—print, radio, motion pictures, museum exhibits, public forums, and others—might be examined in terms of their complicated interrelationships.

The political and social importance of print, radio, and motion picture (with sound television in the offing) has already reduced each to a highly specialized science. Each science is occult, to the student of social forces. What society (and therefore sociology) needs is a fair overview, a body of evidence that will indicate the peculiar efficiences and deficiences of each art for the popular dissemination of different sorts of ideas. It is possible, though unlikely, that any one group in our national society contains both the imagination and the resources to create such an institute.

APPENDIXES

APPENDIX A

DISTRIBUTING AGENCIES IN ST. LOUIS, 1934
(Supplement to Chapter IV)

The following tables show what publications were supplied by each agency to different groups of readers in St. Louis. The data apply to residential districts receiving unusually good service from the public library, and well above the South Chicago sample (Chapter IV) in education and in wealth. The two communities in combination thus offer a better picture of depression conditions than either one alone.

Table 1A of this appendix shows the percentage of magazines and books supplied by the public library to each sex, to each of four age groups, and to three educational groups, and Table 1B shows similar data for six occupational groups. Wherever the data permit similar percentage distributions are presented for the other sources, namely, friends, Table 2; drug stores, Table 3; newsstands, Table 4; and subscriptions, Table 5. Table 6 presents a summary picture of the sources of magazines and books for each sex, age, and occupational group. The data are based on an unpublished study of 3,543 persons from residential districts in St. Louis, in the fall of 1934.

TABLE 1A

PERCENTAGE DISTRIBUTION OF SELECTED CATEGORIES OF BOOKS AND MAGA-
ZINES BORROWED FROM PUBLIC LIBRARIES, BY SEX, AGE, AND EDUCATION
OF BORROWERS: ST. LOUIS, 1934

SELECTED CATEGORIES	SEX		AGE				EDUCATION		
	MALE	FE-MALE	10–19	20–29	30–44	45 AND OVER	0–8	H. S.	COLLEGE
Magazines									
Detective and adventure . .	2.0	1.6	—	—	—	—	—	—	—
Weekly news	—	—	1.9	2.7	1.4	.9	1.5	1.7	2.1
Movie and radio	.2	.6	.6	—	.7	—	—	.6	—
5¢ weeklies	2.3	.7	2.3	1.2	—	.4	1.0	1.7	.4
Monthly story	3.2	2.8	2.0	2.0	4.4	5.5	7.5	2.5	1.4
Religious	—	—	—	—	—	—	—	—	—
Parents', women's, home . .	1.4	5.1	1.9	5.1	5.1	5.5	8.5	2.6	3.5
All others	22.8	7.6	18.4	12.1	3.4	13.3	6.0	15.5	12.6
Total magazines	31.9	18.4	27.1	23.1	15.0	25.6	24.5	24.6	20.0
Books									
Good fiction	13.8	21.8	17.1	18.8	22.8	17.9	17.5	17.5	22.8
Other fiction	25.0	40.1	37.7	32.4	31.6	25.5	37.0	37.4	17.2
Juvenile	3.1	1.9	4.2	.8	.7	.4	—	3.3	.4
Psychology	2.1	3.1	.5	2.3	5.4	7.2	4.0	1.8	5.3
Biography, travel	5.2	4.0	3.9	4.7	4.8	6.0	3.0	4.2	6.3
Social problems	2.9	1.0	1.1	1.9	4.4	.4	1.5	1.6	2.5
Literature	1.2	2.2	1.9	1.2	2.4	1.3	.5	1.7	2.8
All others	14.8	7.5	6.5	14.8	12.9	15.7	12.0	7.9	22.7
Total books	68.1	81.6	72.9	76.9	85.0	74.4	75.5	75.4	80.0
Total	100	100	100	100	100	100	100	100	100
Number of magazines	209	170	215	59	41	57	46	274	54
Number of books	444	758	566	179	247	161	149	824	212
Number of publications . . .	653[a]	928[a]	781	238	288	218	195	1,098	266

[a] Includes publications read by persons of unknown age, education, and occupation not reported
separately

TABLE 1B

PERCENTAGE DISTRIBUTION OF SELECTED CATEGORIES OF BOOKS AND MAGA-
ZINES BORROWED FROM PUBLIC LIBRARIES, BY OCCUPATION OF BORROWERS:
ST. LOUIS, 1934

SELECTED CATEGORIES	UNEM-PLOYED	UN-SKILLED LABOR	CLERKS, STENOG-RAPHERS	SHOP-KEEPERS, SALES-MEN	SKILLED TRADES	HOUSE-WIVES	STU-DENTS	PROFES-SIONAL
Magazines								
Detective and adventure .	—	1	—	—	—	—	—	—
Weekly news	1.3	—	3.6	1.9	—	.7	2.2	1.6
Movie and radio	1.3	—	—	—	—	.3	.7	—
5¢ weeklies	1.3	—	.7	—	—	1.0	2.3	—
Monthly story	1.3	1	2.9	5.6	3.4	5.7	2.0	1.6
Religious	—	—	—	—	—	—	—	—
Parents', women's, home .	2.7	1	8.0	3.7	.9	7.7	1.9	1.6
All others	5.4	1	6.8	11.0	11.3	7.3	19.6	13.5
Total magazines . . .	13.3	—	22.0	22.2	15.6	22.7	28.7	18.3
Books								
Good fiction.	20.0	6	19.0	18.5	20.7	20.5	16.1	24.6
Other fiction	41.3	14	35.7	14.8	35.4	32.3	37.6	13.5
Juvenile	—	1	—	1.9	—	1.0	4.4	—
Psychology	5.3	1	2.9	1.9	3.4	6.1	.4	6.3
Biography, travel	4.0	1	5.1	7.4	.9	4.4	4.2	8.7
Social problems	1.3	—	.7	3.7	3.4	1.7	1.3	4.0
Literature	2.7	—	1.5	1.9	3.4	1.7	1.7	.8
All others	12.1	3	13.1	27.7	17.2	9.6	5.6	23.8
Total books	86.7	—	78.0	77.8	84.4	77.3	71.3	81.7
Total	100	—	100	100	100	100	100	100
Number of magazines . . .	10	4	31	12	19	68	211	23
Number of books	65	26	109	42	98	229	531	102
Number of publications . .	75	30	140	54	117	297	742	125

ᵃ Percentage distribution not presented to base with less than 50 cases. Numbers presented in this
column represent actual cases

TABLE 2

PERCENTAGE DISTRIBUTION OF SELECTED CATEGORIES OF BOOKS AND MAGA-
ZINES BORROWED FROM FRIENDS, BY SEX, AGE, AND EDUCATION
OF BORROWERS: ST. LOUIS, 1934

SELECTED CATEGORIES	SEX		AGE				EDUCATION		
	MALE	FE-MALE	10–19	20–29	30–44	45 AND OVER	0–8	H.S.	COL-LEGE[b]
Magazines									
Detective and adventure . .	7.4	1.1	6.1	2.6	—	1.2	2.8	4.6	—
Weekly news	4.2	1.8	2.6	2.6	1.2	6.1	5.1	2.5	1
Movie and radio	3.2	8.5	6.1	10.5	4.7	4.9	9.1	6.5	—
5¢ weeklies	14.7	11.7	12.7	15.8	5.9	18.3	18.2	13.3	—
Monthly story	8.9	12.1	8.7	9.2	12.9	15.9	11.1	10.5	6
Religious	.5	1.1	—	—	9.4	2.4	—	.3	3
Parents', women's, home . .	4.7	25.6	12.7	11.8	28.2	23.2	29.3	13.6	8
All others	20.6	7.5	16.5	10.6	4.2	8.5	6.5	15.8	5
Total magazines	64.2	69.4	65.4	63.1	66.5	80.5	82.1	67.1	—
Books									
Good fiction	4.7	8.2	4.8	9.2	9.4	7.3	4.0	4.2	11
Other fiction	14.2	14.9	16.2	17.1	17.6	4.9	9.1	15.0	8
Juvenile	2.1	3.2	5.7	—	—	—	—	4.0	—
Psychology	.5	1.1	—	—	2.4	2.4	1.0	.6	1
Biography, travel	2.6	1.4	3.1	1.3	1.2	—	1.0	2.2	1
Social probems	3.2	.7	2.2	2.6	1.2	—	1.0	1.5	2
Literature	.5	—	.4	—	—	—	—	.3	—
All others	8.0	1.1	2.2	6.7	1.7	4.9	1.8	5.1	3
Total books	35.8	30.6	34.6	36.9	33.5	19.5	17.9	32.9	—
Total	100	100	100	100	100	100	100	100	—
Number of magazines . . .	122	197	151	48	48	61	75	214	23
Number of books	68	86	77	27	31	17	18	110	26
Number of publications . . .	190[a]	283[a]	228	75	79	78	93	324	49

[a] Includes publications read by persons of unknown age, education, and occupation not reported separately

[b] Percentage distribution not presented to base with less than 50 cases. Numbers presented in this column represent actual cases

TABLE 3

PERCENTAGE DISTRIBUTION OF SELECTED CATEGORIES OF MAGAZINES SE-
CURED FROM DRUG STORES, BY SEX, AGE, EDUCATION, AND OCCUPATIONS
OF READERS: ST. LOUIS, 1934

SELECTED CATEGORIES	SEX		AGE				EDUCATION		
	MALE	FE-MALE	10–19	20–29	30–44	45 AND OVER	0–8	H.S.	COL-LEGE
Detective and adventure	15.6	.5	7.8	1.9	3.6	5.9	7.3	4.3	6.6
Weekly news	2.5	3.5	3.0	1.9	4.6	1.9	.7	3.5	6.6
Movie and radio	5.0	17.4	18.3	17.5	8.3	8.8	13.2	15.5	3.9
5¢ weeklies	35.2	28.6	30.4	21.4	31.4	39.2	31.6	32.0	22.4
Monthly story	8.0	15.3	7.0	20.4	16.5	12.8	13.2	11.8	19.7
Religious	—	—	—	—	—	—	—	—	—
Parents', women's, home	3.5	27.7	14.3	23.3	22.7	24.5	23.8	17.5	23.7
All others	30.2	7.0	19.2	13.6	12.9	6.9	10.2	15.4	17.1
Total	100	100	100	100	100	100	100	100	100
Number of magazines	200[a]	429[a]	231	94	179	88	135	408	68

SELECTED CATEGORIES	OCCUPATION							
	UNEM-PLOYED[b]	UN-SKILLED LABOR[b]	CLERKS, STEN-OGRA-PHERS[b]	SHOP-KEEPERS' SALES-MEN[b]	SKILLED TRADES[b]	HOUSE-WIVES	STU-DENTS	PROFES-SIONAL[b]
Detective and adventure	1	—	1	1	9	.4	9.0	—
Weekly news	—	1	3	—	—	3.6	3.6	—
Movie and radio	3	6	6	1	4	10.8	18.0	1
5¢ weeklies	11	1	14	13	20	30.5	27.9	4
Monthly story	2	3	7	5	3	18.4	8.1	3
Religious	—	—	—	—	—	—	—	—
Parents', women's, home	5	3	7	3	2	30.0	14.0	8
All others	—	1	11	6	10	6.3	19.4	5
Total	—	—	—	—	—	100	100	—
Number of magazines	22	15	49	29	48	223	222	21

[a] Includes publications read by persons of unknown age and education not reported separately
[b] Percentage distribution not presented to base with less than 50 cases. Numbers presented in this column represent actual cases

TABLE 4

PERCENTAGE DISTRIBUTION OF SELECTED CATEGORIES OF MAGAZINES SE-
CURED FROM NEWS-STANDS, BY SEX, AGE, EDUCATION, AND OCCUPA-
TIONS OF READERS: ST. LOUIS, 1934

SELECTED CATEGORIES	SEX		AGE				EDUCATION		
	MALE	FE-MALE	10–19	20–29	30–44	45 AND OVER	0–8	H. S.	COLLEGE
Detective and adventure	5.6	1.7	3.9	3.8	2.7	2.9	2.2	4.0	2.3
Weekly news	6.4	5.3	6.2	3.8	6.8	5.3	5.5	5.6	6.2
Movie and radio	3.4	11.7	14.1	12.2	6.8	4.9	8.3	10.7	3.1
5¢ weeklies	36.7	25.4	28.1	33.6	27.1	31.1	29.3	29.1	32.6
Monthly story	13.5	15.8	7.8	13.7	21.7	12.6	14.9	14.7	15.4
Religious	—	.2	—	—	—	.5	—	—	—
Parents', women's, home	9.0	30.1	17.2	18.3	19.5	29.6	29.3	20.3	16.2
All others	25.4	9.8	22.7	14.6	15.4	13.1	10.5	15.6	24.1
Total	100	100	100	100	100	100	100	100	100
Number of magazines	269	417[a]	125	124	211	188	168	377	124

SELECTED CATEGORIES	OCCUPATION							
	UNEMPLOYED[b]	UN SKILLED LABOR	CLERKS, STENOG-RAPHERS	SHOP-KEEPERS, SALES-MEN	SKILLED TRADES	HOUSE-WIVES	STU-DENTS	PROFES-SIONAL[b]
Detective and adventure	1	—	1.9	6.6	4.8	1.2	3.5	3
Weekly news	2	—	8.5	8.2	6.5	4.8	5.3	—
Movie and radio	3	—	9.4	1.6	11.3	7.3	13.3	—
5¢ weeklies	8	—	33.0	36.1	40.3	26.2	26.5	15
Monthly story	3	—	20.8	23.0	11.3	16.5	8.0	5
Religious	—	—	—	—	—	.4	—	—
Parents', women's, home	10	—	12.3	8.2	12.9	35.9	16.8	5
All others	6	—	14.1	16.3	12.9	7.7	26.6	19
Total	—	—	100	100	100	100	100	—
Number of magazines	33	—	104	61	62	249	112	47

[a] Includes publications read by persons of unknown age, education, and occupation not reported separately

[b] Percentage distribution not presented to base with less than 50 cases. Numbers presented in this column represent actual cases

TABLE 5

PERCENTAGE DISTRIBUTION OF SELECTED CATEGORIES OF MAGAZINES SE-
CURED BY SUBSCRIPTION, BY SEX, AGE, EDUCATION, AND OCCUPA-
TIONS OF READERS: ST. LOUIS, 1934

Selected Categories	Sex		Age				Education		
	Male	Fe-male	10–19	20–29	30–44	45 and over	0–8	H. S.	College
Detective and adventure	.7	—	.8	—	.2	.1	—	.4	.2
Weekly news	10.8	6.0	8.1	8.5	7.8	7.0	5.1	8.0	10.3
Movie and radio. . .	1.0	1.8	—	—	—	—	—	—	—
5¢ weeklies	21.8	15.5	18.7	21.6	19.8	13.3	19.9	17.7	16.0
Monthly story. . . .	17.6	15.9	14.0	18.3	16.2	17.9	16.5	17.3	15.6
Religious	3.1	3.4	1.8	1.3	3.6	5.2	5.3	3.1	1.7
Parents', women's, home	18.5	46.5	32.3	38.7	36.5	41.7	41.8	37.3	34.0
All others	26.5	10.9	24.3	11.6	15.9	14.8	11.4	16.2	22.2
Total	100	100	100	100	100	100	100	100	100
Number of magazines	1,355[a]	2,746[a]	723	743	1,270	1,116	954	2,153	814

	Occupation.							
	Unem-ployed	Un-skilled Labor	Clerks Stenog-raphers	Shop-keepers, Sales-men	Skilled Trades	House-wives	Stu-dents	Profes-sional
Detective and adventure	—	—	.2	.7	.3	—	.9	—
Weekly news	7.7	7.1	6.2	9.1	12.1	5.8	8.3	12.3
Movie and radio. . .	—	—	—	—	—	—	—	—
5¢ weeklies	16.7	22.6	20.2	22.7	19.6	16.4	18.9	14.3
Monthly story. . . .	13.6	11.9	16.1	20.3	17.3	17.5	14.8	15.2
Religious	5.0	11.9	4.0	2.8	4.1	3.9	.4	2.3
Parents', women's, home	40.3	30.0	43.0	26.9	26.2	47.3	29.7	23.2
All others	16.7	16.5	10.3	17.5	20.4	9.1	27.0	32.7
Total	100	100	100	100	100	100	100	100
Number of magazines	227	86	427	289	375	1,677	670	349

[a] Includes publications read by persons of unknown age, education, and occupation not reported separately

TABLE 6

PERCENTAGE DISTRIBUTION OF MAGAZINES AND BOOKS BY AGENCY
OF READERS: SAMPLE

SEX, AGE, EDUCATION, AND OCCUPATION OF READERS	PUBLIC LIBRARY	FRIEND	DRUG STORE	NEWSSTAND	RENTAL LIBRARY	BOOK STORE	SUBSCRIPTION	ALL OTHERS	TOTAL	NUMBER
Sex:										
Male	6.5	3.8	6.2	8.4	.1	.5	42.3	8.2	76.0	2,438
Female	3.0	3.5	7.7	7.5	.1	.2	49.1	8.7	79.8	4,463
Age:										
Not given	1.5	2.4	8.2	8.4	—	—	54.9	9.7	85.1	386
10–19	9.3	6.5	9.9	5.4	.2	.6	31.1	4.8	67.8	1,575
20–29	3.7	3.1	6.0	7.9	—	.1	47.1	10.7	78.6	1,238
30–44	1.7	2.0	7.4	8.8	.1	.2	52.7	9.4	82.3	1,982
45 and over	2.8	3.0	4.3	9.2	.1	.4	55.0	9.9	84.7	1,720
Education:										
Not given	1.9	2.6	6.7	6.4	—	—	67.4	4.9	89.9	240
0–8 years	2.5	4.1	7.3	9.1	—	.1	51.7	10.8	85.6	1,579
High school	5.4	4.2	8.0	7.4	.1	.5	42.4	8.0	76.0	3,863
College	3.4	1.4	4.2	7.7	.1	.1	50.8	8.3	76.0	1,219
Occupation:										
Not given	2.3	5.8	4.3	6.8	—	.4	47.2	10.7	77.5	375
Unskilled labor . . .	2.2	3.9	8.3	8.8	.6	—	47.5	7.7	79.0	143
Clerks and stenographers	3.3	2.3	5.4	11.0	—	.9	45.0	9.8	77.7	736
Shopkeepers and salesmen	2.2	2.0	5.1	11.0	—	—	52.1	11.9	84.3	467
Skilled trades . . .	2.5	3.9	6.3	8.1	.1	.3	48.7	8.5	78.4	602
Housewives	2.3	2.6	7.5	8.4	—	.1	56.2	10.0	87.1	2,595
Students.	9.6	6.3	10.2	5.1	.2	.6	30.5	4.8	67.3	1,477
Professional	3.3	.9	2.9	7.1	.3	—	50.7	8.3	73.5	506
Total	4.3	3.6	7.2	7.8	.1	.3	46.7	8.5	78.5	—
Number	379	319	629	686	8	27	4,101	752	—	6,901

Column group header: PERCENTAGE — MAGAZINES

ª Less than .05

TABLE 6

FROM WHICH SECURED FOR SEX, AGE, EDUCATION, AND OCCUPATION
FROM ST. LOUIS, 1933

Public Library	Friend	Drug Store	Newsstand	Rental Library	Book Store	Subscription	All Others	Total	Number	Total Percent	Total Number Magazines and Books
13.9	2.1	.3	—	1.6	1.1	.3	4.7	24.0	769	100	3,207
13.6	1.5	.1	—	1.1	.7	.2	3.0	20.2	1,126	100	5,589
10.8	.4	—	—	.4	.4	.4	2.4	14.8	68	100	454
24.3	3.3	.1	—	1.4	.4	.1	2.6	32.2	750	100	2,325
11.4	1.7	.3	—	2.4	.7	.3	4.6	21.4	337	100	1,575
10.0	1.3	.2	.1	.8	1.0	.3	4.1	17.8	430	100	2,412
7.9	.8	.2	—	1.1	1.3	.3	3.7	15.3	310	100	2,030
6.3	.4	—	—	—	.4	—	3.0	10.1	27	100	267
8.0	1.0	.1	.1	.8	.7	.3	3.4	14.4	266	100	1,845
16.2	2.2	.1	—	1.5	.7	.2	3.1	24.0	1,219	100	5,082
13.2	1.6	.3	.1	1.4	1.4	.3	5.7	24.0	383	100	1,602
13.6	1.7	.4	—	1.7	1.2	.6	3.3	22.5	109	100	484
13.7	1.1	1.1	—	1.7	.6	—	2.8	21.0	38	100	181
11.5	1.0	—	—	3.1	.6	.4	5.8	22.4	212	100	948
7.6	1.3	.2	—	1.1	.9	.5	4.2	15.8	87	100	554
12.8	1.4	—	—	1.4	.5	.3	5.2	21.6	166	100	768
7.8	.9	—	—	.7	.7	.2	2.6	12.9	384	100	2,979
24.3	3.6	.1	—	1.3	.6	.1	2.7	32.7	717	100	2,194
14.8	1.7	.6	.2	.7	2.2	.3	6.0	26.5	182	100	688
13.7	1.8	.1	ᵃ	1.3	.8	.2	3.6	21.5	—	100	—
1,202	154	13	2	113	72	21	318	—	1,895	—	8,796

APPENDIX B

Available Data on Community Reading in 1933-1934

List of South Chicago and St. Louis Data Tabulated and Available for Reference in the Library of the Graduate Library School, University of Chicago

Some 500 manuscript pages of tables show each of the following items in relation to each of the others wherever the relation has meaning:

Census Tract
Sex and Marital Status
Age
Education
Number of Children
Religion
Employment
Nationality
Number of Years in America
Dominant Language
Secondary Language
Club Membership
Activities
Favorite Radio Program
Number of Books Read Last Two Weeks

Number of Magazines Read Last Two Weeks
Number of Newspapers Read Regularly
Newspaper Titles
Parts of Newspaper Read
Number of Books in Home
Library Card
Reasons for Not Reading
Books Read Past Two Weeks
Magazines Read Past Two Weeks
Source of Books
Source of Magazines
Non-Readers

Forty tables show the number and percentage of each of eight types of books obtained from each of five sources by persons of specified sex, age, years of schooling, and type of occupation. The eight types of books are as follows:

Good fiction
Other fiction
Juvenile fiction
Psychology

Biography and travel
Books of social significance
Literature
Other non-fiction

214

The five sources are public library, friends, purchases, rental library, and all others.

Forty-eight tables show the number and percentage of each of eight types of magazines obtained from each of six sources by persons of specified sex, age, years of schooling, and type of occupation. The eight types of magazines are as follows:

Detective and adventure	Medium quality fiction monthlies
Movie and love story	Parents', women's, home
5¢ weekly miscellanies	Religious
Weekly news	All others

The six sources are public library, friends, subscription, drug store, newsstand, and all others.

DAILY NEWSPAPERS IN THE UNITED STATES: 1920-1935
A Comparison of Three Sources

YEAR	ALL DAILY NEWSPAPERS			
	TOTAL DAILY (U. S.)		TOTAL DAILY (U. S. & CANADA)[a]	
	Editor & Publisher		*Ayer's Directory*	
	NUMBER	CIRCULATION	NUMBER	CIRCULATION
1920	2,042	27,790,656	2,324	31,000,000[b,c]
1921	2,028	28,423,740	2,331	31,000,000[b,c]
1922	2,033	29,780,328	2,313	33,000,000[b,c]
1923	2,036	31,453,683	2,310	33,000,000[b,c]
1924	2,014	32,999,437	2,293	33,000,000[b,c]
1925	2,008	33,739,369	2,283	33,000,000[b,c]
1926	2,001	36,001,803	2,281	33,000,000[b,c]
1927	1,949	37,966,756	2,222	33,425,000[b]
1928	1,939	37,972,592	2,215	40,175,000[b]
1929	1,944	39,425,615	2,248	44,110,094[b]
1930	1,942	39,589,172	2,219	45,106,245[b]
1931	1,923	38,761,187	2,241	44,448,325[b]
1932	1,913	36,407,679	2,008	38,862,000
1933	1,911	35,175,238	1,902	35,836,000
1934	1,929	36,709,010	2,032	36,540,000
1935	1,950	38,155,540	2,027	38,450,000

| YEAR | TOTAL DAILY (CANADA) | | TOTAL DAILY (U. S.) | |
| | *Editor & Publisher* | | *Census of Manufactures* | |
	NUMBER	CIRCULATION	NUMBER	CIRCULATION
1920	—	—	—	—
1921	—	—	2,335	33,741,742
1922	112	1,755,383	—	—
1923	103	1,673,278	2,271	35,471,070
1924	106	1,763,981	—	—
1925	105	1,797,316	2,116	37,406,615
1926	103	1,844,323	—	—
1927	105	1,930,961	2,091	41,368,320
1928	107	2,006,416	—	—
1929	106	2,182,943	2,086	42,015,461
1930	106	2,093,091	—	—
1931	107	2,103,122	2,044	41,293,659
1932	104	2,043,654	—	—
1933	102	1,998,093	1,903	37,630,345
1934	102	2,015,828	—	—
1935	101	2,141,527	2,038	40,871,246

[a] Calculated from the summary of totals given in the front part of the annual volumes of *N. W. Ayer & Son's Directory of Newspapers and Periodicals.* The number of newspapers is for the United States only; *Ayer's* gives the number of dailies in the U. S. and Outlying Territories together and in the Outlying Territories alone. The above is the difference. The circulation is for the U. S. and Canada together since *Ayer's* gives no separate circulation for Canada.

	SUNDAY EDITIONS OF ALL DAILY NEWSPAPERS			
YEAR	SUNDAY (U. S.)		SUNDAY (U. S. & CANADA)	
	Editor & Publisher		Ayer's Directory	
	NUMBER	CIRCULATION	NUMBER	CIRCULATION
1920	522	17,083,604	—	15,000,000[b,o]
1921	545	19,041,413	—	15,000,000[b,o]
1922	546	19,712,874	—	19,000,000[b,o]
1923	547	21,463,289	—	19,000,000[b,o]
1924	539	22,219,646	—	19,000,000[b,o]
1925	548	23,354,622	—	19,000,000[b,o]
1926	545	24,435,192	—	19,000,000[b,o]
1927	526	25,469,037	537	28,300,000[b]
1928	522	25,771,383	532	26,608,000[b]
1929	528	26,879,536	554	29,427,991[b]
1930	521	26,413,047	527	26,810,600[b]
1931	513	25,701,798	506	28,260,000[b]
1932	518	24,859,888	499	26,236,000
1933	506	24,040,630	442	24,654,000
1934	505	26,544,516	536	26,075,000
1935	518	28,147,343	536	28,300,000

| | SUNDAY (CANADA) | | SUNDAY (U. S.) | |
| YEAR | Editor & Publisher | | Census of Manufactures | |
	NUMBER	CIRCULATION	NUMBER	CIRCULATION
1920	—	—	—	—
1921	—	—	537	20,110,206
1922	7	270,439	—	—
1923	5	276,949	602	24,511,693
1924	5	214,187	—	—
1925	5	301,191	597	25,630,056
1926	4	276,683	—	—
1927	4	290,461	511	27,695,859
1928	4	303,892	—	—
1929	4	315,254	578	29,011,648
1930	5	377,853	—	—
1931	5	432,029	555	27,453,465
1932	5	348,233	—	—
1933	3	240,109	489	25,453,894
1934	3	306,155	—	—
1935	4	369,766	520	28,684,152

[b] Title does not include the term "English language." It reads "Aggregate Circulations of Daily and Sunday Papers in the United States and Canada (Estimated)." Since 1932 the title has read "Aggregate Net Paid Circulations of English Language Daily and Sunday Papers in the United States and Canada (Estimated)."

[o] The word "estimated" is not included in the title although the figures are obviously estimates.

APPENDIX D

New York City Market Analysis, 1933

Compiled and Copyright by New York Herald-Tribune, *the* News, *and the* New York Times

Figures concerning each of the following items are supplied for each borough:

Area, square miles
Population (U. S. Census, 1930)
Families (U. S. Census, 1930)

Manufactures (U. S. Census, 1929)
Number establishments
Number wage earners
Value of manufactured products
Value added by manufacture

Leading Industries
Bread and bakery products
Boots and shoes (excl. rubber)
Foundry and machine shop products
Knit goods
Paints and varnishes

Wholesale Trade (U. S. Census, 1929)
Number establishments
People employed (yearly average)
Net sales volume

Leading Wholesale Groups
Food products
Groceries and food spec.

Tobacco and its prod. (excl. leaf)
Electrical
Mach., equipment, and supplies

Retail Trade (U. S. Census, 1929)
Number outlets
People employed, total
Proprietors
Full time employees
Part time employees
Net sales

Leading Retail Groups
Food
Apparel
General merchandise
Automotive
Furniture and household

Miscellaneous Market Data
Passenger car registration, 1933
New passenger car sales, 1933
Families having radio sets, 1930
Marriages, 1933
Births (by residence of mother), 1933
Individual income tax returns, 1931

218

Savings deposits, April 1934
Residence telephones, January
    1934
  Area, sq. mi.
  Population
  Density, per sq. mi.
Native white
Foreign-born white
  Negroes
  Others
  Families
    in owned homes
    in rented homes
    tenure unknown
  Estimated annual family expen-
    diture

Median
Average
Families spending annually
  $9,000 and up
  6,000–8,999
  4,500–5,999
  3,000–4,499
  1,800–2,999
  under 1,800
  unknown
Total dwellings
  one family
  two family
  three or more

Index

221

duction to amount of reading, 189; on distribution and reading, 191; on technical problems, 192

International Year Book, 119

Journalism as related to research in reading, 55
Juvenile books, new titles published during depression, 67
Juvenile Research, Institute of, University of Chicago, 127; *see also* Chicago, University of

Kohn-Bramstedt, Ernst, 58n

Language study, as related to research in reading, 55
Lasswell, Harold D., 22, 45n; and Casey, Ralph D. and Smith, Bruce Lannes, 35n, 195n; *see also* Waples, Douglas and Lasswell, Harold D.
Law as related to research in reading, 55
Lazarsfeld, Paul F., 94, 190n; *see also* Stouffer, Samuel A. and Lazarsfeld, Paul F.
Leary, B. E., *see* Gray, W. S. and Leary, B. E.
Lewis, Sinclair, 179
Lewis, Wilmott, 125
Libraries, 105-16; 125-30; reading behavior as recorded by, 2, 16, 160; public, circulation of books in, 5, 10, 15, 97ff, 104ff, 108, 110ff, 129, 135ff, 142; rental, circulation of books in, 5, 10, 15, 108, 113, 128ff, 130, 135ff; studies of readers, 15, 16, 135-45, 160, 161-71, 179-82; an-

nual patronage, 16; distribution problems, studies of, 37-39; adaptation of services to readers' preferences, value of, 39; increase in number of, 97; school, college, and university, 102, 108-12, 142, 191; annual changes in budgets, book expenditures, circulation volumes and borrowers, 105, 108; study in South Chicago, 127-45; publications supplied, 129ff; patrons, 132ff; use by patrons, 135ff; problems for study, 143; Dewey system of classification, 167, 173; sex differences in loans, 130, 169, 171, 173; study of New York branches, 161-74, 177ff; patrons, 161ff; relation of registration to circulation, 162ff; rate of borrowing: borrowings by type of book, 165ff; changes in reading, 177; relation of loans to economic differences, 179
Life, 5, 6, 72
Literature as related to research in reading, 55
London, Jack, 179
Lorge, Irving, *see* Brunner, Edmund deS., and Lorge, Irving
Lumley, Frederick H., 47n
Lynd, Robert S. and Helen M., *Middletown in Transition,* 44n, 186n, 200

McMurry, Robert N., 94n
Magazines, 72-79; distribution and sales, 11, 25, 39, 98, 130; changes in character of, 12; directories, 12; categories and types, 12, 75; advertising, volume of, 72ff, 75ff, 89; new publications during depression years, 62, 63; production (1929-1935), 62, 73-79; categories producing greatest number of copies in 1929, 78; factors affecting editorial policies, 89;

Studies in the Social Aspects of the Depression

AN ARNO PRESS/NEW YORK TIMES COLLECTION

Chapin, F. Stuart and Stuart A. Queen.
Research Memorandum on Social Work in the Depression. 1937.

Collins, Selwyn D. and Clark Tibbitts.
Research Memorandum on Social Aspects of Health in the Depression. 1937.

The Educational Policies Commission.
Research Memorandum on Education in the Depression. 1937.

Kincheloe, Samuel C.
Research Memorandum on Religion in the Depression. 1937.

Sanderson, Dwight.
Research Memorandum on Rural Life in the Depression. 1937.

Sellin, Thorsten.
Research Memorandum on Crime in the Depression. 1937.

Steiner, Jesse F.
Research Memorandum on Recreation in the Depression. 1937.

Stouffer, Samuel A. and Paul F. Lazarsfeld.
Research Memorandum on the Family in the Depression. 1937.

Thompson, Warren S.
Research Memorandum on Internal Migration in the Depression. 1937.

Vaile, Roland S.
Research Memorandum on Social Aspects of Consumption in the Depression. 1937.

Waples, Douglas.
Research Memorandum on Social Aspects of Reading in the Depression. 1937.

White, R. Clyde and Mary K. White.
Research Memorandum on Social Aspects of Relief Policies in the Depression. 1937.

Young, Donald.
Research Memorandum on Minority Peoples in the Depression. 1937.